READING COMPREHENSION

READING COMPREHENSION

Strategies for Independent Learners

SECOND EDITION

Camille Blachowicz
Donna Ogle

THE GUILFORD PRESS
New York   London

Library of Congress Cataloging-in-Publication Data
Blachowicz, Camille L. Z.
    Reading comprehension : strategies for independent learners / Camille Blachowicz, Donna
Ogle. — 2nd ed.
        p. cm.
    Includes bibliographical references and index.
    ISBN 978-1-59385-755-4 (pbk.: alk. paper) — ISBN 978-1-59385-756-1 (hardcover: alk. paper)
    1. Reading comprehension—Study and teaching (Elementary)—United States.   2. Reading
(Elementary)—United States.   3. Individualized instruction—United States.   I. Ogle,
Donna.   II. Title.
    LB1573.7.B53 2008
    372.47—dc22
                                                                            2008007820

To my coauthor—C. B.
To Bud—D. O.

About the Authors

Camille Blachowicz, PhD, is Professor of Education at National-Louis University, where she also directs the Reading Program and the Reading Center. She is the author of several books and numerous chapters, monographs, and articles on vocabulary and comprehension instruction and on working with at-risk readers. Dr. Blachowicz was a Fulbright Fellow to Italy and is active in professional organizations and staff development nationally and internationally. She is in the sixth year of codirecting the Literacy Partners: Advanced Reading Development Demonstration Project (ARDDP), a project on coaching and school literacy improvement, in the Chicago Public Schools. In 2003 she was named to the roster of Outstanding Teacher Educators in Reading by the International Reading Association.

Donna Ogle, EdD, is Professor of Education at National-Louis University, a member of the Reading Hall of Fame, and a past president of the International Reading Association (2001–2002). She currently is directing two multischool projects in the Chicago Public Schools: Project ALL (Advancing Literacy for Learning) and the Transitional Adolescent Literacy Leadership (TALL) Project. She is also Senior Consultant to the Chicago Striving Readers Research Study. Dr. Ogle is the author of many publications related to the topic of comprehension development and has particular interest in informational reading and learning. She works internationally in professional development projects and is an editorial reviewer for *Lectura y Vida*, the Spanish-language journal of the International Reading Association.

Preface

As authors of this book, we are excited to share with you our experiences in classrooms, working with students and teachers to develop good models of reading comprehension instruction. Our thinking has been formed by many years of observing students as they negotiate their own comprehension and learning in a wide variety of settings. We are constantly impressed by how much students learn and how capable they become in contexts that support, challenge, and develop their learning and journey toward independence. Another thing we know is that we also learn by observing good teachers . . . and good teachers learn by watching their students, and other good teachers, as they fine-tune their instruction. Furthermore, good teachers know they have been effective when their students become independent and can take responsibility for their own learning. These experiences explain our subtitle—*Strategies for Independent Learners.*

In this edition, we have added information reflecting new learning in informational literacy, in content and academic vocabulary development, and in comprehension with multiple texts—print and electronic. Current examples of field-tested independent reading programs, updates on federal initiatives such as Striving Readers and the National Assessment of Educational Progress (NAEP), and new strategies and teaching ideas provide a rich collection for teachers' use.

Chapter 1 sets the stage by presenting some examples of "good comprehension" embodied in students we have known and watched. We hope that you will find their stories as interesting and informative as we found the actual students. They represent many ages, ethnic groups, and settings (urban, suburban, and rural); they exemplify both the similarities and differences among "good comprehenders"; and they provide living examples of the model for comprehension that underpins this book. Chapter 2 relates these observations of students in action to the research on comprehension, sets forth our model of comprehension, and ends with a model of good instruction with ideas for diversification for a varied student population. Taken together, these two chapters form the theoretical and "best-practices" bases of the book.

The next two chapters present topics that are prerequisites for good instruction. Chapter 3 describes the classroom and instructional organizational issues that have to be considered for good instruction to take place. Chapter 4 deals with finding a starting point for instruction—using assessment to help set appropriate goals for instruction. These are the "nuts-and-bolts" practical issues that can make or break a good comprehension development program.

Chapters 5–9 describe instructional and learning strategies for some common comprehension goals: reading for information; reading fiction; developing vocabulary; engaging in research; and performing tasks, studying, and taking tests. Chapter 10 caps off the book by talking about the encouragement of lifelong reading and learning—every teacher's goal. Each of these chapters refers back to the models of comprehension and of good instruction and differentiation presented in Chapter 2.

We suggest that you start to use this book by reading Chapters 1 and 2 to ground your thinking. Then you can dip into the other chapters in any order that makes sense for your own learning and teaching. To make this book as interactive as possible, each chapter starts with a "graphic organizer," which is intended to help you see the topics and issues that we feel are important. Also in each organizer is a chart of important strategies and other resources and their location in the chapter in case you want to use the chapter as a "handbook." Finally, in the "Putting It All Together" section of each chapter we highlight some of the instructional and differentiation issues that relate to the topic presented.

After working on this book for several years—years full of discussion, argument, laughing, and learning—and then having the chance to revise it with the suggestions and examples from so many readers, we look forward to *your* input. We'd like to hear your comments and suggestions by e-mail or snail mail.

CAMILLE BLACHOWICZ
DONNA OGLE
National College of Education
National-Louis University
5202 Old Orchard Road, Suite 300
Skokie, IL 60077

cblachowicz@nl.edu
dogle@nl.edu

Acknowledgments

What makes it possible for us to do our work is the wonderful support of our colleagues, friends, students, and families. Each and every one of our colleagues in the Department of Reading and Language at National-Louis University is an outstanding teacher and researcher. Their support, encouragement, constructive criticism, and friendship have been priceless and meaningful well beyond the scope of this book.

We would also like to thank the hundreds of teachers and students with whom we have worked for their intelligence, dedication, and generosity. After over 30 years in the classroom for each of us, we are still exhilarated by the quality and dedication of those who choose to be teachers, and thankful that they let us share in their work. Special thanks go to the members of the Reading Leadership Institute—a group of master teachers, administrators, and curriculum directors with whom we maintain an ongoing relationship that includes the sharing and testing of ideas. Their influence has been formative in all the parts of this book, and many of their ideas are contained and credited within. Donna gives particular "thank yous" to the Project ALL team with whom she has worked in refining ideas for content literacy, especially Amy Correa and Debbie Gurvitz. Camille sends kudos to Char Cobb, Kristin Lems, Ann Bates, and all our ARDDP partners for their contributions, along with the many colleagues whose examples are cited in the book. Anne Horton and Tracy Pawluk have provided substantial help in putting together the manuscript and dealing with many crises and emergencies in their ever-capable ways. Our editors at The Guilford Press, Craig Thomas and Chris Jennison, as well as Natalie Graham and Fred Bernardi, have been stalwart and insightful during the production process. Also, many thanks to our husbands, families, and closest friends, who have had to put up with the "emotional overload" that putting thoughts into writing entails. Their encouragement and support are much appreciated.

Contents

READING COMPREHENSION

CHAPTER 1

Learning about Comprehension from Good Readers

We begin our book by introducing some children who have become real readers, rather than by describing instruction or even a theory of reading comprehension. Then we look more broadly at what readers need to do to be considered "good comprehenders" in our society. Indeed, we can almost equate "reader" with "comprehender," for we know that reading is comprehending—making sense of what is read. (Figure 1.1 is a graphic organizer illustrating the topics we cover in this chapter.)

What *do* good comprehenders look like? Pause for a moment and see whether you can picture a good reader in your mind's eye. If you are a teacher, it may be one of your students. If you are not yet a teacher think of yourself or a classmate. Then think of another good reader who is different. That's just what we have done in beginning this book. We hope that by creating images of what good readers are like, we can more easily consider what our responsibilities are as teachers to create classrooms full of these empowered, confident readers. The students are our bottom line; they shape our instruction and are the reasons we make innumerable adjustments in our teaching on a daily basis. In later chapters, we discuss ways to reach children who are not able readers. But, for now, let's think about some active readers we know. From these descriptions, we want to develop a shared understanding of the depth and breadth of the deceptively simple term "reading." As we think about the many students with whom we have worked and who we know in personal ways, their individuality stands out. At the same time, so do many commonalities. A rich group portrait begins to emerge.

1

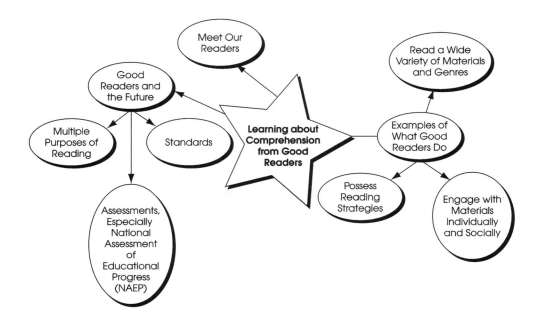

Resource Locator—Strategies and Resources Discussed in Chapter 1

FIGURE 1.1. Graphic organizer for Chapter 1.

Meet Our Readers

Sara loves to read. She spends free time in the school library helping the librarians shelve books. She orders books from a book club regularly and has her own collection of prized books at home in her room. Her favorite authors right now are Cynthia Voigt and Paula Danziger. In class she readily takes part in book discussions. This year she even persuaded her teacher to add two books to the selections the teacher had planned for a unit on "Growing Up in America." Sara demonstrates good comprehension of story plot and great sensitivity to characters. She often makes comparisons between fictional situations and those she has experienced personally. Sara also writes prolifically; she is in the process of composing her first novel. As much as she thinks of herself as a reader and writer, however, when it comes time for science and social studies, Sara does not show the same enthusiasm for reading or for the textbooks and resource materials the teacher provides. She gravitates to fiction and postpones the expository reading that is assigned in class. Her teacher this year has noted that Sara does not seem to think of ways to organize what she is learning from informational materials, as she can when she is reading fiction.

Ken is a different reader. His family has moved frequently, and he is interested in geography and history. He keeps *Cobblestone* and *Muse* magazines in his desk and will pick up books about states and locales where he has been when he is asked to read longer texts. He doesn't read a lot in his free time but enjoys reading during assigned reading periods. Ken takes a leadership role in his class when the integrated science/social studies units are underway. He knows how to navigate the Internet and prints out articles that help the team he's on collect the information they need. He loves to ponder maps and charts of the rainforest areas of the world and to trace the effects of El Niño. In the class study of sub-Saharan Africa, Ken brings in articles from *National Geographic* and *National Geographic World* that extend learning. Ken doesn't write much but will illustrate and make computer charts of concepts the group is working on to present in their reports. He is also good in helping his classmates connect pieces of information they gather from various resources. He has a clear idea of how to chunk information, develop categories that reduce the discrete items of information, and connect them together. He sometimes enjoys helping his social studies team prepare their group presentations, and he provides creative suggestions for ways to represent their findings.

Carlos is in a traditional school and must use the textbooks that form the core of "reading" in all curriculum areas. Last year in sixth grade, Carlos had a teacher who taught him how to read textbooks by mapping each chapter's main ideas in a graphic organizer. He gained confidence in using this strategy and now regularly maps assigned chapters and fills in information on "graphic organizers," akin to the ones we use at the beginnings of the chapters of this book, while he reads. His mother helps him review his chapter maps before exams, and he feels successful in reading for learning. He also likes to use the computerized encyclopedias that are available and makes good use of the headings and subheadings by turning them into questions to guide his reading—a strategy that his teacher recently explained to the class. In literature, his teacher has introduced the genre of mysteries and for the first time he has found some fiction that he really enjoys reading. He is even taking some of these books home to read independently. His teacher has encouraged him to write to the author of several of the books he likes, and he is drafting a letter on his computer. Because the literature curriculum is basically genre-based, Carlos's performance seems very uneven. When he likes a novel or short story, he puts much effort into reading it and adds much to class discussions. However, at other times he can be hard to motivate. At home he reads the sports page of the local newspaper with his dad, and he devours each issue of *Sports Illustrated for Kids* the day it arrives at his house. He also does a lot of reading in the Boy Scouts manual, as he is working on merit badges and has many projects to complete. Carlos finds he has to read this material carefully and reread it many times in order to follow directions accurately. He often stops and gets help from one of his parents, because the vocabulary is tough. His dad noted in the teacher conference how persistent Carlos can be when he is motivated to finish a project. On weekends Carlos gets on the computer and plays games, some of which involve reading and figuring out puzzles.

LaToya is the real writer and poet in her class. She would rather do her own writing than spend lots of time reading. She plays with words and likes to create poems and raps for special occasions. She is also theatrical and a good speaker, so when the class turns stories into Readers' Theater, she is the first to volunteer. Her parents report that she has always liked words and that she began to speak at an early age. Her reading interests are varied, but when she wants to just "escape-read," she generally reads realistic fiction. She has favorite poets and transcribes poems into her own "private" journals. Sometimes she is impatient when the class engages in book discussions; she would rather work alone. However, LaToya is an active participant when the class compares stories to movies and video productions or when they engage in discussions to compare books she likes. Her interest is often sparked by the other students' comments, and she sees details and notices subtle differences in interpretations. She also brings reports of her family's discussions of movies and TV programs. Sometimes she also reports on talk at home about stories that make headlines in the newspaper. It is clear that LaToya gains a great deal from oral communication both at home and at school, despite her impatience.

Maria, a fourth grader, likes reading material that is very graphic. Her choice of books and magazines depends on the number and quality of their illustrations. The first books she remembers as being really engrossing were *The Magic School Bus* books. She vividly recalls poring over Ms. Frizzle's escapades inside the earth and in the water treatment plant. More recently she has discovered graphic novels and is building a collection that she shares with her close friends. When the teacher reads aloud to the class, Maria likes to draw pictures, so that she can really "see" what the author is describing in words. She uses the same strategy of drawing and illustrating when she needs to read for social studies and science; she can get more out of pictures and maps than many kids can from the running text. This year her teacher had Maria create a collage of the characters and setting of the core novels they read in literature. Other classmates really admired her work, and the collages stimulated good talk about the stories. Everyone enjoyed looking at the pictures she found, and several other students started collecting pictures that they put in their journals. On standardized tests, Maria sometimes does not score as high as the teacher thinks she should. Either short, disconnected passages pose problems for her, or she doesn't put effort into them. Her comprehension scores on individual assessments are better and reflect what she can actually do. The computer has also helped Maria read more, because the text and illustrations are both important. At home, she does read newspapers, comics, and books about her favorite TV characters, the Simpsons.

The dictionary and encyclopedia are friends to Jamie both in book form and online. Everyone else in his sixth-grade class thinks this is weird, but he doesn't care. His family likes to play "Pictionary" and other word games; he has grown up in a word-filled environment. Crossword puzzles and jokes with word play tickle this emerging adolescent and he often does puzzles online for fun. Keeping print material short and concrete is another value Jamie holds. His teacher has tried hard to find books that he will read and has resorted to "skinny" chapter books. His favorites are short mysteries, especially the Donald J. Sobol books. When the class is reading a regular novel and discussing it, Jamie has a hard time staying with the book. The teacher notices that he brings little emotional engagement to the discussions; questions that ask for personal connections don't elicit much response from him. Recently she has tried to get him to do more writing with his reading, so that he comes to discussions with thought-out answers. This is helping to some extent, but Jamie still is very concrete in his reading responses. He does like to read music, both at church and in his clarinet lessons; he finds reading music and also singing lyrics to songs relaxing. His sight reading is strong, and he picks up both the music and the lyrics easily. His collection of music on his iPod is important to him and he uses it with Garage Band. His facility with words helps him in classroom work. He doesn't put much energy into studying but finds he can remember well and often links things he has to learn with music he hums to himself. His first choice for information learning is the Internet and he is a master of Google. He doesn't mind doing worksheets and other homework assignments that are short, and he usually finishes the homework that is assigned quickly in his free time. He does well on these assignments and doesn't show any problems with detailed kinds of tasks. When his class is engaged in small-group work, Jamie takes part but is not a leader. He has a few close friends and feels comfortable in these relationships and with some of the friends he has made online.

Nikki enjoys reading in her fourth-grade class but doesn't want to risk taking a book home because her little brothers and sisters are likely to tear it up or ruin it in many "creative" ways. She particularly likes it when her teacher reads aloud in class: She can see the images in her head, and enjoys closing her eyes and visualizing the scene. When the teacher asks for predictions of what will happen next in stories the teacher reads orally, Nikki often volunteers good ideas; she follows a plot well and is sensitive to characters and their motives. The teacher notes, however, that Nikki does not make as many predictions in her own reading, as evidenced by her bland responses to written questions. This causes some concern because she wants Nikki to become more personally engaged as she reads. Nikki enjoys learning lists of new and difficult spelling words. She enjoys street rhymes, jingles, rap, and poetry, and after school she teaches friends jump-rope and clapping routines with complicated lyrics. Cooking from recipes is something she likes to do with an older woman who lives in her building. She reads carefully, knowing that she must be exact with the ingredients she uses. Nikki does well in school and is proud of her ability as a reader. Just this year her teacher has introduced many new links between novels and the social studies units they study. Nikki became very interested in the Birmingham, Alabama, bombings of 1963 from the way the teacher connected them to *The Watsons Go to Birmingham—1963* (Curtis, 1995), which the teacher read to them as part of their study of the United States and the racial issues in the South. She hadn't thought much before about how many stories can be grounded in real events, but she has begun to ask these questions and look for connections.

A Look at These Readers

All of the students described above are successful in school and are considered to be good readers by their peers, by their teachers, and by themselves. Yet it is clear that they are very different from one another. Before you read further, you may want to reflect on how you would describe the similarities and differences among these good readers. What are some of the qualities they possess that make them "good readers"? Below we discuss some of the major areas we think are important in differentiating these good readers. We also raise some issues that come from these comparisons for us to think about as teachers. The three categories we discuss are these: the readers' preferences in materials, their preferences in styles of engagement in reading, and their use of strategies.

Readers' Preferences in Materials

First, we can see that good readers have preferences. The most obvious is that different readers like to read different things. Traditional realistic fiction is one genre that Sara chooses for her personal reading, but Ken, Carlos, Maria, and Jamie all gravitate toward different forms of nonfiction, and LaToya and Nikki resonate to poetry. For Jamie, the Internet is an important source of information. Even these distinctions are very broad, since there are enormous varieties within any basic kind of reading preference. For example, Sara doesn't like to read all works of fiction. She has particular kinds of books and specific authors that she enjoys more than others, and these preferences change periodically. She is influenced by her friends and by what the librarian highlights as new and interesting. A look at her reading log for the past 3 years illustrates her range of reading. Her favorite authors have changed periodically. Three years ago she read several books by Beverly Cleary. The next year she indicated that her favorite was E. L. Konigsburg. Then she discovered Cynthia Voigt, and she continues to read from this author's series. Sara does not like adventure or animal stories but regularly selects contemporary realistic fiction about children, especially when it involves issues with which she can identify and make personal connections. Luckily Sara has had teachers and librarians who have listened to her and helped her find the "right" books for her interests and abilities. They have also tried to broaden her reading interests and to introduce her to books set in other places and times, as well as books in other genres (e.g., fantasy and historical fiction).

Recognizing the variety of interests these good readers have underscores the need to provide a broad range of materials for reading instruction. We know children learn to love reading when they find their own interests and "themselves" represented in the materials they read. There are materials available at all grade levels on a wide range of topics. One of our responsibilities as teachers is to make sure that our selection includes some of each student's favorites.

Many children have not had experiences that make them "love" reading. For these children who are not as interested in reading as those described above, the need to take time to help link their interests to reading is even more important. We, as teachers, need to listen to our students and find some clear entry points for their reading. We can do this in several ways. We can confer with children about their interests and find connections between these interests and print materials. We can use interest inventories that help students identify their own experiences and preferences. We can read to children from a variety of materials and pique their curiosity about the world of literature and language. Most important, we can listen to and watch our students to find the right moments to connect them with reading materials. During the Olympics children generally get excited about the sports and about particular athletes. One whole school decided to learn about and follow the Olympic events. Children selected the athletes and events they wanted to study, and a daily TV news program was developed by the students to share their informative reporting. During the devastating tornado season of 2008, several teachers used this current event to introduce children to books and news articles about tornadoes, and many became engrossed in reading and learning. When one family had a new baby, another teacher found two books that helped ease the child's apprehensions and emphasized the wonder and mystery of new life. By listening carefully to students, we teachers can bring interests and print together for children.

Like Carlos's teacher, we must not only recognize students' preferences but help them expand the range of genres and materials they read through exposure and motivational experiences in our classrooms. We can do this in many ways. Some teachers have a list of genres they use each year and build units around them. Others have students independently select books and materials to read from a "genre wheel" and guide students to read from a wide variety of materials. Still other teachers do book talks and bring in interesting materials regularly to show students all the varieties of materials available. In many schools the librarians are wonderful resources in helping students expand their reading. They, too, often do book talks and introduce students to the range of materials available on whatever topic is selected. Librarians have been known to find just the right book for just the right occasion almost miraculously!

We address this whole topic of selection of materials for instruction more fully in a later chapter, but there are some basic considerations that we can hold in mind. First, because children have such varied interests, we need to make a wide variety of high-quality materials available to our students. This means that we need to introduce these materials to students and help them find their own preferences. Then we need to extend those preferences and deepen them. A major underutilized source of reading material is children's magazines. If we think of our adult reading, we often spend more time reading magazines and newspapers than any other materials. Second, many current materials include a high proportion of the content presented in visual form—in pictures, charts, cartoons, graphs, or tables. Publishers have shifted the ways they present information in response to the much more visual orientation and short span of children's interests. How do we read these "texts" where much of the content is presented in captions and diagrams? We need to help children become familiar with reading in this new mode, where attention to visual presentation of ideas is central to the comprehension of the whole text. Books like *The Magic School Bus* series are illustrative of this new type of presentation.

Children also need to learn to read from and with multiple sources on the same topic if they are to be successful in our society. With so many interesting informational books now available to young readers, as well as so much material on the Internet, we need to help children get in the habit of reading several sources to verify and clarify information. None of the information on the Internet has been reviewed for accuracy in the way material printed in books is. Any point of view or idea can be included on a website that children may find. Therefore, they need to learn to check information in multiple sources and to evaluate the more authoritative ones. We suggest ways to do this in Chapter 8 of this book. The habit of reading more than one source is also valuable when reading fiction. Comparing how different authors handle the same topics or themes gives young readers a deeper understanding of and respect for point of view and perspective in human experience, as well as commonalities across cultures.

Readers' Preferences in Styles of Engagement

The readers described above all have differences in the ways they engage best with print, in addition to their obvious preferences in genres and in kinds of materials. Some students fall into their books and become part of whatever the author has created, like our reader Sara. During silent sustained reading she loses herself in her reading and seems to forget where she is. Others in the class notice her facial responses to her reading; sometimes she even gasps or laughs audibly. Books take her places!

For other students, like Carlos, time at home is best for getting involved deeply in longer books. In class, he does best when focused on a text with a reading guide to help him. The noises and movements in the classroom distract him easily and he doesn't seem to have the same total identification with what he reads that characterizes Sara. Ken needs a computer at hand to pull together his ideas, and he doesn't seem as willing to lose himself in his reading. He stays outside but is very aware of what happens. Some of the other readers engage more deeply by using other senses. Maria needs to draw, and LaToya needs to turn things into rhyme and poetry, to comprehend print material fully and deeply. So not only do we teachers need different materials for such students, we need some options for reading and responding to print, even when the students are reading core books or working with a core text. Becoming engaged as a reader—understanding deeply and feeling the ideas—means different things for different readers.

Different social arrangements also come into play with our students' learning. Sara likes time alone and enjoys responding in her own journal to what she reads, though she is happy to be part of a response group after she is all done reading if it is a book she likes. Ken like to work in a group but focuses on being the leader, as does Carlos. These boys are good leaders, and other students generally follow their ideas and don't challenge their ideas much. When challenges do occur, they can create some tension in the groups, so their teachers are careful both to make the rules for small-group discussion and projects clear and to monitor the students' participation. LaToya and Nikki like to be active group members, and both share and listen well. LaToya helps draw others into the discussions by giving encouraging feedback when ideas are shared. Both girls like opportunities to create short dramas and Readers' Theater productions, and enjoy being part of a performing group. These children like having their performances and quick word play appreciated, and they need an audience for their efforts. Maria, by contrast, is another solitary learner who likes to get lost in her picture books. The pace of class discussions often causes her to fall behind and get frustrated, though she does like to partner with Nikki when they have chosen the same book. Jamie hardly ever demonstrates his understanding of what he reads well in a group setting. His word-processed papers and responses are much better reflections of his understanding and appreciation. He is likely in a group to try to do other work of his own, or just to drift off.

The ways teachers organize classroom activities and opportunities make a difference in how the students grow in their comprehension, too. We see how our good readers learn from and with each other. Ken helps others learn about the computer and how to use it to build knowledge and check their ideas against other sources. His ease with the computer helps others enjoy this form of learning. Because his teacher encourages students to work together and learn from each other, he has become a real resource. Students learn that they can value each other and do not have to depend solely on the teacher. In LaToya's classroom many visitors come and share their ideas about books. By hearing older students and adults who like reading talk about their experiences and favorites, the students acquire models for their own developing tastes and for their identification as parts of a literate community. The school itself has a commitment to "visible literacy," and ever since she was in the primary grades LaToya has enjoyed adults and older students who share their own reading. She even remembers a policeman who read to them in first grade. Each year the third graders have a special day when they dress up like their favorite book characters. The younger and older students get to guess who they are and can ask questions about the characters as the third graders visit each class. All of these experiences help create a community where reading and comprehending are valued and enjoyed. LaToya and her fellow students have learned a great deal from these regular shared experiences.

These students, like all others, have preferences in how they engage with other students in class. Some do better with discussion and verbal exchanges, some prefer individual engagement, and some need more teacher guidance and direct explanation. Their stamina and attention span for reading also vary; some need to be more physically active or socially engaged to make reading meaningful. So in a "good-comprehension classroom"—that is, a classroom where the teacher is ensuring that all students can develop their ability to read and comprehend with confidence—various groupings for learning must exist, both to let students work where they are strong and to help them develop new skills and stamina. Even though students clearly have preferences, a teacher's job is both to honor these preferences and to broaden the students' horizons. All students need to know how to become self-regulating readers. There will always be times when students must do work or read alone. Readers also must know how to participate in group discussion and work together. They will comprehend more fully as they learn to listen to classmates, extend discussion by sharing personal ideas, and participate positively in exchanges. Even the opportunity to summarize what one has read (like telling about a TV program or movie one has seen) is important, and this skill improves with practice. Oral reading, dramatic reading, and forms of interpretation provide powerful ways to help students connect the emotions and perspective of characters. Therefore, in teaching we must assess how our students engage most naturally and easily with reading, and we must support all of our students so they can feel comfortable and confident when operating in many ways as readers in and outside our classrooms.

Strategies Readers Possess

The students we have described vary in the types of strategies they employ when engaging with print material, just as they vary in the kinds of materials they like to read regularly. They are also in the process of developing different repertoires of strategies to fit different reading needs, purposes, and materials. Sara has a good understanding of story structure and characters and can engage personally and emotionally with a story. Her discussion skills and social sensitivity in discussion are well developed, and as a reader she identifies with adults, such as the librarian she admires. She is limited sometimes in her work with nonfiction and class text-books. Both her lack of motivation in these areas and her possible lack of skills need to be recognized and worked with, so she can become a fuller reader.

Ken sees the "big picture" in his work. He can formulate questions and orga-nize information from many sources to answer his own questions. He has also learned to create graphics that depict the relationships among ideas; he seems to work well with images. We don't know whether he uses these same imaging and organizing strategies when he reads fiction. He may, but his teachers need to find out more about ways to connect his various interests and extend his strategic pro-cessing. He is good at leading his group in inquiry and so has developed ways to describe what he does and how to engage others in the process. This probably means that he is developing metacognitive control over his reading.

Unlike Ken, Jamie focuses on details. He loves to amass esoteric information on all sorts of topics. However, he needs instruction on seeing the overall ways in which these details connect. His teacher is using graphic organizers to help round out his comprehension and also is focusing the critical reading of websites.

Carlos excels at school task reading. He has learned from instruction how to map chapters and apply this strategy to textbook learning. His basic comprehen-sion is always strong. He's a good student and learns quickly, but he needs adult or teacher input to get moving. He is just beginning to develop interest in and awareness of the fictional genres that are already familiar to his classmates. Under his teacher's guidance, he is now making more personal connections to what he reads and thinking of authors as people who share ideas. Carlos has also learned the importance of rereading when using printed material to perform tasks. He knows how to "fix up" his understanding when something does not make sense; he has learned to ask his parents for help. Now the teacher wants to find out whether he can turn to other resources (e.g., glossaries and dictionaries) to clarify ideas on his own.

LaToya and Nikki thrive on word play and performance but are less patient with genres that don't lend themselves to this exploration. Like Maria, they re-spond best to shorter text, shorter assignments, and opportunities to transform standard texts into nontraditional formats. They can use this interest in creating their own "texts" as a way of reviewing key ideas they read in other textbooks and stories. LaToya also makes personal connections with what she reads. Her habit of writing about her reading in her personal journal is a powerful strategy that she can elaborate on as she grows as a reader.

These students illustrate why we as teachers must provide instruction on read-ing comprehension strategies that can be applied to many different types of mate-rials, and must continually guide even good readers to broaden their strategies to meet the many needs of contemporary literacy. Ken can't always be the leader; Sara needs to deal with informational material, not just poetry or pictures. All the readers must deal with the structure and vocabulary of many genre and content areas. Our first task as teachers is to determine what strategies students use regularly and successfully and then to develop an instructional program that broadens their repertoires of strategies to include those useful for the major purposes of reading.

Good readers approach reading actively. First, we prepare before actually letting our eyes fall on the page. We reflect generally on the kind of material we are about to read. We think of the genre; perhaps something about the author has attracted us to the text. We may read the book's dust jacket and think about the summary provided there. We begin to activate our own information and experiences connected to the text. In this generally very rapid prereading activity, we also begin to form questions that will guide our reading: What is Dicey's problem? Where did the Great Pyramids come from? When did South Africa begin apartheid, and what really brought it to an end? What do girls in Native communities in Canada do to indicate their maturity? What teams won the games last night? How can we really deal with conflicts in our families among siblings? These are just brief examples of the kinds of questions that come to us as we begin to read.

The second general phase of reading occurs as we connect with the words and illustrations provided by the author. At this time, we are actively connecting ideas while reading and monitoring the meaning-making process. We connect ideas across sentences and paragraphs; we form images and predict where the author is taking us. We revise our ideas as we take in new information. When there is confusion, we may engage in ways of "fixing up" problems so that comprehension is ongoing.

During and after reading, we readers engage in reflection about what we have read. We usually connect it to other texts, events, and experiences in our own life. We reflect on the author's point of view and compare it with other experiences we have had: Does this make sense? Are there other ways of describing, explaining, or interpreting this? In this process we both summarize, reflect, and extend what we have read, making the act of reading our own and using what we have gained in a more global way.

An active, constructive process characterizes most reading. However, specific strategies are particularly suited to specific materials and purposes. For example, reading for a course in which where there will be an examination of the depth of our mastery of the material we may need to employ strategies that deepen our understanding and memory. In some cases, visualizing what we read helps create a deeper understanding. In other cases, underlining with a pen and/or making notes in the margin or on a separate sheet of paper helps us sort out very dense texts and create a sense of the relatedness of different parts. If there are many characters in a novel, then keeping a chart of names, relationships, and so on can deepen the reading. Rereading, note making, and rehearsing key ideas are just a few strategies for absorbing difficult content. Students need to know how and know when to use strategies that are most appropriate for particular tasks and materials. As teachers, we cannot simply define what our students already do well or what we like to teach. We need to have a clear sense of the range of strategies all readers should have at their disposal and to ensure that our students develop these. We need to begin with where our students are, and then to extend their strategic knowledge until they are competent with multiple types of texts and the various purposes for which we read.

Later in this book, we describe in detail several very useful strategies students can develop to increase their effectiveness as comprehenders. These include brainstorming and predicting before reading, visualizing, making maps and graphic organizers during reading, various forms of note making, writing two-column notes and double-entry journals, and many more. The number of ways to describe this active reading process is almost overwhelming, and most of us find some strategies we prefer over others to use in our teaching. What is most important is that we share with students the nature of reading in its multiple forms and purposes, and that we help them develop a repertoire of powerful strategies so reading is enjoyable and they comprehend successfully. The range of teaching strategies is great and is needed to motivate and interest the range of students in our classes. However, the number of actual reading comprehension strategies students need is much smaller.

Looking to the Future

When we think about our students as readers, we begin with a description of where they are today in their development. We also need to look ahead to see what and how they will need to read in the future. This leads us to an exploration of the various purposes for reading. A look at materials used for reading instruction over the last few decades points out that we have often depended on enjoyment of literature and practice with narratives to become good readers. Now there are so many different varieties of reading, and so many everyday demands, that we must go beyond narratives. Studies of the range of reading done by adults and students demonstrates that less than 25% of reading is done in narrative texts (Snowball, 1995). So, as teachers, we must extend what comes naturally to us—teaching with stories and pieces of literature that exemplify many forms of reading, so that students develop competence with multiple literacies. The range of interests in a normal classroom lends itself to this extension, because students bring so many preferences with them.

As teachers, we need to look at students' preferences in reading but also to consider the "big picture." What counts as literacy in today's society, and what kinds of uses do adults make of reading? From this forward look, it is apparent that literacy fulfills personal goals (pleasure, expression, confirmation of beliefs and religious values, etc.) and also is crucial for daily life (work, interactions at home) and for civic activities (political action, etc.). One of the clearest shifts in reading comes from the technological revolution in the use of the computer. Increasingly, much information and many business and personal communications come from interactions on computers. Readers will do well to be selective—to determine what sources and websites and what aspects of more general topics they want to pursue, and to think critically about what they are gaining in information.

When we think ahead to what children will need to be able to do in secondary school and postsecondary education, then our priorities have to include reading to learn. They must be able to comprehend very densely written and abstract material in a wide range of content areas. This leads us to know that we must help young readers develop strategies for dealing with textbooks, tables of contents, maps, and other simple book resources. We must also help them learn to use a variety of expository texts, functional materials, and sets of directions. Comprehension takes on new dimensions when we think of these reading challenges. At upper levels, most of us teachers assume that students can comprehend the basic ideas of texts; what we want is more thinking. We want problem solving and critical responses to ideas; we want students who can form interpretations and defend them. We lay the foundations for this in elementary and middle school, but the fruits of our efforts come throughout life.

Recognition of a broad view of reading comes from many sources and is reflected in the newer forms of national standardized assessments, especially the National Assessment of Educational Progress (NAEP). Most large-scale assessments now have passages that require the reading of narrative, poetry, informational texts, and functional reading (reading to perform a task). This broader definition of reading is also reflected in most state standards and related assessments. These public documents include the expectation that students will be able to read and construct meaning from individual pieces of text, to combine ideas across texts (intertextuality), and then to think critically about what they read. In states like Michigan and Illinois, some test items on the state assessments require students to include open-ended writing in their responses. In addition, several states include in their standards and some in their assessments expectations that students not only will read in more traditional ways but will be able to use technological resources, to select appropriate materials, and to create meaningful products as a result of their research and reading. (Two Illinois state goals, with standards that reflect these expectations, are presented in Figures 1.2 and 1.3. Figure 1.4 is Virginia's Grade Four standards.) Other state assessments, like those in Maryland, have recognized the need to use information and have created problem-solving tasks for groups of children to engage in over a period of 1 week as part of their state evaluation. So, whereas we teachers have traditionally looked at reading in elementary schools as primarily being for enjoyment, we now have to develop more functional

STATE GOAL 1: Read with understanding and fluency.

Why This Goal Is Important: Reading is essential. It is the process by which people gain information and ideas from books, newspapers, manuals, letters, contracts, advertisements and a host of other materials. Using strategies for constructing meaning before, during and after reading will help students connect what they read now with what they have learned in the past. Students who read well and widely build a strong foundation for learning in all areas of life.

A. Apply word analysis and vocabulary skills to comprehend selections.

EARLY ELEMENTARY	LATE ELEMENTARY	MIDDLE/JUNIOR HIGH SCHOOL	EARLY HIGH SCHOOL	LATE HIGH SCHOOL
1.A.1a Apply word analysis skills (e.g., phonics, word patterns) to recognize new words.	**1.A.2a** Read and comprehend unfamiliar words using root words, synonyms, antonyms, word origins and derivations.	**1.A.3a** Apply knowledge of word origins and derivations to comprehend words used in specific content areas (e.g., scientific, political, literary, mathematical).	**1.A.4a** Expand knowledge of word origins and derivations and use idioms, analogies, metaphors and similes to extend vocabulary development.	**1.A.5a** Identify and analyze new terminology applying knowledge of word origins and derivations in a variety of practical settings.
1.A.1b Comprehend unfamiliar words using context clues and prior knowledge; verify meanings with resource materials.	**1.A.2b** Clarify word meaning using context clues and a variety of resources including glossaries, dictionaries and thesauruses.	**1.A.3b** Analyze the meaning of words and phrases in their context.	**1.A.4b** Compare the meaning of words and phrases and use analogies to explain the relationships among them.	**1.A.5b** Analyze the meaning of abstract concepts and the effects of particular word and phrase choices.

B. Apply reading strategies to improve understanding and fluency.

EARLY ELEMENTARY	LATE ELEMENTARY	MIDDLE/JUNIOR HIGH SCHOOL	EARLY HIGH SCHOOL	LATE HIGH SCHOOL
1.B.1a Establish purposes for reading, make predictions, connect important ideas, and link text to previous experiences and knowledge.	**1.B.2a** Establish purposes for reading; survey materials; ask questions; make predictions; connect, clarify and extend ideas.	**1.B.3a** Preview reading materials, make predictions and relate reading to information from other sources.	**1.B.4a** Preview reading materials, clarify meaning, analyze overall themes and coherence, and relate reading with information from other sources.	**1.B.5a** Relate reading to prior knowledge and experience and make connections to related information.

(continued)

FIGURE 1.2. Illinois state goal 1 for English and language arts, and its accompanying standards. From Illinois State Department of Education (2007). Copyright © 1997–2008, Illinois State Board of Education, reprinted by permission. All rights reserved.

1.B.1b Identify genres (forms and purposes) of fiction, nonfiction, poetry and electronic literary forms.	**1.B.2b** Identify structure (e.g., description, compare/contrast, cause and effect, sequence) of nonfiction texts to improve comprehension.	**1.B.3b** Identify text structure and create a visual representation (e.g., graphic organizer, outline, drawing) to use while reading.	**1.B.4b** Analyze, interpret and compare a variety of texts for purpose, structure, content, detail and effect.	**1.B.5b** Analyze the defining characteristics and structures of a variety of complex literary genres and describe how genre affects the meaning and function of the texts.
1.B.1c Continuously check and clarify for understanding (e.g., reread, read ahead, use visual and context clues, ask questions, retell, use meaningful substitutions).	**1.B.2c** Continuously check and clarify for understanding (e.g., *in addition to previous skills*, clarify terminology, seek additional information).	**1.B.3c** Continuously check and clarify for understanding (e.g., *in addition to previous skills*, draw comparisons to other readings).	**1.B.4c** Read age-appropriate material with fluency and accuracy.	**1.B.5c** Evaluate a variety of compositions for purpose, structure, content and details for use in school or at work.
1.B.1d Read age-appropriate material aloud with fluency and accuracy.	**1.B.2d** Read age-appropriate material aloud with fluency and accuracy.	**1.B.3d** Read age-appropriate material with fluency and accuracy.		**1.B.5d** Read age-appropriate material with fluency and accuracy.

C. Comprehend a broad range of reading materials.

EARLY ELEMENTARY	LATE ELEMENTARY	MIDDLE/JUNIOR HIGH SCHOOL	EARLY HIGH SCHOOL	LATE HIGH SCHOOL
1.C.1a Use information to form questions and verify predictions.	**1.C.2a** Use information to form and refine questions and predictions.	**1.C.3a** Use information to form, explain and support questions and predictions.	**1.C.4a** Use questions and predictions to guide reading.	**1.C.5a** Use questions and predictions to guide reading across complex materials.
1.C.1b Identify important themes and topics.	**1.C.2b** Make and support inferences and form interpretations about main themes and topics.	**1.C.3b** Interpret and analyze entire narrative text using story elements, point of view and theme.	**1.C.4b** Explain and justify an interpretation of a text.	**1.C.5b** Analyze and defend an interpretation of text.
1.C.1c Make comparisons across reading selections.	**1.C.2c** Compare and contrast the content and organization of selections.	**1.C.3c** Compare, contrast and evaluate ideas and information from various sources and genres.	**1.C.4c** Interpret, evaluate and apply information from a variety of sources to other situations (e.g., academic, vocational, technical, personal).	**1.C.5c** Critically evaluate information from multiple sources.

FIGURE 1.2. *(continued)*

1.C.1d Summarize content of reading material using text organization (e.g., story, sequence).	**1.C.2d** Summarize and make generalizations from content and relate to purpose of material.	**1.C.3d** Summarize and make generalizations from content and relate them to the purpose of the material.	**1.C.4d** Summarize and make generalizations from content and relate them to the purpose of the material.	**1.C.5d** Summarize and make generalizations from content and relate them to the purpose of the material.
1.C.1e Identify how authors and illustrators express their ideas in text and graphics (e.g., dialogue, conflict, shape, color, characters).	**1.C.2e** Explain how authors and illustrators use text and art to express their ideas (e.g., points of view, design hues, metaphor).	**1.C.3e** Compare how authors and illustrators use text and art across materials to express their ideas (e.g., foreshadowing, flashbacks, color, strong verbs, language that inspires).	**1.C.4e** Analyze how authors and illustrators use text and art to express and emphasize their ideas (e.g., imagery, multiple points of view).	**1.C.5e** Evaluate how authors and illustrators use text and art across materials to express their ideas (e.g., complex dialogue, persuasive techniques).
1.C.1f Use information presented in simple tables, maps and charts to form an interpretation.	**1.C.2f** Connect information presented in tables, maps and charts to printed or electronic text.	**1.C.3f** Interpret tables that display textual information and data in visual formats.	**1.C.4f** Interpret tables, graphs and maps in conjunction with related text.	**1.C.5f** Use tables, graphs and maps to challenge arguments, defend conclusions and persuade others.

FIGURE 1.2. *(continued)*

reading that takes in all of the various purposes for which our students read now and will need to read in the future.

At the same time that reading assessments are changing to reflect new expectations, the national educational standards movement has also embraced a broad sense of what is important for good readers to be able to accomplish. Across the United States, groups of educators have spent a great deal of time discussing what is most important for students to know and to be able to do. The results of these discussions have been written in statements of standards and then benchmarks either at specific grade levels or for a few grades at a time. (For example, in Illinois, we have established benchmarks for the early elementary/primary level, up to and including grade 3; the intermediate level, for grades 3–6; and the middle/junior high level, for grades 6–8.)

As we worked to develop state standards, we had long discussions about the intermingling of process in Illinois statements (e.g., "make predictions") and content or outcome statements (e.g., "understand basic concepts or identify basic structure of the text"). We also felt that students should be aware of their own progress in making sense of text. Successful readers need this ability to self-monitor and to engage in effective "fix-up" strategies. Finally, we chunked many of our specific ideas under three key standards: "comprehend," "read strategi-

STATE GOAL 5: Use the language arts to acquire, assess and communicate information.

Why This Goal Is Important: To be successful in school and in the world of work, students must be able to use a wide variety of information resources (written, visual and electronic). They must also know how to frame questions for inquiry, identify and organize relevant information and communicate it effectively in a variety of formats. These skills are critical in school across all learning areas and are key to successful career and lifelong learning experiences.

A. Locate, organize, and use information from various sources to answer questions, solve problems and communicate ideas.

EARLY ELEMENTARY	LATE ELEMENTARY	MIDDLE/JUNIOR HIGH SCHOOL	EARLY HIGH SCHOOL	LATE HIGH SCHOOL
5.A.1a Identify questions and gather information.	**5.A.2a** Formulate questions and construct a basic research plan.	**5.A.3a** Identify appropriate resources to solve problems or answer questions through research.	**5.A.4a** Demonstrate a knowledge of strategies needed to prepare a credible research report (e.g., notes, planning sheets).	**5.A.5a** Develop a research plan using multiple forms of data.
5.A.1b Locate information using a variety of resources.	**5.A.2b** Organize and integrate information from a variety of sources (e.g., books, interviews, library reference materials, websites, CD/ROMs).	**5.A.3b** Design a project related to contemporary issues (e.g., real-world math, career development, community service) using multiple sources.	**5.A.4b** Design and present a project (e.g., research report, scientific study, career/higher education opportunities) using various formats from multiple sources.	**5.A.5b** Research, design and present a project to an academic, business or school community audience on a topic selected from among contemporary issues.

B. Analyze and evaluate information acquired from various sources.

EARLY ELEMENTARY	LATE ELEMENTARY	MIDDLE/JUNIOR HIGH SCHOOL	EARLY HIGH SCHOOL	LATE HIGH SCHOOL
5.B.1a Select and organize information from various sources for a specific purpose.	**5.B.2a** Determine the accuracy, currency and reliability of materials from various sources.	**5.B.3a** Choose and analyze information sources for individual, academic and functional purposes.	**5.B.4a** Choose and evaluate primary and secondary sources (print and nonprint) for a variety of purposes.	**5.B.5a** Evaluate the usefulness of information, synthesize information to support a thesis, and present information in a logical manner in oral and written forms.

(continued)

FIGURE 1.3. Illinois state goal 5 for English and language arts, and its accompanying standards. From Illinois State Department of Education (2007).

5.B.1b Cite sources used.	**5.B.2b** Cite sources used.	**5.B.3b** Identify, evaluate and cite primary sources.	**5.B.4b** Use multiple sources and multiple formats; cite according to standard style manuals.	**5.B.5b** Credit primary and secondary sources in a form appropriate for presentation or publication for a particular audience.

C. Apply acquired information, concepts and ideas to communicate in a variety of formats.

EARLY ELEMENTARY	LATE ELEMENTARY	MIDDLE/JUNIOR HIGH SCHOOL	EARLY HIGH SCHOOL	LATE HIGH SCHOOL
5.C.1a Write letters, reports and stories based on acquired information.	**5.C.2a** Create a variety of print and nonprint documents to communicate acquired information for specific audiences and purposes.	**5.C.3a** Plan, compose, edit and revise documents that synthesize new meaning gleaned from multiple sources.	**5.C.4a** Plan, compose, edit and revise information (e.g., brochures, formal reports, proposals, research summaries, analyses, editorials, articles, overheads, multimedia displays) for presentation to an audience.	**5.C.5a** Using contemporary technology, create a research presentation or prepare a documentary related to academic, technical or occupational topics and present the findings in oral or multimedia formats.
5.C.1b Use print, nonprint, human and technological resources to acquire and use information.	**5.C.2b** Prepare and deliver oral presentations based on inquiry or research.	**5.C.3b** Prepare and orally present original work (e.g., poems, monologues, reports, plays, stories) supported by research.	**5.C.4b** Produce oral presentations and written documents using supportive research and incorporating contemporary technology.	**5.C.5b** Support and defend a thesis statement using various references including media and electronic resources.
		5.C.3c Take notes, conduct interviews, organize and report information in oral, visual and electronic formats.	**5.C.4c** Prepare for and participate in formal debates.	

FIGURE 1.3. *(continued)*

Grade Four

The fourth-grade student will communicate orally in large- and small-group settings. Students will read classics and contemporary literature by a variety of authors. A significant percentage of reading material will relate to the study of math, science, and history and social science. The student will use text organizers, summarize information, and draw conclusions to demonstrate reading comprehension. Reading, writing, and reporting skills support an increased emphasis on content-area learning and on utilizing the resources of the media center, especially to locate and read primary sources of information (speeches and other historical documents) related to the study of Virginia. Students will plan, write, revise, and edit narratives and explanations. The student will routinely use information resources and word references while writing.

Oral Language

4.1 The student will use effective oral communication skills in a variety of settings.
- Present accurate directions to individuals and small groups.
- Contribute to group discussions.
- Seek the ideas and opinions of others.
- Begin to use evidence to support opinions.

4.2 The student will make and listen to oral presentations and reports.
- Use subject-related information and vocabulary.
- Listen to and record information.
- Organize information for clarity.

Reading/Literature

4.3 The student will read and learn the meanings of unfamiliar words.
- Use knowledge of word origins; synonyms, antonyms, and homonyms; and multiple meanings of words.
- Use word-reference materials including the glossary, dictionary, and thesaurus.

4.4 The student will read fiction and nonfiction, including biographies and historical fiction.
- Explain the author's purpose.
- Describe how the choice of language, setting, and information contributes to the author's purpose.

Writing

4.7 The student will write effective narratives and explanations.
- Focus on one aspect of a topic.
- Develop a plan for writing.
- Organize writing to convey a central idea.
- Write several related paragraphs on the same topic.
- Utilize elements of style, including word choice, tone, voice, and sentence variation.
- Edit final copies for grammar, capitalization, punctuation, and spelling.
- Use available technology.

- Compare the use of fact and fantasy in historical fiction with other forms of literature.
- Explain how knowledge of the lives and experiences of individuals in history can relate to individuals who have similar goals or face similar challenges.

4.5 The student will demonstrate comprehension of a variety of literary forms.
- Use text organizers such as type, headings, and graphics to predict and categorize information.
- Formulate questions that might be answered in the selection.
- Make inferences using information from texts.
- Paraphrase content of selection, identifying important ideas and providing details for each important idea.
  Describe relationship between content and previously learned concepts or skills.
- Write about what is read.

4.6 The student will read a variety of poetry.
- Describe the rhyme scheme (approximate, end, and internal).
- Identify the sensory words used and their effect on the reader.
- Write rhymed, unrhymed, and patterned poetry.

4.8 The student will edit final copies of writings.
- Use subject-verb agreement.
- Avoid double negatives.
- Use pronoun "I" correctly in compound subjects.
- Use commas in series, dates, and addresses.

Research

4.9 The student will use information resources to research a topic.
- Construct questions about a topic.
- Collect information, using the resources of the media center.
- Evaluate and synthesize information for use in writing.
- Use available technology.

FIGURE 1.4. Virginia state standards document.

cally," and "use word analysis and decoding skills." However, we also knew that how readers use their reading abilities is critical. We crafted another standard for inquiry and research, indicating our recognition that readers read differently when they want to find information to create some persuasive or informative product. Because multimedia presentations are a key to successful communication, we embedded use of technology in how students access and present information. Individual districts are also concerned that students develop and use technology in their literacy experiences. (See Figure 1.5 for an example of a local district's standards in this area.)

In reviewing other states' standards, we have found many similarities. No longer is reading a single narrative all that we want students to be able to do. Reading across different texts, reading critically, and reading that enables students to synthesize and represent ideas are all important comprehension outcomes. This certainly does raise the stakes in literacy. There is also new emphasis on the processes

Technology Scope and Sequence—6-7-8

Keyboarding

- Locate Home Row
- Use two hands when typing
- Type 20 wpm in keyboarding program
- Consistently use Home Row

Painting/Drawing

- Use the floor fill (paint bucket)
- Use the pencil tool
- Create rectangles/ovals
- Resize/scale graphic
- Use the paintbrush/adjust paintbrush size
- Save/retrieve paint or draw document
- Know the difference between paint and draw
- Import a graphic into a paint/draw program
- Use group/ungroup/lock/unlock

Multimedia (MM)

- Understand purpose of multimedia
- Add test to MM presentation
- Import/create graphics to enhance MM presentation
- Add sound to MM presentation
- Add motion to MM presentation

Telecommunications

- Navigate the Internet with use of a browser
- Perform search for specific information
- Understand acceptable-use policy
- Understand modem vs. network connection
- Compose e-mail
- Retrieve e-mail
- Send e-mail

Research Tools

- Use electronic research tools
- Use an online catalog
- Gather data with computerized sensory measuring devices (probes)
- Evaluate the value, authority, and quality of reference resource
- Choose most appropriate reference sources
- Use appropriate search techniques to search for information (CD-ROMs, Web)

FIGURE 1.5. An example of a local district's standards for development and use of technology in literacy experiences. Used by permission of Northbrook (Illinois) District 27.

of reading, matching strategies with text structure and purpose, and demonstrating comprehension in a variety of ways—from recognition of important author ideas to interpretation and application of these ideas in new forms. Many also include critical evaluation of ideas and the creative use of information in new ways.

Workplaces also require literate performance and have become concerned in recent years about the level of literacy of high school graduates. As an indication of their concern about the preparation needed for workers in the future, they have created statements of what they think citizens need to be able to do. The SCANS Report (U.S. Department of Labor, 1991) (developed to reflect business needs) emphasizes that we must prepare citizens for the work force who can communicate, solve problems, work on teams, and read and think critically. This report stresses that our society will need young people who can identify problems, ask appropriate questions, locate resources and information, and formulate and test solutions to the problems. The ability to communicate effectively what they find is also valuable.

Think about what you consider essential for your students to do well if they are to be good comprehenders. Are their personal selection of reading materials and engagement in reading important? Is the ability to discuss with others what they like about a story essential? Is flexible vocabulary development one of your concerns? Where does the use of informational, especially expository, text enter into your expectations? Do you watch for and evaluate strategy use and flexibility in your young readers? Do you expect your students to be able to monitor their own comprehension and correct themselves when meaning goes awry?

Putting It All Together

We have begun our book by focusing on particular students in classrooms and then have introduced the perspective of the larger society, with an emphasis on how standards and assessment demands are changing. We want to get you to think about the richness and complexity of the terms "good reader" and "good comprehender" from both of these important perspectives. As teachers, we always need to balance what we know about children and their individual development with what we know about the social context and expectations in which they live and grow. Our jobs are to create classrooms in which both perspectives are reflected. By thinking of the larger picture—the picture of the world beyond the individual learner—we can make wiser decisions about the use of our time and the ways we scaffold for learning. Our vision becomes clearer.

As teachers, we must think about our students as individuals, too. We hope that the students described in this chapter can help us focus on the need to think about the wide variety in the individuals we want to nurture and help develop into competent and flexible readers and thoughtful members of society. As we have looked at some typical good comprehenders, we have recognized both their commonalities and their differences. We have discussed these as differences in preferences for materials, differences in engagement, and differences in strategies. We realize that all these students are likely to be found in any one classroom. This variety does not mean that for us as teachers, the task is an impossible one. Rather, it means that in an organized and planned curriculum, we need to account for each of these issues and to plan for variety.

As we recognize individuality and honor it in how we provide activities in the classroom, we also know that part of our role as teachers is to extend our students' knowledge and skills to ensure their success in the future. We need to begin by discovering the different preferences of our students, and then find materials that will stimulate them to read more deeply in their areas of interest. We also need to extend their reading to a much broader range of materials and genres. We must observe students' preferred styles of engaging with reading, noting where and how they read most effectively and how they like to share their responses to their reading. When these varieties are made public within the classroom, all students can learn from each other and develop a more flexible repertoire of styles of engagement. As teachers, we also need to watch our students to determine what strategies they use while reading. These strengths can then be built on both individually and for the whole class. New strategies can be introduced to extend students' successes with the broadening range and difficulty of print materials and books students encounter in literacy-rich classrooms.

Teachers regularly do a great deal to create reading comprehension programs that work for their own students. Much of this comes almost automatically after a few years of experience. At first it may seem overwhelming. We hope it won't feel that way for long! Focusing on major priorities and involving the students in creating their own reading programs can make teaching a most exciting and enjoyable collaboration. The books, newspapers, technological resources, and magazines available today are outstanding. To make our task more manageable in this book, we have focused on the three major dimensions of program planning that correspond to the three aspects of differences among readers.

The first dimension of planning is providing a rich variety of materials. In Chapter 3 we provide practical examples of ways in which your materials collection can provide the appropriate variety for your students. This doesn't necessarily demand a bigger budget, just a wiser way of thinking about what you purchase and how to locate other resources. A good thing to remember is that a teacher doesn't need to teach directly with all these materials. Building in self-selection and personal reading time ensures that students will be exposed to a variety of materials. Teacher-guided instruction can expose them to the genres that are appropriate for each age level.

The second dimension is to consider varieties of engagement with text. We know that students vary in their preferences. What we as teachers need to do is to scaffold their learning so that they can become effective in a few key structures. These should include individual reading, such as that done in sustained silent reading or in Readers' Workshop. The students also need to participate in paired and small-group reading experiences. And, finally, they need to participate in teacher-guided reading on a regular basis.

Third, we have seen that students naturally choose from a variety of strategies when engaging in reading. Maria makes cartoon notes; LaToya writes down fragments in her journal; Ken uses the computer to record; Carlos uses study guides. Classrooms can make use of these naturally chosen strategies by having students make their preferred strategies visible in group work. This also allows teachers to introduce new strategies that can be effective alternatives and to discuss when a preferred strategy may not be useful in a particular instance. In later chapters, we look at strategic reading in general (Chapter 4) and through specific lenses, as varied by genre and purpose.

Purpose is the last issue we have raised in this chapter. It's clear that we all read for our own purposes, and that these are many and varied. For the classroom, we want to look both at purposes that emerge naturally and at those that our curriculum and school learning dictate, that match our standards, and that prepare kids for the future. This means not only reading literature for personal aesthetic response, but also reading for information, reading to solve problems, and reading to perform tasks. We also recognize that society and schooling demand their own purposes for reading. Therefore, what need to be included in our classrooms are not only what students themselves have as personal purposes, but also what we as educators know the students will need to be able to do to successfully negotiate the variety of reading tasks they encounter as they grow.

Think, now, of what you most want and need to learn. After you read Chapter 2, look over the rest of the book and find chapters that will be most helpful as your starting points. Then fill in additional information and consider alternatives suggested in the book. We hope that as you are reading, you will try the general ideas against what you are doing now. We also hope you will engage in using some of the specific teaching ideas with children you are teaching to read well. It is as you make the vision real that comprehension and implementation come together.

CHAPTER 2

A Closer Look at Comprehension
Context, Processes, Strategies, and Instruction

In Chapter 1, we introduced you to a variety of good readers, to illustrate the fact that the term "good comprehender" is wide enough to describe a variety of different reading behaviors. Just as we all look a bit different, so each of us puts a slightly different "spin" on what we understand, based on the experiences we bring to reading, our own interests and inclinations, and our strengths and learning styles. But in the same way that, underneath all that surface variety of human appearance and performance, all human skeletons are organized in a similar way, so the process of reading and "big moves"—the big strategies that underpin good comprehension—have some similarity. In this chapter (see the graphic organizer in Figure 2.1), we examine the "skeleton" of comprehension—what strategies readers need to master for good comprehension. We focus on the strategic and constructive aspects of our model of reader-based comprehension.

What Carlos, Ken, Jamie, Maria, LaToya, Sara, and Nikki (see Chapter 1) all have in common are a solid underpinning of reading strategies and the persistence and stamina to complete their reading tasks, both personal ones and school ones, successfully. Let's look further at Maria to examine the concept of comprehension as a strategic process in more detail. Maria watched a program on PBS that really captured her interest. It was about the migration of the monarch butterflies to Mexico. She became intrigued and went online where she found a lot of good information at both the *bsi.montana.edu/web/kidsbutterfly/* and the Callaway Gardens Butterfuly Center at *www.georgiaencyclopedia.org/nge/Multimedia.jsp?id=m-3977*. She also went to her school library and found the books *Monarchs* (Lasky, 1993) and *The Life Cycle of a Butterfly* (Kalman & Reiach, 2002) in her classroom library. As she read, she enjoyed the texts and pictures, which con-

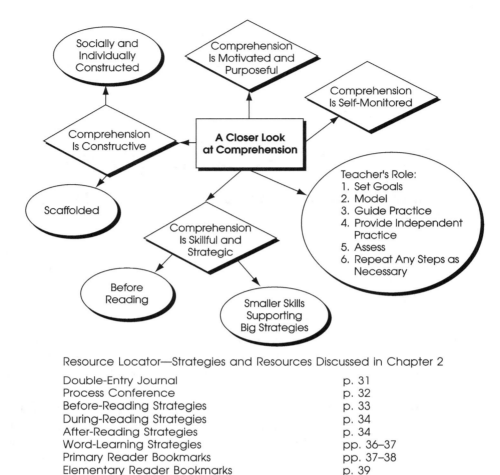

FIGURE 2.1. Graphic organizer for Chapter 2.

firmed what she had learned on TV and added new knowledge to what she had already learned. She developed a personal interest as she constructed her own knowledge base. She thus became "engaged" in the process of learning about butterflies. Engagement has several characteristics: motivation, purpose, skills and strategies, knowledge, and self-regulation. It is also a social activity as well as an individual one. Let's look at each as we think about Maria.

Comprehension Is Motivated and Purposeful

Maria started looking for books on butterflies every time she went to the library, and her fascination made it easy for her family and friends to buy her birthday presents. Soon her room was full of butterfly books and butterfly posters; she wore butterfly clips in her hair and drew butterflies on all her folders. Gradually, as she became a butterfly expert, her questions became more specific. For example, she decided that she wanted to know more about the monarch's life cycle. In *An Extraordinary Life: The Story of a Monarch Butterfly* (Pringle, 1997), she looked at the table of contents and saw a chapter titled "An Extraordinary Life." Rather than thumbing through the whole book, she went immediately to that chapter and found that it *was* a detailed description of the monarch's mating habits, birth, development, and life cycle. She started looking at the indices of new books for this information, and looked on the World Wide Web as well.

Maria began a notebook of drawings, with descriptions of the different types of butterflies she knew. Her girlfriend, Nikki, started to look at some of the books and began writing poems with the first letter of each line starting out with a different variety of butterfly. The two pals were called "the butterfly girls" by their classmates, and they shared some of their learning with the first-grade class when they visited their "reading buddies" in that class. When their own class went on to its next unit, which was on New Zealand, the girls carried over their interest to this new topic as well.

Thinking about Maria, and the many kids who become "hooked" on dinosaurs, American Girl dolls, or other topics, we can see that comprehension is an interest-driven process where the purpose for reading can change over time. Maria had an interest in what she was reading and had questions she wanted to answer. At first, her question was just to know "more." Later her questions became detailed, specific, and sophisticated. After reading the Lasky (1993) book and *Where Butterflies Grow* (Ryder, 1989), she became interested in the monarch's life cycle, leading her to the Pringle (1997) book. Her search process also changed as her purpose changed. Rather than looking at titles alone, she moved to examining tables of contents for likely chapters and read part of books or determined her own order for reading depending on her purpose. Finally, as her interest grew and she went beyond monarchs to other butterflies, she would consult the index first when she wanted information on particular butterflies and moths. Maria, always the artist, also looked for excellent illustrations and gravitated toward books in which the illustrations and diagrams carry a significant amount of information, such as *Amazing Butterflies and Moths* (Still, 1991).

Comprehension Is a Process That Is Constructive

What we have seen Maria doing is what researchers have found most good comprehenders do. Comprehension doesn't "happen" at one point; rather, it is a process that takes place over time. During this time, good readers are active in constructing meaning through the processes of interacting or transacting with what they read and integrating this knowledge with what they already know (Harvey & Goudvis, 2007; Anderson, Hiebert, Scott, & Wilkinson, 1985; Paris & Oka, 1986; Rosenblatt, 1985). Our knowledge and experiences, as well as our present context, influence how we understand, value, and remember what we read (Pearson, 1985; Rumelhart, 1975). Even perception is affected by knowledge and context. If you were shown Figure 2.2 and were then asked, "What letter is this?," most likely you would say "B." But if the question was "What number is this?," then you would probably interpret the same marks on the page as "13." We react in this way, attributing different meanings to the same physical signs, because our knowledge is organized into structures called "schemata" (plural for "schema"). A schema is a "mental information organizer" that helps us make sense of what we see, hear, or otherwise experience. We fit new information into an existing schema, which also "fills in the blanks" of what we may not directly perceive. For example, if you are walking down a street and see a flashing sign "La Casa de Ramón" over a glass-fronted room with tables, chairs, and flatware, you will probably think "restaurant," activating your schema for "restaurant" and all your prior knowledge. You know that if you go in, someone will take your order, you'll eat, and you'll pay for your dinner. Even though no one tells you this directly, activating the "restaurant" schema allows you to construct this understanding, using what you experience and what you already know.

Schemata are linked as well. "La Casa de Ramón" will activate your "Mexican" schema, and you won't be expecting Italian food. But schemata are changeable as well. If you go into the Helman Afghan Restaurant, you will find that some cultures use bread, not flatware, to pick up and eat food. So you expand, refine, and change your schemata as well. And, because of our cultural differences, we have differently tuned schemata that give rise to different predictions and interpretations. Sometimes these can lead to misconceptions, as when (after agreeing "Let's go out to eat") you dress for a fancy French restaurant and your date shows up to take you to Ye Local Greasy Spoon.

But let's go back to Maria and her butterfly learning. First we can think about the *process* Maria was engaged in. Her comprehension was a result of building knowledge, reading actively for specific purposes, and doing something with her knowledge. The process of full comprehension involved her in strategic actions before, during, and after reading. Before reading, she formulated some questions and

FIGURE 2.2. The knowledge- and context-dependent nature of perception: Is this the letter "B" or the number "13"?

made some predictions about content. For example, after Maria looked through *Amazing Moths and Butterflies* just to find out a bit more about monarchs, the mention of butterfly migration for egg laying stimulated her desire to know more about this process. So she went to *An Extraordinary Life: The Story of a Monarch Butterfly* with these questions: "What is the life cycle of the butterfly like? How long does it take to become an adult?" These questions became her purposes for reading and caused her to use the table of contents to decide where to begin reading—in this case, the fourth chapter of the book.

During reading, she answered some of her own questions and refined or changed her predictions, adding new predictions and questions as her knowledge grew. She had thought that it takes a day or two for a butterfly to mate and lay eggs, and that the eggs mature quickly. After reading, she realized that the mating and egg-storing process takes a long time, and that the migration is for the purpose of finding the right spot to lay eggs. She did this not only individually but in concert with Nikki, her friend and co-investigator, who did a time line of a butterfly's mating and migration for her. But she still didn't know much about the maturation process. So she left this reading with a new question—"How do the eggs mature?"—which led her to look for more books. We can see, then, that for Maria comprehension was built over time, becoming richer and deeper as she engaged with the text and her knowledge in a lot of different ways.

It's also clear that the process Maria was engaged in was *constructive*: She was building knowledge bit by bit, not just storing it away through rote memorization. She knew something about migratory birds to start with, and she thought that the process of butterfly migration might be similar to the migration of birds as part of their life cycle. At first she thought that all butterflies migrate, but she learned through her reading that this is not true of all species. She created categories of knowledge about how butterflies look, whether they migrate, and how they reproduce. She then built on these first categories of knowledge to ask, and try to answer, questions about protective coloration, environmental impact, and other more sophisticated topics. It was a case of "the more you learn . . . the more you learn." For all of us, as we learn more concepts and vocabulary about a topic, we are able to learn more about the topic. This is the idea behind cultural literacy and schema elaboration: We add new information to existing categories, elaborating them; we add categories; and sometimes we discard categories or modify them drastically. Besides how Maria learned and changed, we have also seen that her interest "infected" her pal Nikki. This leads us into the social dimension of comprehension.

Comprehension Is Socially Constructed

We can also learn something about teaching by looking at what happened with Maria and her best friend, Nikki, as they interacted with one another and with the books they were reading. Nikki got "into" butterfly books because of her friendship with Maria. Gradually she started becoming engaged with these books because she liked to talk and spend time with Maria, and she realized that the pictures and vocabulary inspired her favorite type of response. She could use the information to talk to her best friend, and she could respond in a different way, with her poetry.

Even though some of the more sophisticated books Maria was beginning to read were a bit hard for her, Nikki helped her by explaining some of the harder concepts and assisting with the vocabulary. And Maria's ability to draw helped Nikki learn by asking specific questions: "What color is that butterfly? Do the wings have curves? Spots?" This helped her represent her learning in another way. This is an example of what educational theorists call "social construction" (Snow, 2002). The two girls were able to learn more together than they could individually, because they motivated and supported one another. Maria's artistic ability helped Nikki, and Nikki's verbal ability aided Maria. They supported each other in learning things they would be less successful at learning alone—a process sometimes called scaffolding.

Comprehension Is Scaffolded

Anyone who has ever taught a child to ride a bike knows what "scaffolded" instruction and learning is. You don't give the child 10 minutes of skill lessons on pedaling, 10 minutes on balancing, 10 minutes on ringing the bell, and so on; you put the child on the bike so he or she can get the "feel" of the whole activity. The goal is to provide just enough help so that the child can succeed.

But you also don't just go sit on the porch and have a cool drink while the child tries to ride. Rather, you run alongside the bike at first (or use training wheels) and hold on, letting go when the child is riding well, catching on when support is needed. The learner is put on a bike of the right size, set down to practice in a safe spot, and given praise for every little thing he or she learns. This is scaffolded instruction. Learning things with the help of another—things that a child can't learn alone—is called "learning in the zone of proximal development" (Vygotsky, 1978). It is learning that can happen because it is supported by a more knowledgeable other—in this case, a parent who is a skilled bike rider. The parent's support, the training wheels, the right-size bike, and the safe place all help the young bike rider get started and do something he or she would not be able to do alone. As the child can take more control of the process, the parent gradually steps back, removing the scaffolding piece by piece and letting the child take over.

Bike riding instruction is a perfect example of scaffolded instruction and is analogous to what a good teacher does every day. Teachers give their students "right-size" material. They make the learning situation "safe" for the students by allowing them to experiment with the failure and success that entails. In Maria's classroom, her teacher, Susan, provided the scaffold of good instruction (which we highlight at the end of this chapter). Susan also scaffolded Maria's learning in many less formal but powerful ways. One way was by suggesting that Maria keep a double-entry journal for her research (see Figure 2.3), putting questions on one side and information on the other. Susan used small Post-It notes to suggest ideas for questions and information sources in the journal. She also helped Maria locate appropriate books and websites, and even connected her with a local lepidopterist for an interview.

When things Maria found were too difficult for her, Susan helped her with paraphrases, showed her how to break the text into small parts that made more sense, or showed her how to use the diagrams to help understand the text. She presented lessons on paraphrasing, modeled her own paraphrasing process by walking Maria and Nikki through it, and gave them graphic templates to help. Sometimes Susan helped with the vocabulary or read things to Maria that were beyond her reading level but not beyond her comprehension level. And, as Maria and Nikki developed the strategies, Susan stepped back so they could gradually take control of the process. In this stepping back and relinquishing of control, Susan had reasonable expectations for her students, requiring not perfection but gradual development. As any parent knows, learning to make a bed has some messy intervening stages where the parent could do a better job than the child, but the parent has to suffer some ragged corners to give the child enough room to make a transition to the parental standard.

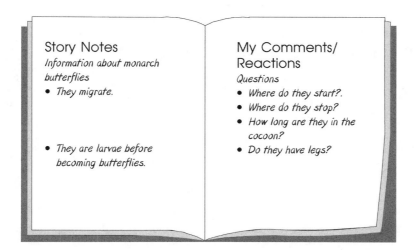

FIGURE 2.3. Maria's double-entry journal on butterflies.

Both Maria and Nikki also had "process conferences" with Susan regularly (Daniels & Bizar, 1999). In these conferences, the questions "What are you working on? How is it going? What are you going to do next?" helped the girls structure their work and keep on track. It also helped Susan determine how she could provide materials, ideas, and guidance for the next step to keep the girls moving forward.

It's clear that the process Maria and Nikki were engaged in was individually as well as socially constructive. Each girl had her own questions and slightly different interests. But this individual learning took place in a rich social context and with the aid of scaffolding. Through their interactions and their responses to one another; Susan's modeling, instruction, questions, comments, and suggestions; and the comments of their other classmates and the adults they talked to, their knowledge was built and elaborated. Figure 2.4 illustrates the model for the process of comprehension in which Maria and Nikki were engaged.

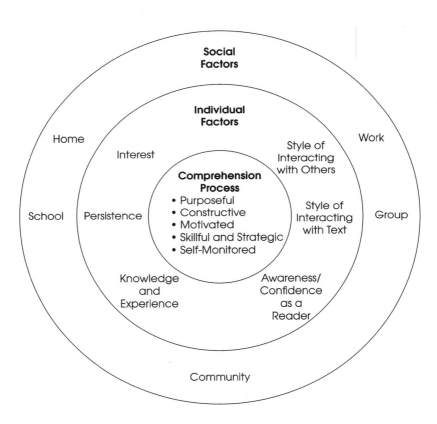

FIGURE 2.4. A model of comprehension as a constructive process strongly influenced by both social and individual factors.

Comprehension Is Skillful and Strategic

A great deal of research has explored and supported the notion that comprehension is a process demanding strategic approaches. Good comprehenders have learned that they have control of the reading process. They actively construct meaning as they read, and they also direct their own comprehending (Pressley, 2000; Snow, 2002; Paris, Lipson, & Wixson, 1983) by using basic strategies and by monitoring their own understanding (Baker & Brown, 1984). They know how reading works because they have knowledge about how sounds, letters, and print work ("declarative" knowledge); they know what strategies to use to help them understand ("procedural" knowledge); and they know when to use which strategies ("conditional" knowledge).

Researchers also suggest that good readers have plans for comprehending, even though these plans can vary for different types of text and different learning tasks. We'll try to begin making sense of these plans by talking about some "big strategies." These strategies are moves and actions that readers of all levels engage in all the time while reading almost all materials. We call them "strategies" because they can be consciously controlled by readers, even though they may be applied almost unconsciously during easy reading and/or when readers are skilled in them. A good way to think of these are as the basic strategies readers use before, during, and after reading.

"Big" Strategies in Good Comprehension

We have looked at Maria and Nikki as cases of engaged readers and good comprehenders. Important components of their reading are the strategies they utilize that lie at the center of our model. Let's review these strategies to see whether we can generate lists that will be useful for the classroom.

Maria and Nikki used some successful strategies before reading. These strategies, which all engaged readers rely on (consciously or unconsciously), are as follows:

- *Previewing the text* by looking at the title, the pictures, the graphics, and other relevant items (chapter headings, summaries, etc.), to evoke ideas, thoughts, and relevant memories and experiences. This starts to activate what a reader already knows; it "primes the pump."
- *Predicting from the preview* what is already known about the topic, content, and/or genre that can help the reader understand, as well as what is known about the form of the reading material. This previewing helps the reader draw on background knowledge about both the content and the type

of reading material. For example, if there are time lines in the material, chronology is important to this piece of reading material. Perhaps it's historical description or biography.

- *Setting purposes for reading by asking questions* that need to be answered.
- *Choosing an appropriate strategy* based on predictions and questions ("I'm going to skim this quickly to find out where he is," or "I am going to read the summary of this physics chapter first to get the overall gist").

Maria and Nikki's actual reading didn't just consist of passively running through the pages. Rather, during reading, "the butterfly girls" were active as they read. The strategies engaged comprehenders pursue during reading are the following:

- *Checking understanding* by keeping track of the gist of the material. This can be done by paraphrasing, by imaging, or by asking, "Does this make sense?"
- *Integrating the new information with what is already known* by making connections, making inferences, creating images, or adding elaborations to what the author says.
- *Monitoring comprehension* by using all cueing systems to figure out unknown words, by determining what is important in the reading material, and by using "fix-up" strategies (such as rereading and reading ahead) when difficulties are encountered.
- *Continuing to predict/question*, to refine those predictions and answer or reformulate the questions, and to ask new questions.

After reading, Maria and Nikki didn't just stop reading; they reflected on and used their new knowledge. These are the strategies good comprehenders employ after reading:

- *Summarizing and synthesizing what has been read* by dealing with the plot and/or central ideas, as well as the author's purpose and perspective. This constructs a meaning for the whole that goes beyond the meaning of the individual parts read (chapters, sections, etc.).
- *Responding appropriately:* personally, critically/evaluatively, and/or creatively.
- *Reading multiple sources and cross-checking information* when appropriate, or making other connections across texts and knowledge types.
- *Checking for fulfillment of the purpose of reading.* Were questions answered? Was the author's presentation adequate? Does the reader need or desire to read or learn more or search further for information?
- *Using what is read* in some application.

All of these sets of strategies—ones used before, during, and after reading—assist readers in being active, constructive readers who can gain and use information.

Smaller Skills Supporting Big Strategies

Along with the big moves that make up the big strategies, there are also supporting moves—the smaller skills that allow the big strategies to work. For example, one big strategy is for readers to keep track of the gist of what they are reading. To do this, they create a model of the story, article, or textbook chapter they are reading as they go along.

A lot of supporting skills are employed in this process. For example, in reading *Amelia Bedelia* (Parish, 1963) and its sequels, a reader needs to realize that language can be interpreted in both a literal and a figurative sense. One instance of this occurs when Mrs. Rogers tells Amelia to "draw the drapes" (see Figure 2.5). The reader's understanding of the literal and figurative meanings of that phrase

So Amelia Bedelia sat right down and she drew those drapes.

FIGURE 2.5. An example of the literal versus figurative meanings of language: Amelia Bedelia "draws the drapes." From Parish (1963, pp. 26–27). Text copyright 1963 by Margaret Parish; illustrations copyright 1963 by Fritz Siebel. Used by permission of HarperCollins Publishers.

helps him or her to create the meaning of the text, to enjoy its humor, and later to generalize across the other *Amelia Bedelia* books.

Similarly, for Maria and Nikki, *The Butterfly Alphabet* (Sandved, 1996) became predictable because each page had the same pattern. They looked at each picture to relate it to a letter of the alphabet, and then looked for the rhythm and rhyme of the poetry on the page. The skill of seeing and using these patterns allowed them to use the structure of the text for understanding. This is another way in which a smaller skill supports a larger strategy.

What else can we learn by looking at Maria's activities? We can see that strategies and skills change and develop over time. As Maria got more curious, she started reading her books differently—looking for specific cues in the index and the table of contents for the categories of questions she had. She also kept a small notebook with her pictures and notes. When she went on the World Wide Web, she often found sophisticated scientific information that was difficult for her. She used the pictures to help her understand, and she started a list of butterfly words that were hard for her, like "lepidopterist." She began to realize that "lepi-" is a word part associated with butterflies when she saw "lepidoptera" as part of so many butterfly names. She was approaching the process strategically, varying what she did depending on her purpose. This is a mark of a true strategic reader.

One thing to note is that these strategies and skills become more sophisticated as readers encounter more sophisticated materials. When Maria's older brother, Hector, helped the girls research butterflies in his high school science text, he needed to use headings and subheadings to locate information on species of butterflies. He also used scientific diagrams to understand and to explain to the girls what a taxonomy is. Strategies become more complex and refined as readers grow.

Comprehension Is Self-Monitored and Self-Regulated

As Maria and Nikki learned more and more about butterflies, they added to their knowledge, refined their own predictions, tried to clarify what they were thinking, and changed their thinking when necessary. When a book was confusing, they worked together to figure out what the author was saying; they would sometimes back up, reread, or look for other information. They would ask their teacher or another student for help when they got totally stuck or would check out their thinking with other media. All of these are examples of "self-regulation"—a metacognitive activity that involves self-evaluation of knowledge and learning and taking steps to "fix up" comprehension when difficulties are encountered.

Self-regulation really was apparent when Maria and Nikki would come to a word they didn't know. They would use the following core word-learning strategy to help them figure it out:

What do I do when I come to a word I don't know?
I think about what might make sense.
I use my word analysis skills, including phonics and structure.
I use the context for meaning.
I propose a word.
I check with the larger context for sense.
I use a reference or try again if I need more information.

They used all their knowledge of phonics, syntax, word structure, and semantics to help them over the hump of an unknown word, applying this strategy both for decoding and for meaning. Knowing that "lepidoptera" is the Latin word for butterfly, and knowing that an artist studies and works in art, the girls could figure out that a "lepidopterist" studies butterflies. This was a small move, but one that helped them create a meaningful interpretation of what they were reading.

Reading specialist Julie Saum Gedgaud, teacher Anne Cochran Kehoe, and their colleagues at Highland School in Downers Grove (Illinois) District 58 use student bookmarks to help remind their students of the importance of self-monitoring and self-regulation. They have created separate bookmarks for primary students (see Figure 2.6) and upper elementary students (see Figure 2.7), to remind them of the strategies for effective comprehension. On the second side of the bookmark for primary students are tips for vocabulary monitoring. The bookmark for upper elementary students covers strategies for both nonfiction and fiction. When these bookmarks are laminated, a teacher can use an erasable pen to highlight a particular strategy for the day or week, or to personalize the bookmarks otherwise for students. Strategy wall charts can serve a similar purpose.

Putting It All Together: The Teacher's Instructional Role

In this chapter, we have used the quest of Maria and Nikki to satisfy their passionate interest in butterflies as a framework for thinking about the strategies good readers need and use and the processes they engage in. We have seen the importance of prior knowledge about butterflies in leading to questions that increased the girls' knowledge. We have also seen that interest, persistence, purpose, and engagement in text led to satisfying reading experiences for Maria and Nikki.

Critical to the girls' growth was their teacher's instruction and scaffolding. Susan made sure that the girls had materials they could use for their learning, and she helped them focus and organize their learning and keep moving. She also organized the classroom so that the girls could confer with her and also with other students; this facilitated their knowledge construction. Within this framework, the girls asked questions, employed different strategies to answer different questions,

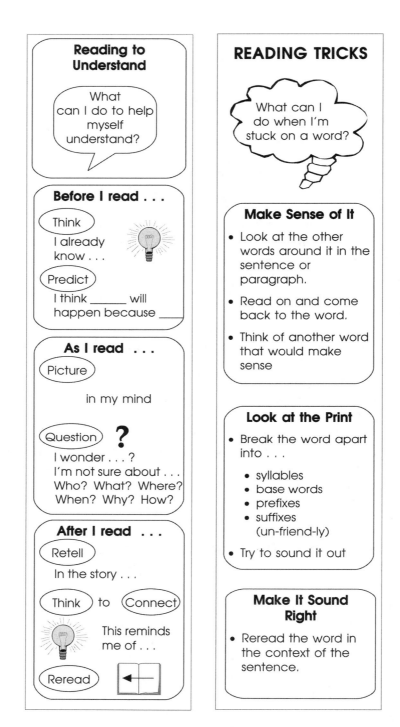

FIGURE 2.6. The two sides of a bookmark created to remind primary students of the importance of self-monitoring in reading (the "Reading Tricks" side contains tips for vocabulary monitoring). Used by permission of Julie Saum Gedgaud, Highland School, Downers Grove (Illinois) District 58.

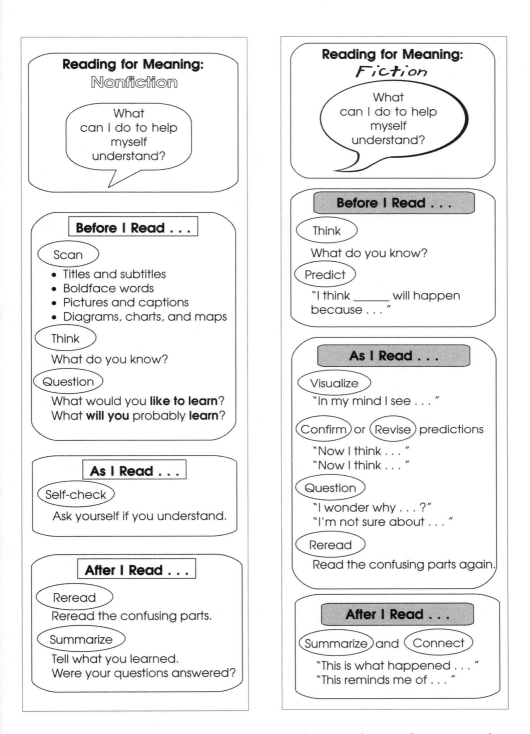

FIGURE 2.7. The two sides of a bookmark created to remind upper elementary students of the importance of self-monitoring in reading nonfiction and fiction. Used by permission of Julie Saum Gedgaud, Highland School, Downers Grove (Illinois) District 58.

made connections, and used their other strategies as they read. When their monitoring showed that they needed more information, they sought other books or da-
tabases. When they needed help, they had the support of "fix-up" strategies (e.g.,
rereading or consulting one another or Susan for help and suggestions).

Along with this general support, Susan used a very specific model of instruction to help all her students learn—a model emphasizing scaffolded learning,
which we have described in a general form earlier in this chapter with the bicycle
example. The goal of this instruction is gradually to release responsibility of the
process to the learners, just as the parent helping a child learn to ride a bike slowly
turns over the control of the bike to the child. Translated into reading instruction
(Pearson & Gallagher, 1983; Pressley & Harris, 1990), the instructional model
has several steps (see Figure 2.8). We discuss the first five of these steps in more
detail below.

1. *Setting goals and diversified performance criteria.* Before starting any instruction, the teacher must have an idea of the goals for instruction and some ideas
of what good performance would look like. State or local standards and school
curricula or other instructional plans can shape these goals. Performance benchmarks help a teacher think about what the signs of success will be for his or her
students. For example, a standard may address the notion that students in sixth
grade should be able to recognize the genre of biography. The teacher may decide
that various performances can be used for assessment of whether or not this standard is met. Students can work on making charts of the common information contained in biographies; they can do Venn diagrams showing the overlapping categories of information in two biographies; they can write a description of the genre;
they can read some simple biographies to third graders and explain to the younger
students what a biography is; and so on. In all of these, or in other performances,
students will have to list the essential elements of biographies. In choosing these

1. Setting clear standard-based goals and diversified
   performance criteria.
2. Modeling.
3. Guided practice, with teacher helping students
   through process.
4. Independent practice, with teacher giving
   feedback, providing diversified support, and
   eventually releasing more responsibility to students.
5. Assessment/evaluation of diversified
   performances, including self-evaluation.
6. Returning to any part of cycle as necessary.

FIGURE 2.8. Teacher's role in scaffolded strategy instruction.

performances and the underlying criteria, the teacher keeps in mind the diversity of students in his or her classroom. Students can work with biographies on many different reading levels, so that there is more than one biography on each level for comparison. They can show their learning in different ways to take advantage of many ways of representing learning. And they can receive different amounts and types of help along the way. Let's look at that instruction in a classroom example.

2. *Modeling.* The next step, which is the first step in the actual instruction process, is modeling by an expert. In many cases this is the teacher, but it can be anyone who is already adept at what is to be learned. One teacher came to class with an autobiography she was reading—*The Road from Coorain,* by Jill Ker Conway (1989)—and modeled a think-aloud process, walking the students through the book and the elements common to many biographies: early life, family life, early challenges, schooling, critical people or experiences, later life, the accomplishments and work that made the subject well known, and the person's philosophy of life or work.

3. *Guided practice.* In this step, the students receive assistance and practice to support them in learning the process, skill, or strategy. The teacher described previously had a stack of third-grade biographies, which she passed out to groups of students. She gave them time to look the books over, especially the tables of contents and chapter headings; she then asked them to look for some of the same elements that she had found in the Conway (1989) book. Students took turns writing key words on the board as they described the biographies and autobiographies they had reviewed. They added a new category of triumphs and tragedies to flesh out challenges and accomplishments.

4. *Independent practice.* After this introduction, the students began their own reading of biographies and autobiographies. Students self-selected their books from those the teacher had provided, and she guided students to various sets to help them make appropriate choices. First, they needed to self-evaluate whether or not a book was on an appropriate level for them. To do so, they used a choice process the teacher had devised, having to do with number of words they found difficult on a page and the rate at which they could read a page. Their job (with their partner or group) was to choose two or more biographies or autobiographies, and to compare and contrast these on the list of characteristics they had created. Some students did most of this reading and thinking with their partners and the teacher encouraged the students who were English learners to take the opportunity to work with a partner so they could practice using the language of their texts orally.

During the 2 weeks the project went on, the teacher assisted the students in various ways. She worked directly with some groups, using a biography frame that they needed to fill out to support the project work. She had some students enter their descriptions in the Biography Project, a computer media space for student work (*www.collaboratory.acns.nwu.edu/neighborhood/mediaspace/*). She did guided reading in some biographies for groups whose members needed extra support. She helped one group of students write a play in which one biography subject met someone from another biography. Another group of students annotated a videotape biography of Babe Ruth by constructing a sheet with the locator numbers on the VCR coded to various parts of the rubric. Such diversified support and performance are essential in the classroom.

   5. *Assessment/evaluation.* At the end of the unit, the students presented their work to the class and to students from another class. Each student then filled out a self-evaluation form the class had designed. It noted whether each element of biographies was represented in their presentation; it also dealt with other issues, such as writing and speaking rubrics. The teacher appended her evaluation as well and talked with some students about reteaching certain elements or having them retry parts of their project in another way.

   This model is only one example of the teacher's role in the learning process we are describing. Good teachers know their students and provide the needed guidance and support as they consciously move from direct instruction to a release of responsibility to their students. Research on effective instruction supports the notion that the instructional elements noted previously play a big part in effective instruction, even though teachers may package them in different ways, may include evaluation and/or self-evaluation at every step, and may skip steps when they are not needed. Though we are focusing on the reader in this book, we highlight these instruction steps throughout the chapters and in the "Putting It All Together" section of each chapter. Teachers are critical in putting strategies into learners' hands. They must ensure choice, feedback, engagement, relevance, and the gradual release of responsibility to students as teachers structure effective instruction.

CHAPTER 3

Creating an Effective Classroom for Comprehension Instruction

Just as a cabinet maker needs good tools and a good place to work, and a schedule for completing that work, teachers and students need classrooms that allow them to do their best work. In order for good comprehension instruction to take place, many different aspects of classroom setup and organization must make it easy for students to learn and easy for teachers to teach. In this chapter we look at some of the things involved in setting up and organizing a classroom for effective comprehension instruction (see Figure 3.1).

The good news from research is that classrooms are *the* critical places for effective instruction, surpassing intervention programs and special-needs programs in their ability to develop good readers (Allington & Walmsley, 1995). In a fascinating study of urban students, Catherine Snow and her colleagues from Harvard (Snow, Hemphill, & Barnes, 1991) reemphasized how powerful the classroom effect is on learning. The researchers looked at the extremes of the range of students we see in school: (1) those who came from high-literacy homes, where reading and writing were valued and emphasized, where there were lots of materials for literacy, and where adults provided encouragement and support to use these materials; and (2) those who came from homes where literacy encouragement and opportunities were low. The question Snow et al. (1991) asked was how these types of students would fare when placed in differing types of classrooms: (1) high-literacy-support classrooms, where there were skilled instruction, a rich literacy environment, and time and encouragement to read; (2) mixed-support classrooms, where instruction and support were not consistent; and (3) low-literacy-support class-

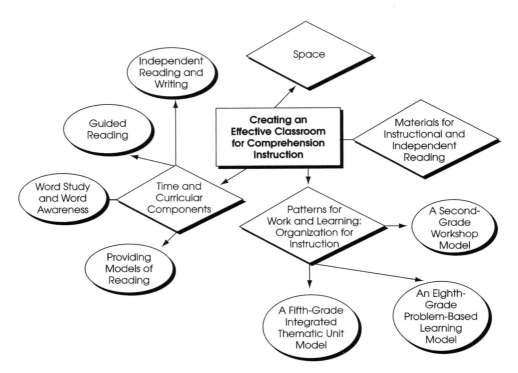

Resource Locator—Strategies and Resources Discussed in Chapter 3

Text Sets	p. 48
Time Allocations for Reading/Writing	pp. 49–50, 56
Conference Cards	p. 50
Scaffolded Independent Level Reading	p. 50
Read and Relax	p. 50
Group Assignment Chart	p. 51
Response Roles	p. 51
Simple Reading Log	p. 52
Complex Reading Log	p. 52
Second-Grade Workshop Schedules	pp. 55–56
Five-Finger Rule for Book Selection	p. 56
Fifth-Grade Thematic Unit Schedules	p. 58
Eighth-Grade Problem-Based Learning Schedule	pp. 59–60
Checklist for Classroom Environment	p. 62

FIGURE 3.1. Graphic organizer for Chapter 3.

rooms, where the instruction was poor or absent and where materials and incentives were few. When Snow and her colleagues examined students who were successful at the end of the primary grades, the achievement rates looked like this:

Percentage of Children Who Achieved Success with Varying Levels of Home and Classroom Support

	High home support	Low home support
High classroom support	100%	100%
Mixed classroom support	100%	25%
Low classroom support	60%	0%

Note. The data are from Snow et al. (1991).

This research dramatically highlighted the effect teachers and classrooms can have on students at different entry levels of literacy and with differing home support systems. Let's think back to our model of good comprehension (see Chapter 2) as an organizer to help us highlight some of the classroom issues that are important to effective instruction. Because learning to be literate has a strong social dimension, the collaborative nature of learning needs to be facilitated by the way classroom space is organized. Nikki and Maria, whose process of learning about butterflies has been described in Chapter 2, needed space to talk about their work and learning, and to work together in order to create that learning. However, they didn't work together all the time, so they needed space for individual reflection and learning, as well as for storing both their work in progress and their finished work.

Materials and their arrangement are also crucial. Interest and purpose play a big part in learning to comprehend; an environment rich in literacy opportunities is a must. Nikki and Maria needed access to lots of books and magazines about butterflies, as well as material in other areas to stretch their interest. They also needed time actually to work on their project, as well as time and instruction to build their learning skills and strategies.

Time alone is not enough; time needs to be well used to reflect a balanced view of literacy. But there must be enough time for students to develop persistence in reading. Furthermore, there need to be organizational structures for the classrooms that will allow students to work and learn in an organized fashion without lockstepping them. Maria and Nikki's teacher, Susan, used regular, planned instruction to build up their strategies as literate readers who could participate in discussions, as independent readers, and as word learners. Let's look at each of these areas in turn: space, materials, time and curricular components, and organizational patterns.

Space

A well-organized and flexible space can make a big difference to instruction. As we have noted in Chapter 2, research on comprehension suggests that it is a constructive process; students become good comprehenders by engaging in lots of reading and writing tasks. Sometimes this is individual learning, but often it is social, with partners and small groups (Tharp & Gallimore, 1988). Regardless of a school building's age, most classrooms can be organized to have constellations of desks arranged in table formations for small-group learning, as well as spaces for individual work. Because teacher instruction, scaffolding, and modeling are also research-based practices (Pearson & Gallagher, 1983), there must also be a space where the teacher can do group guided reading, usually with a blackboard or chart

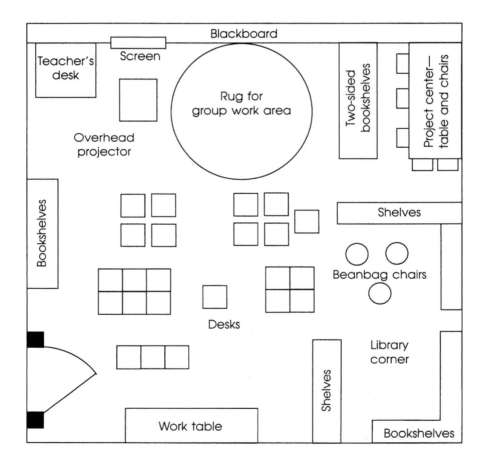

FIGURE 3.2. Map of Susan's fourth-grade classroom.

paper nearby. Finally, work materials must be easily accessible to students and organized for efficient use and cleanup.

Susan organized her fourth-grade classroom as shown in Figure 3.2. The desks of her 24 students were arranged in "tables" of several desks each, so that there was room for a group work area, a library corner, and a project center corner. Books were kept in low bookshelves so they could be easily reached by her students, and the tops of the shelves acted as display centers. The group work area was by the blackboard and the overhead projector and screen, so Susan could use it for small-group instruction or for whole-class lessons.

Materials for Instructional and Independent Reading

A classroom full of materials is essential for growing good readers. Variety in levels of materials and in topics is a *must*. Materials should be chosen for motivational as well as instructional value. The students you have met in Chapter 1 point out that besides books, newspapers, magazines, standard print reference materials, and electronic materials (e.g., CD-ROMs) are necessary to meet the needs of all readers. Many excellent magazines are available for every level, from *Ladybug* to *Ranger Rick* to *National Geographic for Kids*. Magazines devoted to popular youth interests, such as *BMX, Skateboarder, Guitar*, and so forth, are sure hits with older readers. Also, subscriptions to daily newspapers and weekly news magazines provide an ongoing connection to current events and an introduction to adult reading. Magazines in content areas (such as *Contact* for Science or *Cobblestone* for history), regional magazines (such as *Illinois History*), or magazines devoted to student-generated writing (such as *Merlin's Pen*) provide current and motivating material related to the curriculum. Internet news groups and topical forums also require reading and give a "hot-off-the-press" feel to the reading curriculum.

For instructional guided reading (Fountas & Pinnell, 2001; Dorn & Sofos, 2001), classrooms should have small-group and large-group sets of books, novels, or commercial anthologies or readers; sets of short stories; and multiple copies of magazines. These sets permit teachers to provide guided reading instruction using a variety of topical materials, and to introduce students to a variety of text structures for school and personal reading. A book or magazine in hand is much more motivating than a fuzzy photocopy, and it also deals appropriately with copyright issues in the school.

We know it is essential to have materials at a variety of reading levels. Having materials at, above, and below grade level in each category and on each topic can allow for a Readers' Workshop where all kids can read developmentally appropriate materials, as well as for teacher-guided reading on appropriate developmental levels. Not all books need to be put out at the same time; providing books at different times helps to keep the books new and fresh, and teachers can also share reading materials across classrooms across the year. Sometimes these material sets are developed on a schoolwide basis and stored in a central location for teacher checkout and use.

Teachers often like to create "text sets"—sets of related books centering around one topic. For example, for a unit on the sea, a third-grade teacher collected books on several different levels. These included the following:

- *Rescue of the Stranded Whales* (Mallory & Conley, 1989)—interest level 7–9
- *Whales: The Gentle Giants* (Milton, 1989)—interest level 6–8
- *Whales, Dolphins and Porpoises* (Carwardine, 2002)—interest level 8–14

The first book is about at grade level, the second is a bit easier, and the third is a bit more difficult. She used these as core books for the unit, and then allowed students to seek out related materials across these and other levels.

Another teacher created a set of related novels for sixth graders on the theme of survival in nature:

- *Julie of the Wolves* (George, 1972)
- *Hatchet* (Paulsen, 1987)
- *Shipwrecked: The True Adventures of a Japanese Boy* (Blumberg, 2001)

Students were able to choose, with teacher guidance, an appropriate book to use in their literature circles. In this way, all students were reading on the same topic and could contribute to large-class discussions that drew comparisons and contrasts across books and characters and settings; at the same time, however, they were able to read on their appropriate level and have a say in the book selection. Because this was part of a large, integrated unit, students were also choosing resource and reference books for extended personal inquiry projects. These included informational books, magazine articles, other print reference materials, Internet resources, CD-ROMs, and videos.

The group sets were purchased with classroom funds and stored in the school library for use by teachers on a rotating basis. Many of the multimedia materials and some resources were secured by the school librarian and technology facilitator, who were part of the planning process. The one-of-a kind books and magazines were borrowed from a local library, which would loan up to 30 items to any teacher for a 30-day period. (Checking on your local library's lending policy can expand the materials you have available.) Children also participated in putting together these sets by bringing materials from home. One boy in the sixth-grade class doing the survival unit had watched the ending of the Iditarod and brought his family's home video of the race's finish. One girl found several illustrated volumes on the settings of the survival novels and brought them to class, along with her own drawings. Another girl found poetry of the Northwest, and a boy with computer expertise brought in news items off the Internet.

For independent reading, the classroom library is also an important part of the comprehension-building classroom. Students with easy access to books read more than students who have to go down the hall at fixed periods to a school library, or who must fetch books from high, inaccessible shelves. Books attractively displayed (face out) circulate more frequently, and student reviews posted on a reader's bulletin board help students choose. For younger students, books may be organized in bins by subject or author. For older students, a circulating library where the students operate a checkin–checkout system is a possibility. A magazine rack (often stores will donate castoffs) highlights current magazines and newspapers.

When space permits, beanbag chairs or floor pillows (even if stowed away when not in use) can increase the use of the library/reading area. Families can be involved in adding to the class library by being encouraged to donate books on their children's birthdays, and students can do book swaps of their own books to add to the mix. Belonging to commercial book clubs can also help the class library to grow. Bonus books can be ordered based on purchases and can thus expand the collection further. The book-ordering process also students develop personal libraries and is a good way for them to keep aware of new books and authors.

Time and Curricular Components

Besides an organized space and good materials, teachers and students need enough time to enable the students to become good comprehenders, and the time must be used well. A good rule of thumb is to allocate a minimum of 120 minutes per day for reading and writing in grades K–3 and at least 90 minutes for these in grades 4–8. This is time when students are actively engaged in reading, writing, or instructional groups; it can be a single block of time, or it can be organized across the day for integrated instruction.

Even though, theoretically, nine 10-minute intervals of reading equal 90 minutes, we know that students must gradually develop the persistence to read over the grades, so some attention must be given to increasing blocks of work time as students move from primary to upper elementary grades.

Within this time frame, instructional organization should reflect what research tells us is essential for students to become effective readers and writers. Students need independent reading and writing, teacher-guided reading with rich discussion and instruction, and word study to grow as readers. They also need models of good reading and opportunities to use reading for meaningful purposes. These are the foundations of a comprehension-rich classroom. Let's look at each in a bit more detail.

Independent Reading and Writing

We know that students should be engaged in independent reading and writing every day. We know that most of you reading this book will be familiar with a process approach to writing (see books by Donald Graves [1994], Lucy Calkins [1994], and Nancie Atwell [1987] if you want to refresh your knowledge), so we focus primarily on reading in this section. Independent reading can take the form of a Readers' Workshop, sustained silent reading, books chosen as part of an integrated unit, or a variety of other structures. Our perspective on independent reading requires an active and thoughtful teacher who carefully plans and monitors the good work of the students—our acronym is SILR—scaffolded independent level reading (Katz, Polkoff, & Gurvitz, 2005). Though this is termed "independent" reading, the teacher monitors students' progress and has a conference with each student each week on his or her personal reading and writing, scaffolding book selection, and comprehension strategies as needed. Noreen Maro (2001) calls her scaffolded reading time "Read and Relax." During this 30 minutes a day, she circulates helping with book choice and talking with students about their reading. At the end of each period, students share with partners or friends for 3–5 minutes as well. Some teachers like to have an index card for each student and pull out five or six cards each day to select students for conferencing during independent reading time. Others like to assign each child a day of the week for his or her conference. During this time, a teacher can hear each child read, discuss content, do running records, or do whatever else is appropriate for the student's age and accomplishment level. Diane Sullivan, a reading specialist in suburban Chicago, uses a chart with student names on Velcro backing to help students get organized for each reading period (see Figure 3.3).

Response is an important part of this self-selected reading. Response logs are common tools to help students record feelings and responses in relation to their reading. These can be open-ended, or teachers can "prime" students for response by asking them to consider particular issues or play particular roles. Some of the most interesting roles can be unconventional ones (see Figure 3.4). We elaborate on these in later chapters, especially Chapter 6.

Students should also be involved in self-monitoring and recording by keeping reading logs with appropriate documentation of their reading. From simple (see Figure 3.5) to complex (see Figure 3.6), the assignments in these logs show independent engagement and control.

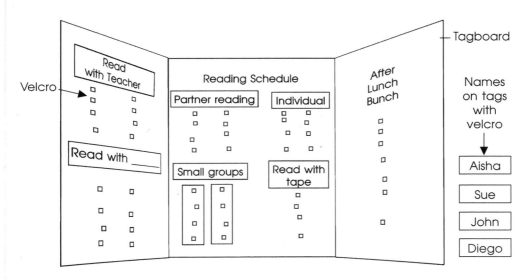

FIGURE 3.3. Group assignment chart.

Guided Reading

Besides independent reading and writing, teachers should do guided reading with small groups two or three times a week on instructionally appropriate materials (Fountas & Pinnell, 2001; Pinnell & Fountas, 1996; Ogle, 2002) . These materials can be drawn from anthologies, short stories, readers, or trade books. We deal with guided reading at length later in this book, but generally it involves working

Response Roles

Artist		Draw a picture of your response and explain it.
Melody Maker	♪	Pick a song that represents your response and explain why you picked it.
Connector		What does this make you think of? (Another selection, book, show, event?) Explain.
Word Splasher	word	Make a "word splash" of related words that represents your response. Explain.

FIGURE 3.4. A list of unconventional response roles.

FIGURE 3.5. A simple reading log assignment.

with students as they read a text, modeling good strategies, involving them in deep critical thinking, doing cross-textual work, and the like. In particular, this is the time when the teacher models good strategies and scaffolds students' attempt to use them. The teacher's goal is to model the types of thinking and engagement that characterize good readers. She does this by making her reading strategies visible through "think-alouds" (Baumann, Jones, & Seifert-Kessell, 1993), and by using instructional strategies such as the directed reading–thinking activity (DR-TA; see Chapter 6) or reciprocal teaching (RT; see Chapter 5), which are designed to build independent strategies for the students. Students in a guided reading group must be able to read a similar level of material—one that allows them a challenge they can meet with the teacher's support, and one that allows them to learn something

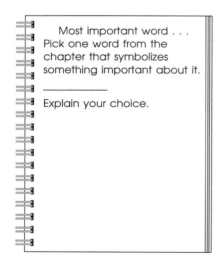

FIGURE 3.6. A more complex reading log assignment.

new about reading and reading strategies. This assumes that the teacher knows how each student functions in different types and levels of materials. In Chapter 4, we share what we know about finding a starting point for instruction.

Discussion is a critical component of guided reading (see Chapter 6), but teachers also need to ensure that students have time to develop the ability to direct their own discussions. Literature circles, book clubs, and reading teams all allow this development, which we highlight in later chapters. What are required are (1) engaging deeply with the text and (2) making that engagement transparent to others through what students talk about, what they write about, or how they express their understanding in other media. Also, students need to think about the strategies they need to approach different kinds of texts for different purposes. Thinking aloud about approaches, showing how to fix up problems, and modeling other good strategies are all components of guided reading. The goal is not just to understand a particular piece of reading material but to talk about ways to understand it and ways to transfer those strategies to another piece of text.

Word Study and Developing Word Awareness

Another component of an effectively organized instructional program is word study. In all grades, this involves developing a strategy for dealing with these questions: "What do I do when I come to a word I don't know?," "What do I do when I want to spell a word and I am not sure how to spell it?," and "How do I remember these new words?" In short, it involves developing an interest in locating and learning new vocabulary. In the early grades, this involves phonics and spelling; in the later grades, this involves vocabulary expansion and spelling.

In all grades, learning about words and how they work involves word play and the development of word awareness. For example, when Jamie was reading about Japan and the 1998 Winter Olympics, *Sports Illustrated for Kids* framed its articles on the Olympics with an introductory article using the word "hello" in Japanese, and a concluding article with the Japanese word for "goodbye," *sayonara*. Jamie thought it was cool to learn and use these Japanese words, and by the end of the Olympics all the students in his class were saying "*sayonara*" to each other at the end of the school day. He knew he had to try out the word whenever he could to make it part of his personal vocabulary. Jamie's teacher recognized this interest and wanted to capitalize on it, to build interest in other students and to give them opportunities to experiment with new words. He helped his students make a bulletin board with Japanese words and expressions. *Ninja* was a favorite, as was *sumo*. As the year went on, this board became a display of words from other languages that have become used in the United States, including *cappuccino* and *latte*. Helping students learn how words work and developing an interest in words and word learning are critical building blocks of literacy. We deal with this topic at length in Chapter 7.

Providing Models of Reading

Finally, an important component of reading instruction is having teachers (and other adults) read to students and share their own reading with them. This can motivate students, engage them in more difficult texts, and model good reading. Students can first be exposed to good strategies when listening to text and can later apply them to what they read. Teachers can read short things—jokes, news articles, sports reports, horoscopes, and other newsy and interest-catching items—to expose students to the variety of adult reading and the variety of purposes for reading every day. Along with reading such "sound bites," teachers need to carefully consider their selection of books to read aloud. If these books are on a level students can read independently, the teachers may want only to introduce the books to pique interest. This can be done by giving a book talk or by reading the first chapter. We discuss these strategies and others in Chapter 10.

Reading at a "challenge level" for students can introduce them to more complicated literate language, so that it can become a part of their own internal voices and help them with later, more difficult materials. We know that by third or fourth grade, the language students encounter in books is more complex and difficult than the language they hear in the world around them (Cunningham & Stanovich, 1997). Reading to students can help to expand their vocabularies and writing skills, as well as to interest them in new ideas. It can also introduce them to new authors and genres of literature that they might not select on their own.

Furthermore, reading to students should stimulate good listening habits. Teachers need to pay attention to the listening behaviors of their students. What do the kids do? Are they active? Does a teacher need to ask for response—to ask the students to visualize, draw, react, question? The stance to encourage students to take is that of active listeners, not passive ones. So, for modeling, for exposure to the richness of print, and for the development of writing awareness and active listening, reading to students is essential.

Patterns for Work and Learning: Organization for Instruction

Besides having time, materials, an understanding of the essential components of a good program, and a well-organized physical space, most teachers find that patterns for work and learning help them plan, help students see the underlying framework for instruction, and help students develop self-control over their own learning. It also allows special education teachers to anticipate and plan for their work with students who are being included in a general education classroom. Brain research suggests that the mind seeks patterns (Jensen, 1998), and this is certainly true of students who are trying to get the hang of how reading works. Most classrooms fall somewhere on a continuum between those that attempt to integrate most reading and writing instruction into thematic instruction and those that maintain a classical division among the content areas and the language arts (reading, writing, spelling, handwriting, grammar, etc.). Variations in school organization and time frames, as well as in individual students and teachers, suggest that many possible models of good instruction share the same commitment to a solid, balanced curriculum.

Good learning can take place in many types of classrooms, and the following three models of organization for reading are illustrated in the work of three teachers considered excellent by their students, their peers, administrators, and the parents of the children they teach. First we'll visit Lucia's classroom; Lucia is a second-grade teacher who uses a reader and trade books in her classroom and employs a workshop model. Then we'll observe Joe's classroom; Joe teaches a fifth-grade departmentalized class, where he uses trade books and a social studies text to integrate reading and language arts with social studies. Finally, we'll spend time with Kathleen, a middle school teacher who uses a project-based learning approach, where the students locate their own reading materials and make heavy use of the World Wide Web.

A Second-Grade Workshop Model

In Lucia's self-contained second-grade classroom, she uses workshops and centers to organize students into guided reading groups and work groups. Students use a commercial reading series for guided reading and trade books for their self-selected reading. Each student belongs to a guided reading group and also to a work group, which has a different composition.

Figure 3.7 presents what the daily schedule for reading and writing time looked like for the 120 minutes of language time. Lucia rotates her presence with her students so that she does guided reading two or three times with each group each week. Figure 3.8 illustrates her schedule for guided reading and other activities for a particular week. To make sure that her time with all students is evenly spent, Becky's and Andrew's groups will meet three times with Lucia, and Jim's and Donna's group twice, in the week following the Figure 3.8 schedule. When Lucia is working on guided reading, Allan, a special education teacher in the elementary school, comes in to work with inclusion students on their project research. The work groups consist of different combinations of students from those in the guided reading groups, so that the latter groups are not fixed groups for all reading. Sometimes the work groups are student selected, based on interest and topic; at other times, Lucia assigns students to work groups for particular reasons. What Lucia is careful to do is to see that each student's guided reading is on an appropriate instructional level each week, and that this level progresses over the year.

1. Independent reading—15 minutes. Students entered the classroom and locate their own books, and teacher circulates, doing short conferences with four students each day.

2. State of the group—5 minutes. Teacher does calendar, talks about special events, teaches a song.

3. Writing workshop—30 minutes. Work on writing process with a minilesson, and then individual and small groups. Teacher circulates.

4. Author's Chair—5 minutes. Sharing of work. Two or three students per day.

5. Reading Workshop—40 minutes. Guided reading. (See Figure 3.8.)

6. Word Workshop—15 minutes. Phonics, vocabulary, spelling.

7. Book sharing, work sharing, reading aloud—10 minutes.

FIGURE 3.7. Daily schedule for reading and writing time in Lucia's self-contained second-grade classroom.

A Fifth-Grade Integrated Thematic Unit Model

In Joe's departmentalized school, he teaches reading and language arts and social studies to three groups of fifth graders. Joe's class works on six thematic units a year. Two are focused on novels that emphasize the topics of challenge and individual responsibility, two relate to topics in the science curriculum (the solar system and inventions), and two relate to topics in the social studies curriculum (immigration and the Holocaust). In addition, there is a short 2-week "bonus" unit on any topic the class chooses. This year the class is researching fads across the 20th century, including dance crazes and popular toys, like Beanie Babies, Webkinz, and American Girl dolls.

For each unit, Joe has text sets of trade books, magazines, and commercial reading materials with related selections. He allows students to choose from three core books and then helps each group find appropriate related material. Joe has taught the students the "five-finger rule" for selecting books. They pick a page in the middle of the book and begin reading; each time they come to a word they don't know, they put down a finger. As long as they don't get beyond five fingers, the book is one they will find readable. Joe also helps students choose and occasionally asks students to consider a particular book for a particular challenge. He retains the right of veto or approval but tries to negotiate with each student so that he or she is reading at an appropriate level of challenge. Each student also has a "pleasure reading" book that he or she is expected to carry at all times.

Figure 3.9 shows Joe's living schedule during his challenge unit (which lasts for 90 minutes a day). Figure 3.10 shows his schedule for guided reading in literature circles during a week of this unit. Rose, a special education teacher at Joe's school, comes into Joe's class during the minilessons to help those students who need more support. In all his units, Joe is careful to have a range of difficulty in the

Day	Reading Center schedule: Guided reading with teacher	Work groups when students are not working with teacher			
		Red	Yellow	Green	Blue
Monday	Jim's group Donna's group	Writing Center Partner reading Project research	Listening Center Writing Center Partner reading	Word Center Partner reading Library	Partner reading Project research Word Center
Tuesday	Becky's group Andrew's group	Partner reading Project research Word Center	Writing Center Partner reading Project research	Listening Center Writing Center Partner reading	Word Center Partner reading Library
Wednesday	Jim's group Donna's group	Word Center Partner reading Library	Partner reading Project research Word Center	Writing Center Partner reading Project research	Listening Center Writing Center Partner reading
Thursday	Becky's group Andrew's group	Listening Center Writing Center Partner reading	Word Center Partner reading Library	Partner reading Project research Word Center	Writing Center Partner reading Project research
Friday	Jim's group Donna's group	Writing Center Partner reading Project research	Listening Center Writing Center Partner reading	Word Center Partner reading Library	Partner reading Project research Word Center

FIGURE 3.8. Weekly schedule for guided reading and other activities in Lucia's class.

1. Teacher reading—5 minutes. Joe reads items of general interest from the newspaper. These include news, sports, and cartoons.
2. Minilesson—15 minutes. This can cover spelling, word study, grammar, some literary genre point all students are working on (e.g., character, etc.).
3. Activities for guided reading and literature circles—50 minutes. (See Figure 3.10.)
4. Workshop—20 minutes. Writing and word study on alternating day. Game day periodically, where word games are played.

FIGURE 3.9. Daily schedule for reading and language arts in Joe's fifth-grade classroom.

books that can be chosen. He and Rose also make sure to give "jump-starts" to students who have chosen books that will be difficult for them, and to offer them extra support during the course of the unit.

An Eighth-Grade Problem-Based Learning Model

Kathleen teaches reading and social studies in a middle school. The social studies curriculum drives the choice of reading materials. The students do six 6-week units a year. Kathleen chooses the overall topics, but students may select their own topics within each unit. For example, the culminating topic each year for the eighth grade is "20th-century America." Each student chooses a subtopic to research, and Kathleen helps them ties these into the overall goals of the unit: realizing the impact of immigration, industrialization, cultural diversity, and burgeoning technology on the American experience.

Each student must accumulate his or her own research materials from the school library, local libraries, personal interviews, and electronic media. Kathleen supplies core readings from the class textbook, periodicals, and chapters of other books, which all students read. For the students who have more difficulty, she meets with them to jump-start them before reading and to make sure they are able to consolidate as they read. Each student is also reading one of a set of core novels on the American experience. Kathleen has several sets at different levels of difficulty, and students must show her that they can handle a particular level of difficulty before they can choose a book at that level. She also has a collection of books for younger students on a large number of topics, which she uses to introduce complex vocabulary and concepts. She introduces the idea of these "concept books" at the beginning of the year, and students help in amassing a library for their own use.

Figure 3.11 displays Kathleen's daily schedule for the 100 minutes allotted per day for social studies and reading. Kathleen carefully monitors her students' progress by having a "state of the project" conference at the beginning of the week and

Group	Monday	Tuesday	Wednesday	Thursday	Friday
Julie of the Wolves (George, 1972)	• Groups disc. with Mr. Z • Response writing	• Read next chapter and discuss without teacher • Writing follow-up to record response • Project group with teacher	• Spelling and word workshop • Project group • Library work for research	• Review prior chapters; read next chapter • Prepare for group discussion with partner-role sheets	• All groups sharing in herringbone fashion across books on issue of character develop-ment • Progress on projects
Hatchet (Paulsen, 1987)	• Review prior chapters; read next chapter • Prepare for group discussion with partner-role sheets • Spelling practice	• Group disc. with Mr. Z • Response writing	• Read next chapter and discuss without teacher • Writing follow-up to record response • Project group with Mr. Z	• Spelling and word workshop • Project group • Library work for research	See above
Island of the Blue Dolphins (O'Dell, 1960)	• Review prior chapters; read next chapter • Prepare for group discussion with partner-role sheets • Spelling practice	• Read next chapter and discuss without teacher • Writing follow-up to record response • Project group with Mr. Z	• Group disc. with Mr. Z • Response writing • Project groups	• Spelling and word workshop • Project group • Library work for research	See above

FIGURE 3.10. Schedule for guided reading in literature circles during a week of the "challenge" unit in Joe's class.

1. Choosing and reading from a newsmagazine on current events—5 minutes. Pupils take turns doing the oral reading for the class.

2. Whole-class work with core reading—30 minutes. Social studies issues and concepts predominate here. Benita, a special education teacher, works with some of the readers who have more difficulty, "jump-starting" them so they can participate more fully in the discussions.

3. Literature circle on core novel—30 minutes. There are three core novels, and the teacher works with one group on Monday, one on Tuesday, and one on Wednesday. On Thursday, the Monday group gets an "extra shot." On Fridays, the students cross groups and share some aspect they have been working on (e.g., the geographical differences in the settings of their novels and what this tells about the kind of immigrant groups who settled there). Each group works on the strategy of analyzing point of view to help comprehension. (On Monday through Thursday, students not in the discussion group work on their own research and research notes at this time.)

4. Research updates—30 minutes. The teacher meets with individuals and groups on their research. During this time they enter new vocabulary and spelling words into personal dictionaries and lists, some on computers. During this time students also deal with writing related to their research. The special education teacher also sometimes comes in during this time to give extra help.

5. Closure and assignments—5 minutes.

FIGURE 3.11. Daily schedule for reading activities in Kathleen's eighth-grade classroom.

another time during the week for each student. She has approximately 25 children in each of her social studies and language arts classes, so each day she pulls five index cards for each class and has a personal 2-minute conference with those five students. She dates each card and writes notes to help her remember what is happening. Students also chart the conference in their log and list specific action items. When students are struggling, she remembers to come back to these students, to go over their materials, to suggest easier resources, to suggest partner reading, or to ask Benita (a special education teacher in the middle school) to support their learning. By the end of each week, Kathleen has talked to each student and used that dialogue to help her plan the next week's instruction.

For example, when students are having trouble extracting the main points and supporting details from their reading, she uses their core readings for the next week as examples for think-alouds. They use the computer program Inspiration (Helfgott & Westhaver, 1997) to chart the ideas and then to relate them in hierarchical fashion. Then the conferences for each student that week focus on the main ideas of the resources being read and the supporting details. Kathleen, a veteran teacher, finds this type of instruction challenging but also rewarding. It is tailored to the project-focused learning she finds matches her teaching style, the expertise she has developed over the years, and the needs of her students.

Putting It All Together

In this chapter we have shared with you our ideas on how space, materials, time and curricular components, and good instructional organization are important variables in developing comprehension. In order for a model of good instruction to be implemented, the class must be organized so that teachers have sufficient time to spend in instruction. During that time, students working independently and in groups must also be learning productively. Finally, teachers need a framework to provide differing types of instruction and learning experiences for students with different needs and at different levels of performance.

You may wish to use the checklist provided in Figure 3.12 to evaluate your own classroom, or to support a new or student teacher in thinking about how the field must be plowed before the seeds can be planted. Also, for staff developers, the grade-level specific books in our series "Tools for Teaching Literacy" (*www. Guilford.com*) offer more ideas for the issues we have highlighted in this chapter.

Checklist for Evaluating My Classroom Environment

Time—I have enough of it and use it well (minimum time, not including content reading):

_____ K–3: I allocate 120 minutes.

_____ 4–8: I allocate 90 minutes.

_____ My students are engaged (involved in reading, writing, project work, instruction).

Instructional organization reflects the basic, research-established avenues to reading:

_____ I do guided reading and instruction to develop comprehension and strategies (two to four per week) on developmentally appropriate material.

_____ Students do independent reading practice (sustained silent reading, book clubs, lit. circles) in my class every day on independent-level material and are involved in response activities.

_____ Students write every day, using a process model and doing appropriate editing (grammar, usage, mechanics).

_____ I teach word study (phonics, spelling, vocabulary) three to five times per week. (Note that half of the instructional time involves students in reading, both guided and independent.)

Materials are thoughtfully chosen for motivational and instructional value:

_____ I have materials at students' developmental (instructional) levels to use for guided reading.

_____ I have a wide range of independent-level materials (above and below grade level).

_____ I use fiction and informational materials along with poetry, drama, newspapers, other print, references, electronic resources.

_____ We have a classroom library that contains the material above, as well as magazines, guides, almanacs, and other motivating materials.

_____ Materials are attractively displayed and available for students' independent use.

Effective instruction and research-based practices are used in my classroom:

_____ I know the developmental level of each student in my class through quick, curriculum-based assessment.

_____ I guide reading on an appropriate developmental level and jump-start students who need more help.

_____ My main goal is helping students develop strategies that will make them independent readers.

_____ I make the strategies and skills clear and explicit by combining discovery, modeling, and clear instruction, so students learn the "secrets" and the systems of language.

_____ I motivate, guide, instruct, and facilitate during all instructional time.

_____ I read aloud and/or discuss my own reading every day.

_____ I believe I am responsible for helping each student in my class become a better reader.

FIGURE 3.12. A self-evaluation checklist for evaluating the classroom environment.

CHAPTER 4

Finding a Starting Point

Ways to Assess Comprehension

As teachers, we need to assess comprehension for many different purposes. Standardized tests provide one type of information. The National Assessment of Educational Progress (NAEP; 2005), for example, provides national information on reading on a 4-year cycle and is the touchstone to which many state assessments are keyed. The NAEP Reading Framework reflects research that views reading comprehension as a dynamic, interactive process. The major national assessment that must be given in all of the states in 4th, 8th, and 12th grades is the NAEP. In 2009 a new Framework will be used for the first time, replacing the earlier Framework that was developed in 1992. This new NAEP Reading Framework includes two types of texts: literary and informational. Poetry will be included at all three levels of testing. An important shift in the assessments is the inclusion of more informational texts recognizing the shifting nature of reading in our society. By the 12th grade the majority of the reading will be in informational material. (The fourth-grade test will have equal passages of literary and informational texts; the 8th-grade test will have 45% literary and 55% informational; by 12th-grade the distribution will be 30% literary and 70% informational. The assessments will also include items that measure vocabulary knowledge as an aid to comprehension:

1. *Reading literary texts.* Literary passages will come from three categories of literary texts: fiction, literary nonfiction (i.e., essays, speeches, and biographies and autobiographies), and poetry.

2. *Reading informational texts.* Informational texts will come from three categories: exposition, argumentation and persuasion, and procedural texts and documents. The documents may include graphic representations that ask readers to draw on information presented in varied formats. Embedded documents will be used in grades 4 and 8 and free-standing documents in grade 12.

3. *Reading multiple texts.* Reading and integrating information from more than one text is a common task for students at all grade levels. Therefore, the test includes intertextual passage sets to approximate the normal type of reading schools require.

Four cognitive tasks will be assessed:

1. Forming a general understanding of text.
2. Developing an interpretation of text.
3. Making reader–text connections.
4. Examining content and structure of text.

comprehension

NAEP grounds state assessments and makes available a framework for thinking about what the assessments can provide.

An important part of developing good readers is having them read materials of increasing complexity and difficulty. Assessment helps us to make informed decisions regarding the level of materials our students can handle. But knowing *what* they can read is only the first step. We also need to know *how* they read, so we can build on strong strategies and introduce new ones. Assessment thus both alerts us to the ways in which our students are capable comprehenders and strategy users and helps us to see their instructional needs. This type of assessment is a starting point for instruction. Finally, when we assess, we also teach. Assessment focuses on what's important in reading; it can model for developing readers the ways in which good readers monitor and fix up their own comprehension.

In this chapter (see the graphic organizer in Figure 4.1), we present several different types of assessment that relate to comprehension and to our comprehension model. If you reflect on the model of comprehension presented in Chapter 2, you will be reminded that we have characterized comprehension as having social, individual, and process dimensions. Our discussion of assessment starts with a way to look at students as members of their school social group, the classroom. We describe the "classroom fluency snapshot" (CFS; Blachowicz, Cieply, & Sullivan, 2001)—a quick way you can "scan" your class at the beginning of the year to get a baseline for thinking about instruction and the materials you might use.

As well as looking at each student as part of the class, you also need to look at each student as an individual, to find out what level of materials the students needs and what initial goals for instruction can be set. We'll describe some stan-

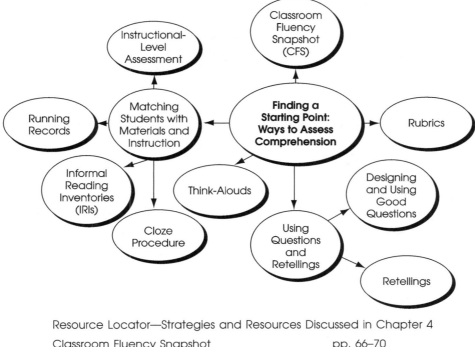

Resource Locator—Strategies and Resources Discussed in Chapter 4

Classroom Fluency Snapshot	pp. 66–70
Running Records	pp. 71–72
Informal Reading Inventories	pp. 72–75
Cloze Passages	pp. 75–79
Story Map/Selection Map	p. 81
Story Map/Selection Map Questions	p. 82
Retelling Checklist	p. 85
Think-Alouds	pp. 86–87
Double-Entry Journal	p. 87
Comprehension Rubrics	pp. 88–90

FIGURE 4.1. Graphic organizer for Chapter 4.

dard ways for matching students with materials—running records, informal reading inventories (IRIs), and the cloze procedure—to make sure you have your students at the right level of challenge in their instructional reading. Finally, we hone in on the processes of comprehension by looking at three different ways you can tap students' ongoing comprehension strategies for gaining a general understanding, developing an interpretation, making reader to text connections, and reflecting on ther content and structure of a text (NAEP, 2007). These include use of good questioning, retellings, and think-alouds, which are assessment methods that reveal how students are building meaning over a text, over multiple texts, and over time. Also, we briefly mention some rubrics developed for structuring observations about students' reading comprehension.

The Classroom Fluency Snapshot

At the start of the school year, or whenever you are meeting a new group of students, it is often helpful to take a quick "snapshot" of your class to establish starting points for more detailed reflection. Just as a class picture on the first day of school can help you learn your students' names and faces and give you an initial point of reference, so a CFS can help you get a sense of the class. The CFS is "curriculum-based" because you use a regular piece of classroom text to collect a short sample of each student's oral reading. It uses correct words per minute as a measure of fluency—that is, a student reads a particular passage at a good rate, with prosody (i.e., sounds like language), and with accuracy.

At this moment you might be asking yourself, "Fluency measures in a book about comprehension?" We know that fluency is highly correlated with comprehension. A fluency measure can tell you whether students can handle the word level and prosody demands of a text. A CFS can be used for gathering different types of information and has four basic goals:

1. To help you get a quick sense of the class baseline in the fall.
2. To identify those students who may need special support and/or more time when working with grade-level material.
3. To help you in the selection of independent reading material.
4. To enable you to chart the progress of students' fluency over the year as a measure of overall progress.

However, this type of assessment is meant to supplement, not to be a substitute for, richer data that are collected anecdotally and through other authentic means throughout the year. Fluency can also be measured on an IRI and in running records, which are more detailed and labor intensive. Still, a teacher needs a quick "thermometer reading" to guide later, more detailed assessment.

How to Do a CFS

The first thing you need to do is to select some reading material that is representative of the materials you will actually be using in class. This can be a core novel, an article from *National Geographic World*, or a short selection from a magazine or basal anthology. Try to avoid highly technical material or unusual and exotic vocabulary. Choose a passage that will take the typical student 1 or 2 minutes to read, and make a copy for each student to be assessed and a master copy (which you might laminate).

Each student is assessed individually, but doing this only takes 2 or 3 minutes per student. One good way to manage the process is to place each child's name on an index card. Once you have your class stack, divide it into five piles. Do one pile each day, and you will have your whole class assessed by the end of the week.

Begin each session by sitting in a comfortable place and introducing each student to the process and the text. The directions should go something like this:

> "I would like you to read this passage about [add as much description as necessary to prepare students for the concepts they are going to encounter]. I'd like you to read this at a comfortable rate, as accurately as you can. You may start now [start timing]."

Some teachers begin with the first paragraph. Others let each student read at first without timing or marking. Whatever you choose, begin timing for 1 minute. Each time the student makes a miscue, put a tick mark in the margin or over the word, or mark the exact miscue if you are a skilled marker. At the end of 1 minute, make a mark for the last word and let the student complete the passage. If you like, ask a question or ask for a retelling or major point after the reading.

Count how many words were read in 1 minute, and subtract the number of errors a student has made. This will give you a correct words per minute (CWPM) score. For example, Figure 4.2 shows the record sheet of Alex, a student in Daria's class. (You may add a comprehension question or retelling task.) Also, many teachers make anecdotal notes on each sheet to remind them things they note about each child's reading: "Had to hold paper really close to face. Glasses?", or "Had lots of trouble dropping down each line," or "Very fluent . . . this is way too easy for this child," or "Raced through and couldn't tell me anything about what she had read." Teachers who are experienced in analyzing oral reading also note the types of miscues students make for later probing—for example, "Had trouble with all the multisyllable words."

Displaying and Interpreting CFS Results

Once you have listened to all students and charted their readings, make a class CFS summary. The summary constructed in September by a teacher named Daria for her third-grade students is shown on the left in Figure 4.3.

From this summary, Daria could see that Katie E, Elizabeth C, RJ, Scott H, Diane, and Jean were going to have significant trouble with the novel she had chosen as the unit core book. She would need to support them in their reading, and also to make sure they had extra time. She scheduled each of these children for an IRI to get a more detailed picture of their reading levels, strengths, and weaknesses.

By contrast, Katie F, Jamie, Sara, Jeanette, and Caressa were very speedy readers. Daria resolved to check their comprehension on their next reading. If they were indeed as fluent as they seemed on the CFS, and they understood what they

Amelia Earhart

Amelia Earhart was an adventurer and a pioneer in the field
of flying. She did things no other woman had ever done before.

During World War I, Earhart worked as a nurse. She cared
for pilots who had been hurt in the war. Earhart listened to what
they said about flying. She watched planes take off and land.
She knew that she, too, must fly.   *(counted as one)*

1	START / In 1928, Earhart was the first woman (to) cross the Atlantic in	12
2	a plane. (But) someone else flew the plane. Earhart wanted to be	24
3, 4	more than (just) a passenger. She *went* wanted to fly a plane across the	37
5	ocean herself. For four years, Earhart trained to be a pilot. Then,	49
6	in 1932, she flew *along* alone across the Atlantic to Ireland. The trip	61
7	took *40* over fourteen hours.	65

Flying may seem easy today. However, Earhart faced many   74

dangers. Airplanes had just been *in - -℗* invented. They were/much * FINISH 83

smaller than our planes today. Mechanical problems happened   91

quite often. There were also no computers to help her. Flying   102

across the ocean was as frightening as sailing across it had been * 1 min

years before. Earhart knew the dangers she faced. However, she
said, "I want to do it because I want to do it. Women must try
to do things as men have tried. When they fail, their failure must
be a challenge to others."

Earhart planned to fly around the world. She flew more than
twenty thousand miles. Then, her plane disappeared somewhere
over the huge Pacific Ocean. People searched for a long time.
Finally they gave up. Earhart and her plane were never found.

Name _Alex_____   Total words read __82_____

Date _____   Total errors/mis ___7_____

                            CWPM   ___75_____

FIGURE 4.2. An example of a marked and scored classroom fluency snapshot (CFS),
based on a passage about Amelia Earhart from a fourth-grade social studies textbook. The
passage is from Schreiber and Kain (1985, p. 380). Copyright 1985 by Scott, Foresman and
Co. Used by permission of the publisher.

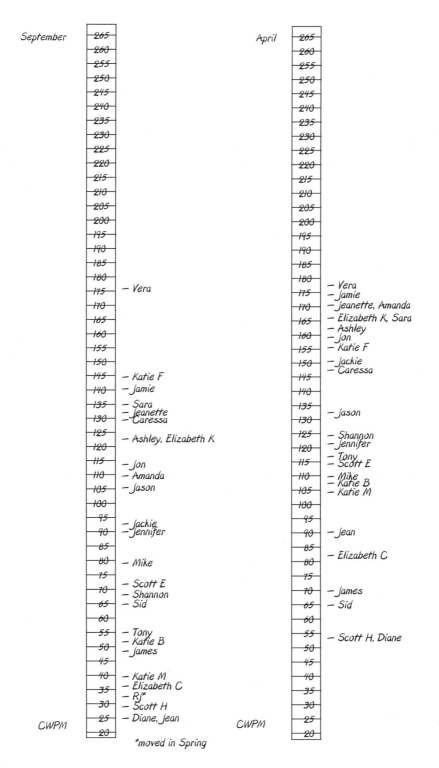

FIGURE 4.3. Examples of class summaries of CFS results for September (left) and April (right).

were reading, she would need to look for some challenging material for them when they finished their regular class assignments. With Vera, Daria suspected that comprehension was often sacrificed to speed. She planned to use the cloze procedure and DR-TAs with Vera, to make sure to model appropriate speed rather than rapid reading. Finally, Daria noted in her anecdotal comments that several students had trouble with multisyllable words, and she decided to schedule a minilesson early to do some diagnostic teaching on this topic.

In April, Daria did another CFS summary for her class (see Figure 4.3, right). From this summary, she could see that most of the class was progressing smoothly, and that Elizabeth C, Jean, and Jamie were making particularly good progress due to the extra work she was doing with them in class. Scott H and Diane still needed the support of Jenna, the inclusion specialist, but she was able to show their parents their improvement in fluency even though they required ongoing support.

Things to Think About

If you use a CFS, you need to use your own expertise and knowledge to make some decisions. For how long a time do you want to have the children read? We know that a short test of reading is like a short test of anything else: Sometimes children do their best, and sometimes they need more time to show what they can do. For some children, the time limit may produce a really skewed impression. Second, should you deduct errors or miscues? Try it both ways and see whether your picture changes. Third, should you have students do a "cold" or a prepared reading? We have found that the profile of a class remains largely the same, but that students do a bit better in prepared situations and when non-meaning-changing miscues are not counted as errors. But because the CFS is only a screen, you have to balance these factors against the time it takes you to do a longer reading and a more detailed analysis. The important thing is to do the same thing with each student and from one testing to the next.

What about norms? The idea of a CFS is to establish your own class norms, but between-class comparisons in a school can help teachers determine which classrooms may need more assistance from other professionals; it can also help explain variation in the standardized test performances of one class in a school or district. Although rates will vary according to the conceptual difficulty and structure of a text, Figure 4.4 provides some common bands to help you think about your class (Morris, 1999).

The CFS makes a great measure to take the "reading temperature" of your class on a regular basis. Often it shows growth where other measures are not sensitive. The CFS can also provide a "reality test" of the materials you choose and can help you plan extra support for students who need it. Moreover, it will suggest to you which students may need a more sensitive choice of learning materials.

Grade level	Oral	Silent
First	30–70	—
Second	60–90	60–100
Third	80–110	90–120
Fourth	95–120	110–140
Fifth	110–140	140–170
Sixth	110–150	160–190

FIGURE 4.4. Typical reading rates (oral and silent) by grade level. Used by permission of D. Morris (personal communication, 1992).

Matching Students with Materials

Instructional-Level Assessment

When selecting materials for use in the classroom, teachers use many different criteria. Content, format, and language are all important elements for establishing whether materials are at an appropriate level of difficulty for a student in reading instruction. Standardized reading formulas using sentence length and word frequency are commonly used to rate commercial materials and trade books for their readability (Weaver & Kintsch, 1991). Yet teachers often make these determinations without a particular child or group of children in mind; their estimations also often do not take into account what the readers already know or don't know about the subject being discussed, or what their prior experiences with reading materials of the type and organization under examination have been.

A more classroom-sensitive concept is that of "instructional-level assessment"—using classroom materials to estimate a level at which a student can comprehend adequately in a challenging but teacher-supported situation. In general, a reading selection is considered suitable for instruction when a student, after reading it, can answer correctly a certain proportion of the questions asked or can retell a majority of the important ideas in the selection (Barr, Blachowicz, & Wogman-Sadow, 1995). Figure 4.5 presents a set of more specific criteria for assessment of whether a student is functioning at an instructional level.

Running Records

A "running record" (Clay, 1993) is an assessment measure that has a student read orally a piece of known readability level, so that the student's instructional level can be estimated. As the student reads the piece, the teacher indicates how well the

Graded word lists . . .	. . . are decoded with at least 75% immediate recognition.
Oral reading of text . . .	. . . is accurate 95% of the time (can fall to 90% if other signs are good).
Comprehension of oral and silent reading . . .	. . . is 75% or higher.
Reading rate . . .	. . . is appropriate to grade level of material (see Figure 4.4).

FIGURE 4.5. Criteria for determining whether a student is functioning at an instructional level.

student reads it by making a mark over each correct word or over each incorrect word. (The latter is easier, but it may make students more conscious of their mistakes.) Figure 4.6 is an example of a marked running record for a student named Sabdt (note that the same passage used for the CFS in Figure 4.2 is used here).

A particular set of marking conventions is used to indicate where a reader mispronounces or substitutes a word, makes an omission or addition, pauses, self-corrects, and so forth (see Figure 4.7). At the end of the reading, the listener may ask a few questions or ask for a retelling to assess understanding. The reading is also timed. Standard criteria for interpreting oral reading are used to determine whether or not this material is appropriate for an individual child. For younger children, rate and prosody are often enough to determine appropriate level.

Although experts have disagreed on functional reading levels, many determinations seem to fall in the range indicated in Figure 4.5. Students whose oral reading accuracy is in the 95%+ range—that is, who have difficulty with not more than 5 in 100 words—can usually handle materials at that level instructionally. Teachers who use leveled books take running records weekly to determine when to move students on to materials of increasing difficulty. Also, analyses of the miscues a student makes can give insights into reading processes at the text level. We'll elaborate on this point as we discuss IRIs next.

Informal Reading Inventories

IRIs are among the most widely used forms of instructionally based reading assessment and are more complex forms of the same type of assessment used in a running record. They consist of sets of graded word lists and oral and silent reading passages with questions, which are used to move a student from those he or she can read most easily (independent reading level) through those he or she can read with the support of a teacher (instructional level), stopping at the level where the materials becomes too hard for the reader (frustrational level).

Amelia Earhart

Amelia Earhart was an adventurer and a pioneer in the field
of flying. She did things no other woman had ever done before.

During World War I, Earhart worked as a nurse. She cared
for pilots who had been hurt in the war. Earhart listened to what
they said about flying. She watched planes take off and land.
She knew that she, too, must fly.

In 1928, Earhart was the first woman to cross the Atlantic in
~~a plane~~ *an airplane*. But someone else flew the plane. Earhart wanted to be
more than (just) a passenger. She wanted to fly a plane across the
ocean (herself.) For four years, Earhart trained to be a pilot. Then,
in 1932, she flew alone *along* across the Atlantic to Ireland. The trip
took over fourteen hours. *40*

Flying (may) seem easy today. However, Earhart faced many
dangers. Airplanes had just been invented. They were much
smaller than (our) planes today. Mechanical problems happened *Many*
quite often. There were also no computers to help her. Flying
across the ocean, was as frightening as sailing across it had been *It*
years before. Earhart knew the dangers she faced. However, she
said, "I want to do it, because I want to do it. Women must try *myself*
to do things as men have tried. When they fail, their failure must *many*
be a challenge to others." / *

	12
	24
	37
	49
	61
	65
	74
	83
	91
	102
	114
	124
	139
	152
	157

* 90 sec

Earhart planned to fly around the world. She flew more than
twenty thousand miles. Then, her plane disappeared somewhere
over the huge Pacific Ocean. People searched for a long time.
Finally they gave up. Earhart and her plane were never found.

Name *Sandy*   Total words read *157*

Date _____   Total errors/mis *13 / 6*

CWPM *92 / 96*   *Good*
INSTRUCTIONAL

FIGURE 4.6. An example of a marked running record, based on the same passage about
Amelia Earhart as that used in Figure 4.2. The passage is from Schreiber and Kain (1985,
p. 380). Copyright 1985 by Scott, Foresman and Co. Used by permission of the publisher.

Omissions	the (big) boy
Insertions	very the ‸ big boy
Mispronunciations/substitutions	box the big ~~boy~~
Reversals of order	It was Chicken ⌐Little ⌐
Long pauses	It was / Chicken Little
Self-corrections	sc the (big) boy

Remember to make qualitative notations, also:

Difference due to dialect   (d)
Attempted correction   (ac)
Repeated error   ◄—————— or   ～～～～～～

FIGURE 4.7. Conventions for marking a running record.

The development of IRIs is commonly attributed to Betts (1946), but similar diagnostic procedures have been used in earlier clinical assessment and in later incarnations, such as the running record. The procedure first called on teachers to construct their own inventories from school materials. Later, graded materials were assembled into commercial, purchasable IRIs. IRIs are closely tied to our real classroom tasks: We teachers ask students to read orally, to read silently, to listen, and to retell and interpret what they read. We also ask them to decode graded word lists of increasing difficulty. In scoring and analysis of IRIs, teachers are encouraged to take control of the decision making about their use and interpretation. Criteria are not norm referenced and look at aspects such as word recognition and comprehension, along with vocabulary. There has been a rich dialogue about the administration, scoring, and interpretation of these instruments (see Johns, 1993), but they remain among the most widely used instruments for curricular instruction. If they are constructed and used for comprehension, the passages ought to represent the type of reading done in the classroom. They should be of good literary quality with language that sounds natural. Topics should be of interest to students, and the selections should be of sufficient length and integrity to stand alone. For comprehension purposes, questions should be clearly worded and should represent both convergent and divergent thinking. They should be "passage-dependent" questions (i.e., the reader should need to read the selection to answer the questions), not questions answerable from prior knowledge, such as "What color was the elephant?" Good questions should call on readers to provide elaborated answers, not simple "yes" or "no" responses. The questions following reading, or the retelling rubrics (which we discuss later), are examined to see whether there is a pattern in the types of questions missed. For example, does a student have a problem with getting the "big picture"? Or are small details often missed? Does vocabulary seem to be a problem?

Similarly, records of the oral reading can provide clues about a student's metacognitive approach to the process. Did the student go back and correct him- or herself when it didn't make sense? Did the student read on and then change interpretation when answering the question? Was the way he or she segmented the sentence in oral reading natural, and did it show understanding? All these things help with comprehension. IRIs can also indicate whether word recognition is a barrier to comprehension when many words are misread. Rate is another indicator of comfort level in reading and correlates with comprehension.

When Daria did IRIs with Katie E, Elizabeth C, RJ, Scott H, Diane, and Jean (the students who placed lowest on her classroom summary of CFS results—see Figure 4.3, left), she found that Katie, RJ, and Scott had poorly developed print skills. They were not able to decode many of the words, which made them dysfluent in their reading. Scott stopped and tried to correct himself; this made his reading even slower but showed his strength in monitoring for meaning. Katie and RJ seldom corrected themselves and just tried to "get through" with the reading. Daria worked on phonics with all three students and used Scott's self-correction strategies as a model for the group. Elizabeth, Diane, and Jean had good decoding skills but poor fluency. In other words, they knew all the "notes," but couldn't play the "tune" so that it was recognizable. Daria worked on repeated readings with them and involved them in Readers' Theater to improve phrasing and flow. In this way, IRIs helped Daria pinpoint what was happening in the CFS.

The Cloze Procedure

Another way to match pupils with materials is to use the "cloze procedure." When good readers read, they use context and what they know about the topic, the world, and language to help them when understanding is tough. For example, if I find a book in a school library with a page totally covered with jelly (as some are) and scrape away a bit to see a four-letter word that starts with the letter "h"—

h _ _ _

—I can think, "help," "home," "hard," "hand," "here," "hear," and so forth. But I probably won't think "hzpq." I know some things about English spelling (the graphophonic system, which translates spoken words into spelled words) that help me predict what the word may be.

If I scrape off a bit more jelly and see this—

the h _ _ _

—my knowledge of sentence structure and parts of speech (the syntactic system) helps me predict that the mystery word is a noun or an adjective before a noun.

If I scrape off even more jelly and see the following—

The velvet glove on the h _ _ _ reached toward me from behind the screen.

—I may predict "hand" as the word, as something that wears a glove and reaches is intended here. I use meaning (the semantic system) to predict.

Besides these cueing systems, which are linguistically and semantically based, I also have a general knowledge about the world that can help me understand. If I'm walking on a rainy night and see a flashing neon sign with some missing letters—

B _ N _ O

—if the sign were over St. Mary of the Lake Church and I saw crowds of people with bags of quarters going in, I would think "BINGO." If the same sign were over the Old Town School of Folk Music announcing the musician Bela Fleck, I would think "BANJO." What we know about the world also helps us achieve closure on meaning when we don't immediately have all the information we need.

The cloze procedure was developed from this knowledge about how we read—how to use all our knowledge and the cue systems in text to reach closure on meaning. In the cloze procedure, words are deleted from a passage according to a word-count formula or various other criteria. The passage is presented to students, who insert words as they read to complete and construct meaning from the text. This procedure can be used as a diagnostic reading assessment technique; it can also tell us whether the material a student is given to read is on an appropriate instructional level. Because it is a silent task, cloze passages can be administered to a group and easily scored, making this a popular assessment process for middle school and above.

Besides matching students with materials, other purposes for using cloze passages are as follows:

• To identify students' knowledge and understanding of the reading process.
• To determine which cueing systems readers employ effectively to construct meaning from print.
• To assess the extent of students' vocabularies and knowledge of a subject.

- To encourage students to monitor for meaning while reading.
- To encourage students to think critically and analytically about text and content.

Preparing and Using Cloze Passages

The cloze procedure should not be used as a diagnostic technique until students are familiar with the procedure. It is advisable to do a passage or two on the overhead projector, so that students understand the process and what is required before using it for assessment.

Select a self-contained passage of a length appropriate for the grade level of the students being assessed. Leave the first and last sentences and all punctuation intact. Carefully select the words for omission according to a word-count formula (e.g., every fifth word). Do not remove more than every fifth word. When preparing the final draft of the passage, make all blanks of equal length, to avoid including visual clues about the lengths of omitted words. Figure 4.8 shows a portion of the same passage about Amelia Earhart as in Figures 4.2 and 4.6, adapted for use in the cloze procedure.

Have the students scan the entire passage before they fill in the blanks, to get clues to the gist and topic. Encourage the students to fill in each blank if possible. Although there should be no time limit for this exercise, the time necessary for completion should be noted. Suggest that students reread the completed passage.

Amelia Earhart

Amelia Earhart was an adventurer and a pioneer in the field of flying. She _____ things no other woman _____ ever done before.

During _____ War I, Earhart worked _____ a nurse. She cared _____ pilots who had been _____ in the war. Earhart _____ to what they said _____ flying. She watched planes take _____ and land. She knew that she, _____, must fly.

In 1928, _____ was the first woman _____ cross the Atlantic in _____ plane. But someone else _____ the plane. Earhart wanted _____ be more than just _____ passenger. She wanted to _____ a plane across the _____ herself. Then, in 1932, she _____ alone across the Atlantic to Ireland. The trip took over fourteen hours.

FIGURE 4.8. Part of the passage about Amelia Earhart (see Figures 4.2 and 4.6), adapted for use in the cloze procedure. The passage is from Schreiber and Kain (1985, p. 380). Copyright 1985 by Scott, Foresman and Co. Used by permission of the publisher.

Scoring the Procedure and Interpreting the Results

There are two ways of scoring the cloze procedure:

1. Only those words that are exactly the same as the deleted words are scored as correct. If exact replacement is necessary, a score of 40% or less indicates that the reader is unable to read the passage effectively or has reached frustration level. A higher score indicates that the material is appropriate for guided and independent reading experiences. Exact-word scoring has been found to be most reliable for assessing reading level (Bortnick & Lopardo, 1973). Figure 4.9 elaborates on this scoring method.

2. Words are scored as correct either if they are the same as the deleted words, or if they are synonyms or words that preserve the meaning of the sentences in which the blanks occur. If the procedure is scored using this method, a score of 70% or lower indicates that the material is inappropriate and frustrating for the reader.

Students should not be penalized for spelling errors if words are recognizable. In either scoring method, scores and completion times can be used to determine the suitability of reading material for a class, small groups, or individual students.

The cloze procedure can give diagnostic information as well. Examination of each student's responses will indicate the need for specific instruction. For example, if a student has replaced nouns with verbs, then syntax is not being used effectively to construct meaning. If deleted nouns have been replaced by nouns

Scoring:

1. Give 1 point for each blank filled in with an acceptable answer.

2. Divide the number correct by the number of blanks to figure out the percentage. (Passage should be 200–250 words in length.)

Percentage correct	Reading level	Appropriate for students?
60% or above	Independent	Should be easy reading.
40–60%	Instructional	Challenging, but readable with instructional support from teacher.
Below 40%	Frustrational	Will be difficult for students even with support.

FIGURE 4.9. Guidelines for scoring the cloze procedure and interpreting the results, according to the first of the two methods described in text.

unrelated to the content of the passage, the reader is not employing contextual or semantic cues, or has minimal knowledge about the topic. Instruction on these specific skills and strategies should be planned. Passages can also be constructed for certain purposes. For example, leaving out connectors can help to see how students predict the use of "and," "but," "or," and "nor."

Daria used the cloze procedure with Vera to force her to slow down and think about what she was reading. At first Vera just filled in the blanks with any word that came to mind, but slowly she began monitoring for meaning and focusing on comprehension rather than speed. When it is used in this way, the cloze procedure is helpful not only for assessment but also for instruction.

Using Questions and Retellings for Comprehension Assessment

The use of questions in instruction has a significant effect on both the development and assessment of students' comprehension strategies. The focus of direct questioning affects the thinking strategies that students develop. Also, when your instructional activities use good questioning and model the process of self-questioning, you help your students develop into effective independent comprehenders (Palincsar & Brown, 1984). Furthermore, strategies directed toward the metalinguistic aspects of asking and responding to the questions "What are they really asking here?" and "How should I go about finding and integrating information in the text with what I know?" are critical to independent content learning (Raphael, 1986) and can be analyzed when using questions for assessment. A bit later in this book, we talk about questioning strategies for developing comprehension.

It is clear that assessment involves asking good questions, interpreting responses to them, and using probing questions to follow free response and recall. You may ask yourself, "Of the many questions that may be asked about any given text or selection of text, which one will assess a reader's comprehension fairly?" This issue of using questions has engaged the attention of experts in reading, and in education generally, for a very long time; much has been written about the kinds of questions teachers should ask. In general, teachers are urged to ask a variety of questions, in order to give students the opportunity to respond in a variety of ways to the materials they read. Teachers are also advised, more specifically, to avoid overemphasizing questions that require only memory for directly stated information. They are encouraged, above all, to focus on questions that require higher-level thinking in order to develop higher-level cognitive processes. In short, questions have traditionally been approached from the standpoint of the mental processes required to answer them.

A major problem with this approach is that it is difficult to implement. A number of question classification schemes based on this approach have been developed over the years, but even the simpler ones require distinctions between levels or types of thought that are both difficult to make and "not warranted by the current state of our knowledge about language and cognition" (Anderson, 1972, p. 149). Moreover, questions that appear to elicit higher-level thinking because they cannot be answered from directly stated information may actually be quite trivial. Sanders (1966) points out that "thinking" questions cannot really be derived from insignificant subject matter. He gives the following examples to illustrate this point from a familiar children's rhyme:

TEXT: This little pig went to market.

QUESTIONS: Why? Did he go to buy or to be bought? . . . If to buy, what and for whom? Is he an informed buyer, the sort who would study the Buyers' Index and Consumers' Guide? . . . If he is to be sold, what price will he bring? What will be the effect on the market price . . . ?

TEXT: This little pig had roast beef.

QUESTIONS: Would you consider roast beef proper food for a pig? Which is better, nutritionally speaking, rare or well-done meat? (Sanders, 1966, p. 171)

Abstracted from the text, these seem to be excellent "higher-order" questions engaging deep thinking. But the quality of "This Little Pig" certainly doesn't support this depth of questioning. Sanders's caution is particularly relevant for the field of reading, where the "instructional diet" of simple story materials may provide little "food for thought." That is, the stories designed for developing basic reading skills do not always lend themselves to thoughtful discussion, and attempts to use them for this purpose may be unproductive.

Another problem with the mental-process or levels-of-thinking approach to questions is that it does not recognize a distinction between literal questions that pertain to important information and those that pertain to incidental detail—a point raised by Beck and McKeown (1981). Guszak (1967) alluded to this problem in his now-classic study of the kinds of questions teachers actually ask. He found that approximately 70% of the questions were of a literal nature, requiring only recognition (locating information in the passage) or recall (answering from memory) of factual information. Although this result is frequently cited as evidence that teachers ask too many literal questions, Guszak (1967) himself did not feel that a 70% proportion of literal questions was necessarily objectionable; his objection was that many of the questions involved "retrieval of the trivial factual makeup of stories." It appeared to him that students were likely to miss "literal understanding" of story plots, events, and sequences "in their effort to satisfy the trivial fact questions of the teacher" (p. 233). But Guszak recognized, at the same time, that teachers could not employ more appropriate questioning patterns without clearer guidelines.

In sum, the traditional focus on levels of thinking in the design of questions does not effectively guard against the trivialization of either literal or inferential questions. Questions need to be considered in conjunction with the responses they elicit and also in relationship to the structure and importance level of ideas in the text.

Writing Good Questions for Assessment

The best way to write good questions for assessment is to start with a selection map that graphically details the important parts of a selection. For a story, it might be a story map of some sort, asking the student about the elements of the story's "grammar"—the setting, characters, problem, resolution, and so forth. As well as structural aspects of the selection, motivational aspects—the "why" of the story—should be included in the story map (McConoughy, 1980). Figure 4.10 provides a map for the well-known story "Cinderella."

Story Map: "Cinderella"

Setting:
A land of castles and princes.

Characters:
Cinderella, stepmother, stepsisters, prince, fairy godmother.

Events:
Cinderella is orphaned.
The stepmother and stepsisters treat Cinderella badly.
The prince is looking for a bride at the ball.
Cinderella is forbidden to go to the ball.
Cinderella is helped by the fairy godmother to attend the ball.
Cinderella and the prince are attracted to one another.
Cinderella leaves as the clock strikes 12, and loses her glass slipper.
The prince searches for the slipper wearer.
The prince finds Cinderella.

Problems/goals:
The prince wants a bride.
Cinderella wants to escape her maltreatment.

Resolution:
The prince and Cinderella marry and live happily ever after.

FIGURE 4.10. A story map for "Cinderella."

Using the story map, questions are then constructed related to the story and to the essential motivation and vocabulary. Figure 4.11 provides a question set for "Cinderella." Some teachers like to begin with a "big idea" question; others prefer to start with a middle-level inferential question and "build" to bigger concepts, backing up when more detailed questions are needed. In either case, probing students' answers ("What makes you say that?") can reveal the processes they use to come to their understanding or misunderstanding.

With an informational piece, as with the story, the piece should be mapped first and then questions should be constructed. The organizational patterns (cause and effect, problem solution, description, etc.) can help you ask higher-level questions. For example, an informational piece on giraffes from *Ranger Rick* magazine was mapped as shown in Figure 4.12 for categories common to informational pieces about animals. Then broad questions for student thinking were generated from these categories, as shown in Figure 4.13. Using a map or other type of analysis of the selection to be read enables important questions on all levels of thinking to be constructed.

Questions: "Cinderella"

Possible "big idea" questions:
Why does Cinderella want to get away?
Why does the stepmother treat her badly?
Is this fact or fiction? How do you know?

Setting:
Where does this story take place? What does this tell you about the story?

Characters:
Who are the characters, and what is the importance of each to the story?

Events:
How does the stepmother try to keep Cinderella from meeting the prince?
How did Cinderella get to the ball?
What does the phrase "the clock strikes 12" mean, and how does it figure into the story?

Problems/goals and resolution:
How does the prince resolve his problem? Does this solve Cinderella's problem as well?
Is any of this story like real life? Not like real life? Explain.

Cross-textual additions:
Do you know any other versions of "Cinderella"? (Possible answers: "Yeh Shen" (Chinese tale), "Mufaro's Beautiful Daughter" (African tale).)
How are they like/different from this one?

FIGURE 4.11. Questions generated from the story map for "Cinderella."

Category-Based Map: "Twiga's First Days"

Description (how Twiga looks)	Where Twiga lives	What/how Twiga eats
Twiga is about 2 meters high. She has a buff-colored hide with big spots. She has two tassels of hair.	Twiga lives with a herd of giraffes in the Serengeti Desert in East Africa. It is so hot there that you can see heat mirages.	Twiga drinks milk from her mother's milk bag. She also eats leaves when the rest of the herd eats.
How giraffes get along with other animals/birds	Other interesting things . . .	
Lions and other predators are dangerous for Twiga and the herd. When Twiga is scared, she hides under her mother. When grown-up giraffes are scared, they run away.	A grown-up giraffe can be over 5 meters tall. Giraffes have long necks so they can eat leaves from trees.	

FIGURE 4.12. A map for an informational selection about giraffes, using categories common to informational pieces about animals.

Retellings

Many teachers prefer retellings (free recollections by students) to asking questions, because a retelling reveals how a student prioritizes and sequences information without the prompts of a teacher's questions. The examiner asks a student to retell the selection, and lists what is said in the order it is presented. Following the student's unprompted recall, the examiner uses probing questions to assess further for any important information the student does not supply. The teacher can assess how the student uses oral language, reconstructs a passage, and prioritizes and sequences information.

You can score recall easily by preparing a checklist based on the same selection maps discussed previously. For example, Figure 4.14 presents a retelling checklist for "Cinderella." (compare this to the story map for "Cinderella" in Figure 4.10). Give a student points for each idea or fact recalled, as you would with questions. Retellings are used extensively as research tools, and less frequently for assessment and instruction. As noted earlier, however, they have the advantage of

Questions: "Twiga's First Days"

Name _____

Write about Twiga. Use as many of the vocabulary words as you can.

Description (how Twiga looks)	Where Twiga lives	What/how Twiga eats
How giraffes get along with other animals/birds	Other interesting things . . .	

FIGURE 4.13. Questions generated from the map for the selection about giraffes.

showing the examiner what the student sees as important without the prompts of a teacher's questions. Furthermore, the sequence in which the student retells the information and the language he or she uses to express it provide more diagnostic information.

Some cautions about retellings are in order here. Morrow (1988) found that students often have trouble with the process of retelling if it is unfamiliar. Students will also often omit important information, because they assume that the examiner has also read the piece and already knows the information (Golden & Pappas, 1987). Moreover, younger children tend to omit information about the goals and motives of story characters but can often answer direct questions about these aspects of a selection (Stein & Glenn, 1979). Finally, Bridge and Tierney (1981) found that poorer readers were less able to offer information spontaneously than good readers. Therefore, some combination of questions and retelling may be opti-

Retelling Checklist: "Cinderella"

Note: Number items in order in which student presents them.

Setting:

_____ In a time long ago.

_____ In a land far, far away.

_____ In a time of castles and magic.

Characters:

_____ Cinderella.

_____ Wicked stepmother.

_____ Two mean stepsisters.

_____ Fairy godmother.

_____ Prince.

Problems/goals:

_____ Cinderella wants to escape stepmother's home.

_____ Stepmother wants one of her daughters to marry prince.

_____ Prince wants a bride.

Event structure (varies according to version):

_____ Cinderella comes to stepmother's home.

_____ Cinderella is treated badly.

_____ She contrives to get to a ball with help of fairy godmother.

_____ She entrances prince.

_____ She leaves at midnight, losing glass slipper.

_____ Prince finds her as the one who fits the glass slipper.

Resolution:

_____ Happily ever after (for the prince and Cinderella).

Comment on:

Organization of retelling: _____

Retelling of important elements: _____

Language/vocabulary used to retell: _____

Interpretation: _____

Engagement: _____

FIGURE 4.14. A retelling checklist for "Cinderella."

mal for getting the "big picture." The retelling indicates how students identify and organize important information.

Think-Alouds: "Online" Monitoring

Not only do we want to assess what students understand, we want to know how they understand. "Think-alouds" (Baumann et al., 1993) reveal how readers are processing the text and the ideas as they read. We discuss the instructional use of these tools in Chapter 6. Here we want to examine how they can provide a window on comprehension, especially into the area of metacognitive strategies.

In the think-aloud procedure, students verbalize before, during, and after reading a selection, revealing not only information but their internal thought processes. A teacher asks a student to reflect on what he or she is reading as the text is read chunk by chunk. Each chunk can be a line, a sentence, a paragraph, or a larger section, depending on the student and the task. Readers commonly comment on what they are reading, summarize it, or predict what is coming next (signaling understanding); indicate what is causing them problems (monitoring for understanding, clarifying); analyze part of the text (analyzing) or verbally try to figure things out (reasoning); relate the author's ideas to their own knowledge (elaborating); or evaluate the author's message or style (judging) (Lytle, 1982). By analyzing this "online" reading, the teacher can often understand why a student is having a difficulty understanding.

A rubric (set of guidelines for interpreting think-alouds) can help a teacher chart the moves a student makes. The teacher listens and records the main ideas remembered, using a checklist such as the one given. Besides noting *what* the reader remembers, the teacher can use this checklist to analyze *how* the student came to understand.

Before reading: Did the reader . . .
- Notice cues for prediction, such as title, picture, heading, author, charts, graphs?
- Make some suitable prediction about the text, topic, genre?
- Bring up something he or she already knows about the genre, topic, author?

During reading: Did the reader . . .
- Comment on what was read?
- Ask questions to be clarified?
- Try to answer his or her own questions and clarify what didn't make sense?
- Relate what was being read to prior knowledge?
- Summarize and/or retell the gist to that point?

- Check guesses or predictions?
- Reread or read ahead when trying to make sense?
- Use context for word meaning?
- Describe visualizations?

After reading: Did the reader . . .
- Summarize or retell?
- Respond?
- Critically reflect?

The checklist can also reveal what students emphasize; whether or not they note or overlook important aspects of a selection; how they make connections to what they know; and how they use such strategies as prediction, visualization, summarization, and self-questioning.

A think-aloud can open a window onto a reader's mind and let a teacher see process in action. One caution is that it is often difficult for children with weaker verbal skills to handle. Some students would rather write their questions as they read. A double-entry journal can be very helpful for this. On one side of the page, students write what they think the author is trying to convey; on the other side, they write their questions, interpretations, and criticisms. Figure 4.15 illustrates the use of a double-entry journal (see also Figure 2.3 in Chapter 2). Other students may want to place Post-It notes at various places in their reading that stimulate an idea or raise a question. Later reflections on these with a teacher can have a diagnostic use as well. Similarly, writing after reading, outlining, mapping, and so forth can give a teacher insights into both what and how students understand.

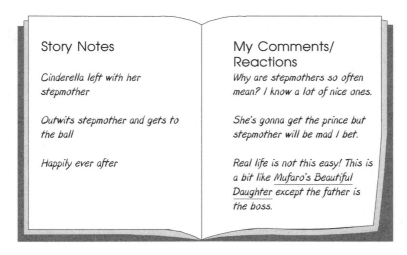

FIGURE 4.15. Double-entry journal for "Cinderella."

Rubrics for Comprehension

A "rubric" is a structured format for evaluating some performance. Rubrics assist teachers in looking at students' talking about or writing about reading, as well as at the ways students use what they read. There are many different ways to structure reading rubrics depending on what is to be evaluated. For example, a holistic rubric for evaluating how well student read to answer a question might look like the North Carolina Rubric (2007; see Figure 4.16). A second rubric (2007; see Figure 4.17) developed by the faculty at Norwood Park School in Chicago is used to evaluate student reading logs. Many other state/provincial and local standards

101 North Carolina General Rubric for Reading and Social Studies
Source: North Carolina Department of Public Instruction

Subjects	*Reading*	**# of scales**	*1*
	Social studies		
Grade(s)	*3–8*	**Scale length**	*4*

Holistic Scale

3 Answer addresses most aspects of the question and uses sound reasons and cites and explains appropriate examples. Uses skills of evaluation as well as analysis and synthesis.

2 Answer deals with most aspects of the question and makes correct inferences, although minor errors may exist. Comprehension is on an inferential level and the key skills are synthesis and analysis.

1 Answer deals with material on a concrete, literal level that is accurate in most dimensions.

0 Answer is unresponsive, unrelated or inappropriate.

Note: Scale points are defined in more detail for each test question. For example, a social studies question that asks the student to draw conclusions about a table comparing information from several countries is scored as follows:

    3 Response draws logical, clear conclusions which are somewhat developed.

    2 Response draws some conclusions but may be brief, somewhat lacking in clarity, or have minor errors in logic.

    1 Response draws at least one conclusion but it may be sparse or confusing.

    0 Response draws no conclusion or is inappropriate or unrelated to the task.

FIGURE 4.16. Example of a holistic reading rubric.

105 Norwood Park Draft Reading Log Rubric

Source: Faculty of Norwood Park Elementary School, Chicago, Illinois

Subject	Reading	**# of scales:**	4
Grade(s)	K–8	**Scale length**	4

Scale I: Frequency of Independent Reading

Distinguished   Daily reading for extended periods.

Proficient   Reads most days.

Apprentice   Occasionally reads.

Novice   Seldom reads.

Scale II: Difficulty Level of Books Selected

Distinguished   Reads at and beyond student's independent level.

Proficient   Reads at independent level.

Apprentice   Reads at and below independent level.

Novice   Reads below independent level.

Scale III: Variety of Genres Represented

Distinguished   Sampling of books from different genres.

Proficient   Willingness to try books from different genres.

Apprentice   Little experimentation with genres.

Novice   Little or no experimentation with genres.

Scale IV: Completion of Books Started

Distinguished   Completes most of the books initiated; completion of class and group books.

Proficient   Completes many of the books initiated; completion of class and group books.

Apprentice   Completes less than half of books initiated; completes some of class and group books.

Novice   Fails to complete many class and group books.

FIGURE 4.17. Example of a student reading log rubric.

committees have developed rubrics for their own charting and exploration of reading. The Chicago Public School shared a Rubric Bank for many subject areas at intranet.cps.k12.il.us/Assessments/Ideas_and_Rubrics/Rubric_Bank/rubric_bank.html. Also, the excellent Kathy Schrock website (http://school.discoveryeducation.com/schrockguide) has many rubrics for examination.

Putting It All Together

One of the important steps in effective teaching, which we discussed at the end of Chapter 2, is assessing and evaluating. In this chapter, we have presented varied models for carrying out this assessment. We have provided instructional strategies to help you do the following:

1. Get a "big picture" of your classroom.
2. Determine the general instructional level of your students.
3. Assess comprehension with questions and retellings.
4. Pinpoint comprehension strategies through think-alouds.

Questioning, retellings, and think-alouds can be used with any strategy you are modeling or presenting for guided or independent practice and are an essential component of the instructional cycle. Before standards-based goals can be set (the first step in the cycle of effective instruction), we need a clear picture of our students and their strengths, needs, and strategies. Similarly, differentiation of instruction and appropriate scaffolding depend on our knowledge of the appropriate developmental level of instruction. Finally, ongoing assessment is as critical a part of the effective instructional cycle as initial assessment.

CHAPTER 5

Strategies for Reading
for Information

Much of the reading we do is for information—sometimes for school purposes and other times for our own. In fact, recent reports of current reading practices by students and adults (Smith, 2000; Snowball, 1995) indicate that the majority of reading done by middle and high school students as well as by adults is informational in nature. For instance, we read newspapers and magazines; we browse the World Wide Web; we read brochures and manuals; and we follow directions on appliances and in recipes. The recognition of this shift in reading needs and preferences has led to significant changes in the published reading programs for elementary and middle school students and in the current state reading assessments. At least 50% of the materials in most programs and tests now involve informational reading. With the development of the new framework for reading for the 2009 National Assessment of Educational Progress (NAEP; American Institute of Research, 2007) there is a clear recognition of the increasingly important role of reading for information. Fifty percent of the fourth-grade assessment will be in informational reading and increasingly large percentages of informational reading are included in the 8th- and 12th-grade tests. In addition, the importance of cross-textual reading is also recognized and several passages on NAEP require this kind of reading and thinking.

All of these changes in materials and assessments reflect the reality that more and more reading is done in informational materials both for functional purposes and for pleasure. The best-seller lists generally have one section for fiction, another for nonfiction, and often yet a third for "self-help" books. One of the real transformations in the last decade has been the explosion of materials available for us to read on an enormous range of topics—both on the World Wide Web and in more traditional publishing, especially in books and magazines. There are thousands of magazines catering to our wide range of interests in sports, hobbies, people, and . . . the list goes on and on.

All of this underscores the fact that much of our reading is motivated by our own interests, and those interests are amazingly varied. We can also look specifically at reading of informational material from the perspective of our purposes. Sometimes we select informational materials because we want to learn more about one of our areas of interest. For example, many of us, as we plan a trip, read widely to gain a better sense of what we will encounter as we travel. At other times we want to be very specific—for example, to find the exact distances between two locations or the river on which our destination is located. At still other times, we are motivated because we want to create something new. We may read to perform a specific operation or task, such as cooking a recipe from our vacation site. Or, after returning from our holiday, we may want to read just to help recreate in our mind's eye what we saw and did, and to enjoy the emotions and feelings associated with those events and places again.

Because purpose has such a powerful effect on reading, when we teachers think about helping our students become better readers of informational materials, we need to begin by thinking of the purposes for which our students will read these materials. We need to provide opportunities for each type of purpose, from learning new information to performing tasks to recreating experiences. We also need to prioritize the importance of learning to read textbooks and the reference materials used heavily in schools. This kind of reading ability often determines whether our students will be successful throughout their schooling. It does not develop automatically and deserves concerted attention from us as teachers.

This chapter on informational reading (see the graphic organizer in Figure 5.1) begins by addressing motivations for such reading and then focuses specifically on the skills and strategies we as teachers can help students develop so they will have the necessary abilities to be successful with this important kind of reading. Informational texts are very different from fiction and poetry in organization and structure. Therefore, we need to look closely at the importance of identifying these differences and helping students use both the external and internal structures as they read and learn.

Because so much of the reading instruction in elementary schools has focused on fiction (Duke, 2000, 2004a, 2004b; Organization of Economic Cooperation and Development, 2001), it may be helpful for you, our readers, to take a few moments to think of what you have been reading recently. Do you read the newspaper or a news magazine regularly? Have you been engaged in reading professional literature in preparation for your teaching this year? Are you taking some course—either in an educational program or to improve your sports ability, skill

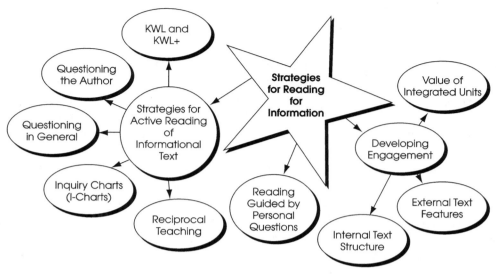

FIGURE 5.1. Graphic organizer for Chapter 5.

with computers, or health? Did you take a trip recently or are you planning one? Make some notes of the kinds of materials you are reading and why you are reading them.

A Personal Example

An example from the personal experience of one of us (Donna Ogle, who is the "I" in what follows) may be helpful here. I think specifically of the amount of reading for information that I did recently, related to my experience as part of the staff development team from the International Reading Association working with the Reading and Writing for Critical Thinking Project. When I was selected as part of the 3-year staff development project in Russia, I became voracious in my consumption of information about that country. One of my first activities was visiting a bookstore and selecting some basic books on the history and current culture of Russia. The possibilities seemed endless, so my husband and I put together a collection that represented a variety of perspectives on Russia and the Russian experience. We tried to fill out our prior knowledge with some history and some interpretation of current events. I also read with curiosity a new computer encyclopedia entry for Russia; it was rich in information, maps, and even snippets of music and dance.

The newspapers seem full of stories of Russia—from the country's current economic plight to the political vagaries of the government. I needed to refamiliarize myself with Russian cultural figures like Anna Pavlova, Baryshnikov, Rimsky-Korsakov, Stravinsky, Dostoyevsky, and Pushkin (to name just a few), who are also, of course, prominent in Western culture in general. I purchased anthologies of Russian folk- and fairy tales and individual trade books, some with sumptuous illustrations, to help fill in my lack of knowledge of the cultural history and story of Russia. Both the texts of the stories and the artwork help bring to life more of this country's rich traditions. I have also read a novel, *Dreams of My Russian Summers* by Andrei Makine (1997), as part of my exploration and "knowledge-building" activity. Language tapes and Usborne's (1989) *The First Thousand Words in Russian* represent another dimension of my reading for information.

As I reflect on how I have tried to build a better knowledge base about Russia, it is clear that "reading for information" involves reading many different kinds of texts. I am not limited to traditional expository texts. In fact, more recently I have read little from traditional historical and encyclopedia-type materials about Russia. Once I reestablished that basic knowledge, I could seek many other kinds of materials to build my knowledge. My "reading for information" has included a wide range of materials. It seems that *purpose*, more than text type, has been central in my own experience.

As I have thought about what the term "purpose" means, I have noted its many different dimensions. My own first purpose, I think, was building a basic knowledge of Russian history. I needed to be refreshed on events and their time frames. For example, what were the stages of the revolution that brought about the Soviet state? Where did most of the revolution take place? What was the relation of this revolution to World War I? Second, I wanted a better sense of Russian geography. Why was St. Petersburg the capital for so long? Which rivers have dominated the landscape and influenced trade and daily life? What different ethnic groups are important? Who are the Cossacks and White Russians, and where are they from? I had a hard time creating a mental map of Russia, so I turned to my globe and world map.

Once I had a basic sense of history and geography in mind (drawing on a sense of chronology and space), I wanted to fill in information about the Russian people and culture. With our team's focus on critical literacy, it was to the literature and folk literature that I attended. How do I describe this "reading?" It was not for enjoyment primarily, yet I have also found myself enjoying the stories I read. Nevertheless, my basic purpose was "informational." I wanted to get a general orientation to the kinds of tales that young children learn as part of Russian culture. I now know the Baba Yaga tales and "The Firebird," and I rely on Pushkin and Krylov (collectors of traditional tales) as resources. My knowledge of this literary tradition has also helped me understand references in other informational reading. Fiction is the backdrop for many of the illusions about Russia.

My motivation in reading for information was clearly to fulfill a very personal need and desire to learn. I had the questions and used the resources to fill in the pieces I needed. Some of my questions were very general, and others were quite specific. I often read parts of a text or article rather than the whole thing; when my questions were answered, I would stop. Sometimes I would skim over a chapter or article looking for specific information and just focus on one spot. My reading for information sometimes resembled my reading of a novel or piece of fiction, in which I would start from the beginning and read through to the end. At other times I read in very different ways. I might look at a table of contents or at section headings in an article and read from a single section of text.

Now think about the notes you made on your own reading. Did you have some of the same purposes and use some of the same processes? Have you shared with others any "stories" of your pragmatic experiences of reading to learn or reading to be informed? We think that young readers need to hear about the ways adults read across many texts to fulfill their own purposes. With the accessibility of the World Wide Web it has become very common for students to be able to search multiple sources rapidly. They need guidance, however, in using these sources critically, keeping their own purposes central, checking the authority of sites, and cross-referencing information they gain from different sources.

Developing Students' Engagement with Informational Texts

We can use our own insights into how we read for information—in a wide variety of materials and in different ways, depending on our purposes and interests—to help our students appreciate the breadth of materials available to them and the different strategies they can use in reading. One of our best starting places is to share some of our own reading interests with them. We can talk about what we read, share some of our materials with them, and then read aloud to them both from our materials and from good informational texts at their level.

A good guideline is to *read aloud* daily from various kinds of informational materials, beginning with something you are enjoying or learning about. For example, read interesting pieces from the newspaper—often human relations stories, sports, or "this week in history" items. Later in the day, read aloud something related to your topic of study, from a more difficult text than the students would be able to handle themselves—perhaps a biography or magazine article. Bring in materials that encourage students to ask questions or create some new items. For example, the book *Sidewalk Games around the World* (Erlbach, 1997) is an excellent resource for encouraging students to make and play their own games. Finally, read aloud from good informational books just to introduce students to the variety that is available—just as you do with fiction. A good source for quality trade books is the Orbis Pictus award winners and honor books selected by the National Council of Teachers of English (NCTE) each year (*www.NCTE.org*). By reading from a variety of different texts, your students will begin to appreciate the full range of materials that they can read; they may find some particular topics and genres that they will begin to self-select; and they will learn more about the structure and format of exposition.

The Value of Integrated Units

When we organize some of our literacy instruction around integrated units—as Joe does in his departmentalized class, with two units related to science and two to social studies (see Chapter 3)—we give students an opportunity to develop the particular skills and strategies needed for informational reading while they are motivated to learn about an interesting topic or concept. Many teachers are finding that using integrated units provides the motivation for them, too, to attend more fully to informational texts. Students don't automatically know either how to engage in a process of inquiry or how to use the resources available to them. A starting point is learning how to handle and read texts as varied as an encyclopedia entry and a narratively structured informational magazine article. Students need both internal strategies and visible tools to help them integrate information from varied sources. Integrated units also provide supportive contexts for English language learners (ELLs). The more ways a topic or theme is approached the more likely it is that ELLs will be able to build their knowledge of the language and the essential academic vocabulary, the disciplinary foci, and the content that they need to learn (Mora, 2006; Echevarria, Vogt, & Short, 2008). Often in integrated units teachers plan ahead by bringing together a wide range of resources including books and articles with high visual content and video or DVD sources. These more visual sources help English learners access what they already know and also help them build new contextual references to what they will be doing in the classroom.

Within the structure of integrated units teachers also have more time to focus on key vocabulary and language patterns that are foundational to the theme or topic. The more frequently the vocabulary and oral-language patterns are used, the more likely ELLs will be able to appropriate these for themselves.

In our work in Chicago (Chicago Public Schools, Office of Literacy, 2004; Project ALL, 2006) we have built a partner reading process that helps all students in a classroom access the social studies or science content they are learning. Over the last 4 years we have refined the Partner Reading and Content, Too (PRC2) approach to include an initial matching of students as partners based on similar reading fluency and interests. Students are taught through teacher modeling and guided practice to read short informative texts at their instructional or independent reading level. Students begin by surveying the book together attending to the external features. Then they read the text together sharing one book. The student on the left reads the left-side pages; the student on the right reads the right-side pages. Initially we provide a set of four questions that can be used to stimulate talk after each set of two pages is completed. See Figure 5.2 for an example of these questions. At first students are instructed to read each page three times. They begin by surveying both pages so they know the content. Then they reread their page

Name _____	Partner _____
Title: _____	Date: _____ Page _____ to page _____
What was most important? Why? (Explain)	What was most interesting? Why? (Explain)
What connections can you make? (Explain)	What could the author make clearer? How? (Explain)
Vocabulary—What are important words to remember?	

FIGURE 5.2. Sample matrix and questions from the PRC2 (Ogle & Correa, 2006).

and prepare to read it orally. If there are terms that seem unfamiliar they try to determine how to pronounce them using the glossary, their partner, or the teacher as a resource. The third reading is when they read the page orally to their partner. Finally, they select a question they want to ask their partner at the end of their oral reading.

The questions are to stimulate talk, not "stump" the listener. Key to this PRC2 process is that students learn to read academic content material fluently, become familiar with the written and oral sounds of the language, and engage in "academic" talk about the topic. At the end of each PRC2 session the students select two to three words that they think are important to learn and enter these in their vocabulary notebooks. This process has been instrumental in helping many students, not only the ELLs, attend carefully to informational texts and develop their ability to discuss content material confidently. The process, combined with a surrounding rich instructional program, deepens students' knowledge and thinking about content (Ogle & Correa, 2006).

In the rest of this section, we highlight some of the skills and strategies that make reading informational texts comfortable for students. We have organized our description of these into two subsections: dealing with the external features of informational texts and the internal structure of such texts. (We discuss inquiry-based reading and research more fully in Chapter 8.) Then you may want to refer again to Chapter 3 to think of how these skills and strategies can be developed within a time frame and structure that will work for you.

Developing Familiarity with External Features of Informational Texts

One of the first things we notice when we pick up nonfiction or informational materials is that they generally have a different format from fiction. Think of an informational book you have recently read, or of a children's informational book from one of the publishers producing quality short texts that support content instruction like National Geographic, Rosen, and Newbridge. Or ask your school librarian for a copy of one of the recent Orbis Pictus winners like Sy Montgomery's (2006) *Quest for the Tree Kangaroo* or Russell Freedman's (2005) *Children of the Great Depression*. One engaging feature of these informational books is that there are generally more pictures and other visual aids to enhance our engagement and help us understand the concepts. Much of the information is, in fact, often presented in pictures, graphs, diagrams, maps, and cartoons, and in their captions. In surveying the features of books, we note that in addition to a table of contents, these books, generally include a glossary and an index. The chapter titles are worth some attention, because they are often important indicators of how the author has organized the information. Within each chapter there is likely to be a further breakdown of information, with headings and subheadings designed to guide our reading to important content or "main ideas." Many books and articles also highlight key vocabulary with italics, boldface, or marginal notes that provide explanations of the terms. A well-organized informational piece helps us locate the part of the text we want to read when we have particular questions we want answered.

In addition, as timely, accurate information is important, readers need to be aware of both the copyright date and the qualifications of the author. Books for very young readers are just now becoming more complete, so looking to be sure there are chapter divisions is important before selecting books for primary-school students. Even checking to see whether the pages are numbered may be a good idea because it is hard to locate and return to information without some pagination. As we help children use informational books, we need to be sure that we have high-quality books available for them. Sometimes the colored photographs are stunning, but the rest of the important book features are missing.

One group of primary-school teachers in Evanston, Illinois, has been working to build students' confidence and ability to read informational trade books. These teachers have noticed that children can have difficulty relating the pictures and other graphic information to the text content. Some books now have graphics inserted in a wide variety of places over the pages, and often on a two-page spread. The captions are often placed variously, too. Sometimes a caption is beneath a picture, and at other times the captions may be beside or even above the illustrated material. Only by carefully studying the individual pages and mapping the relationship between text and graphics and captions can their relationship be determined. Then it is important to share this process of exploration and what is learned about the text layout with the children. Without support from teachers, much of the richness of these new informational texts can be overlooked by young readers.

Another team of primary-school teachers in Glenview, Illinois, helps young students explore and become familiar with informational texts by including a wide array of books and magazines with each of the monthly science units. These teachers introduce one or more informational books each week. They also have students read informational books as part of their self-selected reading component. As a way to reinforce the special nature of these "true books," the teachers have developed a "Nonfiction Book Report" worksheet that is in the form of four book pages (see Figure 5.3). One page consists of a "Nonfiction Book Checklist." Students fill this out as an essential part of their reports. Other pages ask for what they liked, what they learned, and what would make the book better. When children's attention is drawn to these features of the text in this manner, the students begin to use them more regularly and think of them as "resources."

Intermediate-grade teachers also have children preview expository texts they are using both as textbooks and as other resource materials. At the beginning of the year, it is always good to refresh students' memories of all the ways information is available. Reading aloud to students from magazines and books provides

Nonfiction Book Report	Nonfiction Book Checklist

by
 	
_____
 	
Title of the book:
 	
_____
 	
Author:
 	
_____
 	
1
	_____ 1. Table of contents
	_____ 2. Index
	_____ 3. Photographs
	_____ 4. Realistic, accurate
	        illustrations
	_____ 5. Maps
	_____ 6. Diagrams
	_____ 7. Captions (descriptions of
	        photographs, illustrations,
	        etc.)
	_____ 8. Glossary (words and
	        definitions)
	_____ 9. Page numbers
	_____ 10. Other
	
	2

Something I liked about this book was: Something I learned from this book: 3	This book would be better if: 4

FIGURE 5.3. Four-page format for a nonfiction book report. Used by permission of D. Gurvitz, D. Sheffrin, and J. Kirsch.

Observations about This Book

Fill in the information below as you skim through the book *before* you read.

Your name: _____

Title of the book: _____

Title of the chapter we are reading: _____
_____

I am reading this book because: _____
_____

Two questions I have are:

1. _____
_____

2. _____
_____

Now look through this book. Write down some special features you observe in this book that might help you answer your questions.

1. _____
2. _____
3. _____
4. _____

FIGURE 5.4. Worksheet for previewing an informational book.

further opportunity to focus attention on illustrations, captions, and other presentations of information. Students themselves can also learn to preview texts. A teacher can prepare worksheets similar to the ones in Figures 5.4 (for books) and 5.5. (for articles) to guide students in thinking about the various aids provided. Because so much of students' reading instruction is in fiction and story materials, these worksheets reinforce the need to approach informational materials in a different way.

Intermediate students should begin to anticipate how informative expository material is organized. By third grade, most students should be able to predict what might be in the table of contents of an animal book (description, habitat, food, family, etc.). Before studying regions of the earth in fourth grade, some students

Be a Detective—Survey the Scene in This Article

Name: _____

Title of article: _____

Starts on page _____ and ends on page _____

Look through the article. Put an x next to any of these you find:

_____ Headings   _____ Dates   _____ Pictures   _____ Boldface or italics

_____ Maps, charts, or graphs

Predict what the article will be about:

    After surveying this article, I think

the main point will be: _____

Some major points will be: _____

_____

Some important dates may be: _____

_____

It seems to be organized this way (check any that seem correct):

_____ Sequence of events   _____ Comparison/contrast

_____ Description by categories   _____ Problem and solution

_____ Process description   _____ Cause and effect   _____ Other

FIGURE 5.5. Worksheet for previewing an informational article.

should be able to identify some possible topics that will reoccur with each region studied (plants, animals, geography, human life, etc.). Fifth graders need to know that biographies have some common topics that are used to organize information (early life, education, hardships, accomplishments, etc.). One way to assess students' awareness of these "expert" ways of organizing content information and then use it to prepare for reading and learning is to have them fill out a "Predicting a Table of Contents" worksheet (see Figure 5.6).

At the middle school level, some teachers have students identify and use the external structure of textbook chapters and magazine articles to make notes. They skim through a chapter or article and create a graphic organizer or map of it, with the title in the center and each of the main headings on one spoke of the spider-like map (see Figure 5.7). This map is then used while students read, to help them keep

Predicting a Table of Contents

Wolves	Deserts
Chapter 1. _____	Chapter 1. _____
Chapter 2. _____	Chapter 2. _____
Chapter 3. _____	Chapter 3. _____
Animals/Nature	**Regions of the World**
Chapter 1. _____	Chapter 1. _____
Chapter 2. _____	Chapter 2. _____
Chapter 3. _____	Chapter 3. _____
Ancient Egyptians	**James or Dolley Madison**
Chapter 1. _____	Chapter 1. _____
Chapter 2. _____	Chapter 2. _____
Chapter 3. _____	Chapter 3. _____

FIGURE 5.6. Worksheet for predicting a book's table of contents.

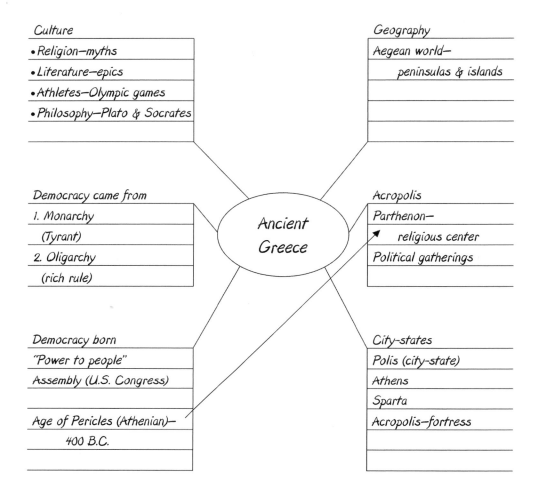

FIGURE 5.7. A graphic organizer or map for a book chapter or magazine article about ancient Greece.

focused on the way the information is related. It can also be used as an interactive guide for reading. The students can brainstorm what they know about each section before reading, write those ideas on the map, and then make notes of new information on the map as they read. This active engagement helps students focus on and retain information while they read.

As part of the PRC2 framework students are introduced to the process of previewing the book's external features by following the steps provided on their guidesheet. For many students, this is the first time that they have taken the time to preview informational texts with some rigor. Working with a partner and talking about the text features helps students understand them as meaningful guides to the main ideas and priorities selected by the author. When they later compare two to three books on the same topic by different authors they become more aware of the choices authors have to make when writing informational books, in terms of both the content to include and the way to organize and prioritize information.

Yet another strategy teachers use to help students utilize the external structure of articles and chapters is to have a class read a chapter in cooperative fashion, in a variation of the "jigsaw" cooperative learning strategy. The class previews the text by identifying the major sections. The teacher writes these on the board. Then the class is divided into teams. Each team of students reads and creates a visual report of the key ideas of just one section of the text (one heading and elaboration). Many informational chapters and articles have such a heavy load of information that asking students to learn just one section from reading makes the task manageable. Each group then reports on its section. Having group members serve as teachers for the rest of the class both enhances engagement in reading and creates a shared environment for learning.

Visually presented information is also critical in many informational texts. For example, in *The Magic School Bus* books by Joanna Cole, information is all around the page—in the captioned dialogues of teacher and students in the center, in the labeled drawings of the classroom or environment where the adventure takes place, and in the slate or notebook information in the upper corners of the page (see Figure 5.8). All this is part of the "text" and needs to be read and assimilated by the student reader. *The Magic School Bus* books are not unique. We have seen greater use in recent years of a variety of visual presentations in good informational books, textbooks in all content areas, and magazine articles. Teachers need to help students read and integrate this information into the rest of the narrative textual input.

How can we do this? First, find out how your students attend to pages of "busy" text. We ask students individually to point to how they read a two-page spread in a book or magazine. As they do so, we listen and make notes of their approaches. Where do they start? Do they read the visually presented information? When do they read it? Do they integrate the visual presentations with the running text? Do they read captions on graphs and pictures? Are they aware of how they approach reading when the materials are presented in a variety of formats? Do they integrate these different sources in notes they make or in summaries they create? All of these are questions that you can use to help you assess students' engagement with text materials.

From this assessment, you can talk with your students about the importance of using all information. Modeling how to approach "busy" text by doing some think-alouds with groups of students can help students use texts more adequately (see Chapter 6). Make a transparency of one or two pages of text. Explain how you survey the page, note the different layout of information and graphics, and raise questions that are stimulated by the text. (You may ask, "Why did the author use this cartoon? What is its role in this section? Let's see, the caption says . . . Oh,

FIGURE 5.8. A page from one of *The Magic School Bus* books, showing the many ways information can be presented in an illustration. From *The Magic School Bus Inside a Hurricane* by Joanna Cole, illustrated by Bruce Degen. Text copyright 1995 by Joanna Cole, illustrations copyright 1995 by Bruce Degen. Reprinted by permission of Scholastic Inc. *The Magic School Bus* is a registered trademark of Scholastic Inc.

yes, I bet it is an example of . . .") You can also cover the text on the transparency and ask students to survey the graphic information. From this survey, ask them to predict what content they think is being highlighted and what questions they think will be answered on the page or two. In this way, the importance of using the visually presented material may become clearer to them. In fact, sometimes this kind of preview can reduce the actual reading time considerably. All of these are strategies we as adult readers use when appropriate. Students often need to hear another person's thinking before they understand how active they need to be as readers.

Developing Familiarity with the Internal Structure of Informational Texts

Another key to reading and learning from materials written to inform is becoming familiar with the way the ideas are organized by the writer. As readers of narrative stories, we have learned—often first by listening to stories our parents read to us— that there is a predictable pattern to these tales. We read to find out who the characters are, what problem they encounter, and how they go about resolving it; then we savor their victory at the end. No similar pattern characterizes informational texts. They can be organized in several ways. This makes predicting and organizing ideas more difficult for novice readers. And it makes it all the more important for us to provide guidance, so students can learn to identify and use these writing patterns for their own reading.

Although different labels are given to these common patterns, there are at least six basic ways writers organize information in expository texts:

1. Description using categories of information with no particular ordering.
2. Comparison/contrast.
3. Sequence of events.
4. Problem and solution.
5. Process description.
6. Cause and effect.

We can introduce students to these patterns by collecting several books on the same topic and guiding students to compare their internal structure. For example, in doing her unit on butterflies, Susan (see Chapter 2) shared several interesting books with her students and focused on how the authors had chosen to organize their information. The first books she brought in was *The Butterfly Alphabet Book* (Sandved, 1995)—a beautiful book with each page devoted to a letter of the alphabet found in the wings of a butterfly.

Information about each butterfly is available in the back of the book, and a poem about butterflies is carried through all the pages from A to Z. After this introduction, she brought in *Monarchs* (Lasky, 1993), and then *An Extraordinary Life* (Pringle, 1997), on the monarch's life cycle and metamorphosis. Next came *Amazing Butterflies and Moths* (Still, 1991), comparing and contrasting the two related groups of insects. The authors of these books had chosen different ways of organizing their information, and students began to see these patterns. When they wrote their own reports, they were reminded of the various ways the information could be organized, and their newly focused interest in writing and reading was solidified.

Susan also used the actual tables of contents from several books to help students understand that there are several ways information can be organized. Look at the four that are shown in Figure 5.9. Each represents one author's way of presenting the ideas about butterflies and moths. The one at right is a life story, told basically in chronological order. The one at top right simply goes week by week through a butterfly's life. The other two have descriptive categories. The one at bottom left begins with a more comparative chapter ("Bright butterfly, dull moth") and only at the end explains the butterfly's life cycle (in the chapter "From egg to butterfly"), with no mention of the moth's life cycle in a chapter title.

Another teacher used the students' weekly news magazine to introduce these internal structures to students. She had them predict from the titles of the articles

KEEPING MINIBEASTS

BUTTERFLIES
AND
MOTHS

Text and Photographs: Barrie Watts

CONTENTS

Contents

Contents

Contents

FIGURE 5.9. Tables of contents from four different books about butterflies and moths, illustrating different ways of presenting similar information.

how they were likely to be organized. For example, one issue dealt with the reentry of wolves to Yellowstone National Park. The headline on page 1 read "Wolves in Yellowstone: Will They Make It?" (problem and solution). On the second page, there was a comparison between wolves and dogs (comparison/contrast). Another short article explained the family pattern, eating, and habitat of wolves (description). When the students' attention was focused on these patterns used by authors to communicate their ideas, they could begin to look for the patterns in other materials.

Following this introduction to ways of organizing ideas, the teacher made a cube with each side containing one of these ways of organizing ideas. As part of their prereading brainstorming, she would periodically ask students to use the cube. If she turned it to "comparison/contrast," the students would need to brainstorm some ways of comparing and contrasting the topic to others. For example, when a unit on immigration was just beginning, the teacher asked students to brainstorm what they knew about immigration. When the cube was turned to "comparison/contrast," students thought hard, and then a few responded:

"It's like animal migration—when butterflies go to Mexico for the winter, since there isn't food for them in the north."
"Immigration and adoption are alike—you don't know for sure what you are going to get, it is very risky, and . . ."

When the teacher turned the cube to "problem and solution," the students again thought hard, and a few responded:

"Sometimes immigrants are not wanted—like some Mexicans coming across the border into Texas."
"Sometimes too many immigrants make it hard to find food—like in Africa now. I read in the newspaper that there isn't food or water in Uganda."

Teachers can also use the internal structure of a text to help students brainstorm the questions they think will be answered when they read. For example, during a unit about planets, Susan asked her students: "If we are going to read a book about the planet Uranus, what questions do you think the author will answer?" The students responded:

"Where it is located in relation to the earth."
"How big it is and what scientists think it is like."
"Moons or special features."
"Temperature."

By introducing the reading of the book in this way, Susan engaged her students in thinking about the big picture of what the author was trying to accomplish in writing this informational text. Then the students could compare their assumptions with what the author actually wrote. After reading a few books or articles about different planets, the children began to have a clear idea of what scientists might consider most important to include in their descriptions of planets. They could use these expectations as readers to predict and chunk information in their memories; they could also use these expectations to compare planets on their own, even if some authors didn't make these comparisons explicitly.

Yet another way teachers can help students think about and use the author's organization of ideas is to have them write using an author's structure. From first grade on, children can create their own informational books using what they have seen in books they have read. See Figure 5.10a for an example of the kinds of informational books students in Kristin Kaczmarek's first-grade class in Northbrook, Illinois, write. Kathy Callaci of Palatine, Illinois, has second and third graders write stories following the pattern of easy books like *Polka Dots* (Tatler, 1996). By writing "like an author," students may become more attentive to organization, and they certainly enjoy using these frames to communicate. Thus, both reading and writing objectives are enhanced. Figure 5.10b shows the book a second-grader produced using the pattern from the *Polka Dots* book that read, "I spot something with polka dots. It's a . . . ."

Reading Guided by One's Own Questions

A clear difference between informational reading and literary or story reading is that in informational reading, we don't have to start from the beginning and read straight through a text. Often when we read informational texts, we aren't interested in reading all the author has provided. We want to find a specific piece of information, or we want to browse at our own initiative. One of the nice aspects of informational text is that we can often read it in our own order—we don't have to start from the beginning and go through the text page by page. Because most informational text does not have a plot, we can read it "out of order." If we want to know how long monarch butterflies live, we can take a book about monarchs, go to the table of contents or the index, and look for a section of the book that addresses this question. We need to help students learn to use these tools for their own purposes. Too many students only know how to begin at the first sentence and read through a text word by word. We need to help them develop the skill of self-directed search and reading. For example, what words should we use to find the indexed page(s) for lifespan in the book about monarchs? What possible words would help us access this topic? (With the increased use of the World Wide Web, this last skill is becoming an essential one.)

It is helpful to students that we discuss these differences. We want them to think about why they are reading and what they want to accomplish. When they

FIGURE 5.10a. Cover, contents, and two representative layouts from *All About Eagles*, an informational book created by Melanie Simon and Tommy Bendewald, first-grade students in Northbrook, Illinois. Used by permission.

FIGURE 5.10b. Child's version of the *Polka Dot* book.

know their purposes, they can decide whether they want to read just a small portion of a text or whether they want to start at the beginning and read through the full article or book. Reading to find answers to specific questions and reading to develop more general knowledge require different approaches. Part of being a mature reader is knowing that not everything has to be read cover to cover, and that some texts can be discarded while others deserve several readings.

We can help students differentiate the strategies they would use for these different conditions. Suppose the students have been studying Russia and have at their disposal four books on Russia. They have been reading and learning about Russia for a while, and they now have specific interests. These interests will shape how each text is read. For example, if the purpose is to find specific information about when Catherine the Great lived and the role she played in St. Petersburg, the reading proceeds in a specific way. Students will want to use aids in the books to locate their topic. First, they might look at the table of contents to see whether the reference material addresses historical periods and leaders. If they can't find a section that seems apparent, then they may need to look at the entry for Catherine the Great in the index. Page references can then be checked out, and the pages can be read. With some brief introduction, students can formulate more specific questions to guide their further reading.

By contrast, if students are only just starting the unit on Russia, they may just want to read to get a general idea of the history of Russia. Then they can preview a book to determine whether it seems to be at their reading level, is attractive to them, and contains resources that will help build their knowledge. They may want to read a short section of the text just to test their choice.

Strategies for Active Reading of Informational Text

As teachers we help students become familiar with the structure of informational text, but we also need to help students develop ways to engage actively with the authors of those texts and to think about the content. Several basic strategies are worth developing to the extent that students can use them on their own. These are the "know, want to know, learn: (K-W-L) and the K-W-L+ strategies, inquiry charts (I-charts), reciprocal teaching, questioning the author, and questioning in general. These strategies have been developed independently, but they often work well when used in consort.

The K-W-L and K-W-L+ Strategies

The K-W-L Process

Students become much more engaged in reading when they and their interests form the starting points for new inquiry and learning. K-W-L (Ogle, 1986) is a process in which the teacher models and guides active engagement with informational texts. It is a group process using the knowledge and information students bring to help each other build a better starting place for learning and to share the results of their reading. The adept teacher weaves together what some class members know and stimulates questions for all to pursue as they read to learn. The process also helps students lacking confidence in both reading and writing, because the teacher is the first one to write on the board. This permits children to see the written forms of key terms they will encounter in text later. It also models what the students will write on their own worksheets or in their learning logs.

The teacher and students begin the process of reading and learning by brainstorming together what they *know* (the K in K-W-L) about a topic. The teacher guides students to probe their knowledge statements and to find conflicting or partial statements of what they know. For example, as members of a group brainstorm what they know about wolves, one student says, "They live in Alaska." Another volunteers, "I think they live in Colorado and Wyoming." The teacher can encourage more student engagement by continuing the thinking: "Does anyone else know something about where they live? Can anyone frame a question that may help us find out more?" The teacher writes on the blackboard, overhead projector, or computer what the students think they know, writing down their ideas just as they volunteer them. If the format of the K-W-L worksheet depicted in Figure 5.11 is used, these ideas are written down in the "K—What We Know" column. The teacher's role is not to correct or evaluate but to encourage and stimulate students to think broadly about what they bring to the study. Through this brainstorming–discussion process, some questions or uncertainties generally surface. These the teacher writes in the center column, "What we want to know."

The teacher's role is to help students activate their knowledge and develop interest in the topic. As ideas are voiced and written down, they may seem random and unconnected. At this point the teacher needs to make a decision. If the group members are engaged and ready to think a little more deeply, the teacher will ask them to think of ways the experts organize information on this topic. This move to a deeper level of thinking can begin by first focusing on categories of information the children already have some intuitive knowledge of. The teacher can initiate reflection: "Look at what we have listed in the 'K' column. Are any of these items connected? For example, I see three items about animals that live in the desert. Can you find other items that go together in this category?" The teacher may also begin simply by asking students to step back and think about the topic generally: "What are the basic categories of information we are likely to need to use?" or "If you were going to write a table of contents on this topic, what would you include?" The ideas students volunteer can be listed separately at the bottom of the "K" column (see the "Categories of Information" box at the lower left of Figure 5.11).

With a variety of ideas being shared, the teacher can easily ask what the students *want to know* (the W in K-W-L). Again, it is the students' role to think of real questions, and the teacher's to write down what they say. These questions form the second column on the worksheet or blackboard. If students are not familiar with the process of generating their own questions, the teacher may need to model some questioning at the beginning. He or she may pick up on some comment made by a class member and extend it into a question. For example, if the

K-W-L Worksheet

1. K—What We Know:	W—What We Want to Know:	L—What We Learned and Still Need to Know:

2. Categories of Information We Expect to Use:

A.   E.

B.   F.

C.   G.

D.   H.

3. Where We Will Find Information:

1.

2.

3.

4.

FIGURE 5.11. The K-W-L worksheet.

class is beginning a unit on the desert region and someone has listed "cactus" as a plant in the desert, the teacher can extend this by asking, "I wonder if there are any uses people make of cactus in the desert?" He or she can write this in the "W—What We Want to Know" column. The teacher can continue to guide students to find questions by suggesting, "Is there anything else we might want to learn about the animals that live on the desert? Do we have to be careful of any of them? If we were hiking, should we watch out?" Until students are able to put themselves into their learning by finding their own questions and level of knowledge, it is unlikely that they will retain much of what is studied. Therefore, the time spent in activating personal and class interest is important. This process puts the students right in the center of any new study. Rather than beginning with a text and previewing it, the teacher begins with the students and becomes an active listener and recorder. This group focusing helps students think about the range of ideas that they and others already have on the topic. It should also help them make new connections and become intrigued by what they don't know. Listening to each other can stimulate new vocabulary and associations; the writing done by the teacher often helps more reluctant readers begin to make associations between oral language and the written forms of words they will encounter as they read.

It may be necessary for the teacher to establish the rules for brainstorming as the process begins: "All ideas are acceptable. Say what first comes into your mind. Later these ideas will be checked and edited or revised." Students need to listen to each other but not to judge the quality of each other's ideas. The goal is to get as many different ideas out as possible in the time allotted.

Once the students have discussed the topic, they are more ready to begin their own reading. It may be useful to have students write down on their own worksheets or learning logs those pieces of information they individually think they know and the questions they want to know more about. In this way, both the group and the individual are respected. Some teachers have students work in pairs to do both the writing and reading, as this is more stimulating and supportive for some children who may lack confidence in writing and taking risks.

Teachers can diagnose from this discussion what texts will be most useful to the students. It may be that what was anticipated as adequate turns out to be inappropriate. One of us (Donna Ogle) remembers doing a lesson on air pollution to prepare students for the discussion of this topic in their fourth-grade science text. By the time the class had brainstormed what the students knew, it was clear that they could have written a more sophisticated text than the one they had before them. Rather than reading that text, I led the class in collecting other materials and they wrote their own chapter for future students in fourth grade. If the text or texts are appropriate, then students can read and make notes on their own of what they learn—both answers to their questions, and unexpected information that they think is interesting and/or important. By this point the students generally have many more questions and can add those to their worksheets.

The K-W-L+ Process

Teachers working with students in content areas know that even with motivation and engagement, the students will not remember much of the new information the first time they encounter it. Therefore, the "Plus" in K-W-L+ (Carr & Ogle, 1987) extends this learning process. Students are asked to do more reorganizing of what they have learned by making a semantic map or graphic organizer of the key information. They select the major categories and list facts under those categories, thus rethinking what they are learning. Finally, they write what they have learned in an essay form, so they have additional opportunities to consolidate their learning. See Figure 5.12 for an example of how a student (in a remedial reading class) engaged in this process. She began by listing what she knew about camels and continued through the process of reorganizing both her prior knowledge that was confirmed through reading and new information she gained (see Figure 5.12a). She chose three major categories under which the information could be grouped: history, survival in the desert, and varieties of camels. She listed all she knew under those three category headings (see Figure 5.12b). She then wrote her own summary on the topic of camels. The result was a coherent, informative essay that pleased her and her teacher (see Figure 5.12c). Engaging actively in such a variety of learning activities gives students a sense of how they can become active learners on their own, even when the teacher is not present. The need to reorganize and rehearse new knowledge and connect it with what was previously known establishes for students the effort needed in learning and reinforces their personal self-esteem, because they possess a productive process for school tasks.

Inquiry Charts for Thinking Critically

Using multiple sources of information is both natural and important in helping students find texts that meet their own levels of knowledge and interest, find answers to their own questions, and compare and contrast authors' points of view. It encourages the critical thinking that is so needed in our world today. Yet many students have a difficult time using more than one source effectively. Studies (Many, Fyfe, Lewis, & Mitchell, 2004; Spector & Jones, 2007; Boyd & Ikpeze, 2007) underscore how important it is that teachers carefully guide students in deepening their understanding so they can make effective use of the variety of sources now available. With the Internet, media dramas, and visual artifacts, as well as the rich resources of magazines and books, the possibilities for reading and learning from varied texts and text types are nearly limitless. Yet, students need help in learning across texts (Spiro, Coulson, Feltovich, & Anderson, 2004). They also need support in developing understanding of different points of view and perspectives that come from reading different accounts of the same events.

What I Know	What I Want to Find Out	What I Learned
Desert is sandy. *Camels drink a lot of water.* *Camels have humps.* *Camels have soft felt.* *Little water in the desert.* *Related to llama.* *Camels can go for days without water.* *Camels resemble horses.*	*How do they survive in desert?* *History of Camels* *1. Are there different kinds of camels?* *2. Where do they live?* *3. How long do they live?* *4. How many people can they carry?* *5. Why do they have humps?*	*1. Different kinds of camels are Arabian and Bactrian. Sometimes people talk about dromedaries. This is another name for Arabian.* *2. Arabian camels live in the Middle East, India, and North Africa. Bactrian camels live in the Gobi Desert of northeastern Asia.* *3. It is designed for life in the hot, dry, and sandy parts of the world. Its long legs help the camel do more than walk.* *4. They usually carry one person and their belongings. One-humped camels are used to carry things.* *5. The hump is filled with fat. This fat could be more than 80 pounds. The fat is used for energy when food is not available.*

FIGURE 5.12a. One student's engagement in the K-W-L+ process: (a) A basic K-W-L listing of information about camels; (b) the grouping of information into three major categories; and (c) the student's final essay on the topic of camels.

A good starting place in using multiple texts is the I-chart, developed by Hoffman (1992). This chart enables students to take important questions, select three or four sources of information they want to use to explore those questions, and then come to their own conclusion about the questions they framed initially. Figure 5.13 presents an I-chart.

Once students have used the K-W-L process to activate their knowledge and interest, they select some key questions for more in-depth research, which they can work on together to learn more about. The class or small groups can decide on the questions they want to concentrate on and write these on the chart. Then the best sources of information for the questions are selected, usually with teacher help and

Ship of the Desert

Kinds of Camels	Camel History	How Camels Survive Desert Life
Two kinds: 1. Arabian—one hump. Middle East and India. Also called dromedary. Used for racing and riding. 2. Bactrian—two humps. Asia—Gobi desert.	1. Goes back millions of years ago. 2. First kind of camel was humpless. 3. All spread out because of land bridges. 4. Died out in North America. 5. Llama is present-day cousin of camel. 6. Used to be a sign of worth.	Hump—food, fat, and energy. Long legs, not too close to sand. Padding on knees—to protect them if it falls or lies down. Eyelids and eyelashes to protect from sand storms.

FIGURE 5.12b.

Ships of the Desert

Camels go back millions of years ago. They used to be a sign of wealth. The first kinds of camels were humpless. They were all spread out. Most of them died out in North America. Llama is their present-day cousin.

There are two kinds of camels. They are Arabian and Bactrian. Arabian is also called dromedary. Arabian camels have one hump and they are found in the Middle East and India. They are used for racing and riding. Bactrian camels have two humps and they're found in Asia in the Gobi Desert. Bactrians have short legs and long wool.

Camels have many ways of surviving in the desert. In their hump they have food, fat, and energy, so camels can go without food for awhile. Camels also have long legs, so they're not close to the hot sand. They have padding on their knees if they fall or lie down. Eyelids and eyelashes protect the camel's eyes from sand storms.

FIGURE 5.12c.

Topic	What We Know	Source 1	Source 2	Source 3	Summary
Interesting facts					
New Questions					

Guiding Questions

FIGURE 5.13. A blank I-chart. Adapted from Hoffman (1992). Copyright 1992 by National Council of Teachers of English. Used by permission of the author.

guidance, and are also listed across the top of the chart. This simple framework establishes that in seeking answers to questions, multiple sources are needed. The I-chart is then used to make a systematic search for information. The I-chart also includes a row for "Interesting Facts"; these are pieces that don't fit the basic questions but are still relevant to the students' inquiry. This often becomes an important way to take notes on ideas that can be shared with the class later—ideas that are full of potential for more reading.

The K-W-L and the I-chart are frameworks through which teachers can engage students personally and collectively in thinking about their relationship to a content to be studied and in setting a course for learning. The frameworks do not, however, show students how to actually engage with the text as they read it. That is where the next strategies are most useful.

Text Annotation

While reading a particular text it is helpful to make notes on the information and ideas that help answer the questions that have been asked. It is also helpful to make notes when reading for general information, or when reading a textbook for a particular content area. An easy way to help students engage actively with informational texts that they want to read in some depth is to teach them a simple annotation system, so they can "read with pencil in hand." We like using marks that students can make in the margins with a number 2 pencil and then erase when they are done or marks made with small sticky notes. Some teachers enjoy giving students two to three different colors of notes, one for each kind of annotation. The teacher can introduce and model using a "+" to indicate something that is an important idea. While reading from a text that all share or by reading with a transparency or text on a visual screen the teacher can stop periodically and make a "+" mark in the margin beside an important idea. Explaining why this part of the text is worth marking, students can begin to understand the "thinking" that lies behind the marking. Following the teacher model, students can be asked to work with a partner and read another two to three paragraphs, marking the text, talking with their partner about why they marked the sentences they did, and then returning to the whole group where some partners share some of their markings. Once students are comfortable with marking important ideas they can be introduced to the other basic markings for questions (?) about ideas in the text, and confirmations of what the readers know and consider worth noting (checkmark). Beyond this basic marking classes often add their own markings for other engagements like an exclamation mark for "amazing" ideas; a venn diagram to show connections, or an asterisk to indicate something worth discussing (Vaughan & Estes, 1986).

Another way to help students keep notes of important ideas is to show them how to make note cards. Some primary teachers (McKee & Ogle, 2006) make multiple copies of Amazing Fact Sheets (or Notes to Remember) and put them in a convenient place in the classroom. As students encounter some interesting and worthy information they write it on the Amazing Fact Sheet with their name and the text information. Then, when the class is gathered at some point in the day students can share what they have learned by reading their Amazing Fact Sheets or Notes to Remember. See an example of the Amazing Fact note in the chapter on research.

Both of these strategies help students highlight important ideas they encounter while reading so they don't lose track of them. Being able to engage physically by using a pencil while reading helps many readers be more focused and retain key ideas. Other students may need to draw diagrams of what they are reading or create visual images (Ogle, 2000b). Some teachers encourage students to add notes of what they learn to the large classroom K-W-L charts. Both written information and drawings or diagrams enhance the corporate sense of classroom activity. All of these are tools that students need to try out as they develop their ability to attend to important information while reading and learning These written records also help ELLs and students with special needs because they don't depend on oral discourse and are not time sensitive.

Reciprocal Teaching

One of the most researched group strategies for modeling and developing engaged reading of informational text is reciprocal teaching (RT). Developed by Palincsar and Brown (1984, 1986) to help less able readers handle the demands of exposition, RT includes four different strategies students learn to use during oral discussion of a text being read by all students. First the teacher models each of the strategies, and then he or she turns the teacher role over to the students. The students become teachers for their classmates and guide the continued reading of small portions of text.

The four basic strategies of RT are summarizing, questioning, clarifying, and predicting. The teacher first models reading a short section of a longer text and creating a summary of the main ideas. (Depending on the group and the amount of time needed to teach each of the four strategies, the teacher may need to spend several sessions on a single strategy, or they may model more than one at a time until all four strategies become part of the readers' response to each paragraph or segment.) Students learn to ask good questions of the text, They learn to identify problems that hinder comprehension—vocabulary items that are unclear or unfamiliar, references that are confusing, and other unclear aspects—and seek to clarify these problems posed by the text. Finally, they learn to make predictions of where the text is leading. Students take turns in assuming the teacher role for each segment of text, so that during a single class period many students have the opportunity to lead their fellow students in considering the meaning of a shared segment of text.

This form of guided and shared reading has been effective in helping less able readers make sense of dense text material. The combination of good interactive strategies with a shared teaching and learning approach helps students maintain interest and focus on the material they are studying.

Increasing interest and giving students a sense of power when dealing with difficult and dense reading material is not easy. Both RT and the next teaching strategy, Questioning the Author, give teachers and students supportive alternatives to round-robin reading (a still-too-often-used way to have students read content texts).

Questioning the Author

As opposed to simply memorizing text content, the "questioning the author" (QtA) teaching strategy (Beck, McKeown, Hamilton, & Kucan, 1997) helps students learn to think more about who has written a text and how successful the writer was for them as audience or readers. They develop a dialogue with the author, just as they would with a person talking with them face to face. Students are encouraged to "query" the author, asking questions that get at a writer/content expert's decisions. Basic questions include the following:

- What was the author trying to say?
- What could the author have said instead?
- What was the intent of the author?
- What is the point of view?
- How could something be stated more clearly?

Students are led by their teacher in discussion of short segments of text, just as they are in RT. Only this time they focus on the author, thinking about how the author has written for them as readers/learners. For instance, after reading a paragraph in a sixth-grade history text, students may ask these questions:

- Why do you think the author spent a paragraph explaining the cuneiform writing system?
- What do you think it represents to the author?
- What else about the society might have been more important?
- Was it clearly written?
- Could something have been added to make it clearer?
- How would you have written this?"

By questioning or querying the author, students take a different stance in relation to the text and begin to feel more active as participants in the process of communication about content topics. The teacher's role changes in this kind of discussion; rather than being the one who asks factual questions and then evaluates students' responses, the teacher tries to stimulate students' thinking and search for their own ideas and answers. Teachers withhold evaluative comments and instead guide and shape group discussion. In classrooms where teachers use this approach, they report that the students seem to engage more deeply with the material they are asked to read and become more willing to read "content" textbooks.

Questioning in General

Asking and answering questions are major aspects of school life. The active strategies we have just described all depend on good questions. Teachers ask thousands of questions each week. Questioning is an ongoing process used by teachers to guide instruction and determine what students know. It is also an important active thinking activity learners use while reading and trying to make sense of text. It is a central part of comprehension for students and teachers alike, because both commercial materials and tests rely on questions. At the end of almost every textbook chapter, there is a set of questions to guide student review. Many books also have prereading questions to activate thinking; some have marginal questions that help readers highlight important concepts. These are important models and guides for learners that influence how meaning is constructed. Much controversy has been generated about the quality of questions in materials and in tests that students take (both teacher-prepared tests and large-scale commercial ones). For example, What questions can help evaluate good comprehension of a passage one has read? What does it mean to comprehend a passage one has read? What kinds of questions should teachers encourage to develop comprehension of text?

Moreover, how do we as teachers use questioning? Traditionally, and continuing into today, many teachers use questions to find out how well students have comprehended what they read. A teacher asks a student a question, the student answers, and the teacher gives some evaluative feedback. We have all done this—in our teaching and with our own children. Researchers (e.g., Mehan, 1979) have labeled this form of school dialogue the I-R-E ("initiation, response, evaluation") form and have criticized it because it does not really help students develop comprehension; it simply helps teachers test students. A second criticism is that generally the kinds of questions teachers ask students are very literal. If we want to develop good comprehenders, then we need as teachers to think seriously about the kinds of questions we ask students. Their answers will reflect the types of thinking in which we ask them to engage.

We teachers can also use questioning to model the process of thinking before and during reading. We can begin a lesson or introduce a story by asking students what they already know about a topic. This kind of questioning is not a testing but a modeling and activation of students' own thinking. Many commercial materials also embed questions so that students have a scaffold to help develop ideas.

Most teachers do use questions to help students consolidate what they have read and to reflect on ideas. The nature of these questions can vary considerably. Many studies (see Chapter 4) indicate that generally our questions are quite literal; however, we can ask much more thoughtful and reflective questions. How do we want to focus students' reflections about what they have read? It is useful for us to evaluate the kinds of questions we ask students, as well as the nature of the dialogue we encourage from our questions. Let's address the nature of our questions here. Later you will want to think about how you involve students in reflecting together to deepen their responses to questions you or texts pose.

There are several ways we can identify and categorize our questions. The most widely used is probably one developed by Benjamin Bloom and his colleagues in the 1950s (Bloom, 1956). Bloom's taxonomy was not really developed for use by teachers but as a taxonomy of educational objectives to measure school goals and assessment. However, teachers saw its value and have used it as a tool for reflecting on their classroom questioning patterns. The taxonomy has seven levels of questions: "knowledge," "translation," "interpretation," "application," "analysis," "synthesis," and "evaluation." In research studies of classroom talk, it is not uncommon to see analyses of these levels of teacher questions. Some teachers keep the levels of questions in their teaching manuals or put them on a bulletin board, so both they and their students are more aware of the need to go beyond the literal or memory level.

In some descriptions of reading comprehension and reading assessment, these seven levels have been defined differently. One common way of describing reading is in terms of "literal," "interpretive," "applied," and "critical" levels of comprehension; these levels are used to define kinds of questions in relation to text. Raphael (1986, 2004) has helped students think about sources of information for questions they are to answer by creating four categories of questions. She refers to these as "right there," "author and you," "think and search," and "on my own" (see Figure 5.14). These very practical definitions make it easy for students to become more involved in planning their strategies for responding, as well as to become metacognitively aware of the range of responses they need to be able to make to text.

There has been much criticism of the use of taxonomies to evaluate comprehension. Critics focus on the nature of the *process* of constructing meaning, and they argue that questions should ask students, "What do you predict will happen?," "What else could have been done?," and "What does this remind you of?" instead. Even those who worked with Bloom have now revised their original work to reflect a broader understanding of learning (Anderson & Krathwohl, 2001; see Figure 5.15). The new taxonomy includes both knowledge and process dimensions. The knowledge dimension has four categories: "factual," "conceptual," "procedural," and "metacognitive," knowledge. The process dimension includes "remember," "understand," "apply," "analyze," "evaluate," and "create." These

FIGURE 5.14. Illustrations of ways to explain four categories of responses to questions about reading (QARs) to students. From Raphael (2004). Copyright by the Wright Group/ McGraw-Hill Companies. Used by permission of the author and publisher.

The Knowledge Dimension	1. Remember	2. Understand	3. Apply	4. Analyze	5. Evaluate	6. Create
A. Factual Knowledge	■					
B. Conceptual Knowledge		■				
C. Procedural Knowledge			■			
D. Metacognitive Knowledge						

The Process Dimension

FIGURE 5.15. A revised version of Bloom's taxonomy of questions, including both knowledge and process dimensions. From Anderson and Krathwohl (2001). Copyright © 2001 by Pearson Education. Used by permission of the publisher.

changes create a much richer framework for thinking about the expectations we have for students and about our own instructional priorities.

Some educators don't find this kind of attention to questions as important as others do. They argue that the reader–text interaction should be the focus of attention. Do readers connect and respond personally to what they read? Can they establish a purpose and read to fulfill their own purpose? This focus leads to another range of questions about text construction or engagement. Yet, as long as questions are a critical part of teaching and evaluation in the United States, some attention to them seems necessary. If we consider the nature of questions we as teachers ask and the questions in the materials we give students, we can make them as valuable as possible. They are powerful guides to what students will learn to think about as they read and learn. We can also involve students in evaluating questions, the ways they can respond to them, and the kinds of questions that are useful to their own learning.

Putting It All Together

Reading and learning from content materials, whether textbooks or trade books and magazines, require a different approach than does reading for pleasure with fictional pieces. We as teachers need to take seriously the needs of our students and prepare them for the kinds of reading they will be doing throughout their school careers. Making a variety of informational texts available and guiding students' use of them is part of teaching reading. With regular experiences these texts become familiar and the effort spent providing a variety of ways of engaging with them opens up new worlds to students. It is not a choice but a necessity that teachers themselves know how to read informational texts (both print and electronic) effectively and develop students' independence in this type of reading. They also become more critical readers and thinkers when they learn to look beneath the surface of the material and ask questions about authors' perspectives and purposes and then compare different presentations on the same topic. When we use a variety of informational texts daily and model with our students how to read and think about them, students come to enjoy and know how to select informational materials for a wide range of purposes.

As you think about your own preferences, identify the kinds of informational materials you read most frequently. Bring some of these to class and make them apparent to your students. Talk about them, read from them, and compare and contrast ideas coming from a variety of sources. Bring in easy and moderate as well as difficult texts on the same subject, so students can see that there is a wide range in the level of materials from which they can choose.

Establish opportunities for students to read from a wide selection of informational materials, so that they will become personally involved with them. As you introduce key strategies for reading for information, be sure you involve all your students by using some materials that are of great interest to each of them. You will probably find that boys and girls who have not liked "stories" so well will respond to the beautiful informational materials now being published. If you teach in an urban area, bring in books about city life—like *Urban Roosts* (Bash, 1990), an informational book about the birds that inhabit our cities. Meet students' interests as you teach them strategies. Then be sure to give them many opportunities to practice the strategies under your guidance—first in simple materials, later in more difficult ones. Highlight their work and display it around the room. K-W-L worksheets, the graphic summaries and essays that children write, and I-charts all make good visual reminders of what the students are learning. Enlarged wall charts in the I-chart or K-W-L invite visitors to the classroom to engage in a dialogue about the content you are studying, too. As we learn, we all share and broaden our perspectives; show students how much fun it can be in the way you use your classroom.

CHAPTER 6

Strategies for Reading Fiction

As we begin this chapter, we think of the fun we have reading during the summer. It's then, with the pressures of work a little lighter, that we feel free to let a work of fiction take us to some new, unfamiliar location and introduce us to some interesting, and sometimes challenging, new "friends." Teachers of reading often think of these pleasurable experiences as the *raison d'être* for our efforts to make students readers. Each of you, our readers, may want to pause a few moments and jot down some of your favorite reading memories. Do you remember one of your favorite works of literature, one of those times when you just couldn't put a book down? Or, can you recall some memorable shared reading experience in school— when a teacher read aloud and the whole class wept over the death of Charlotte in *Charlotte's Web* (White, 1952) or Leslie in *Bridge to Terabithia* (Paterson, 1977)? Recently the Harry Potter books have created a whole new generation of young readers who have experienced the joy of losing themselves in books. Emotional experiences like these help instill the love of reading and invite readers to explore their lives and those of others through literature. From research as well as from personal experiences, we know that when children enjoy reading, they read more; and when they read more, they become better readers, explore more genres, and develop an appreciation for authors. Therefore, a major part of our role as teachers is to introduce children to the joy of reading stories and help them develop their engagement in literary experiences.

Finding the right books for each student is important. Luckily, there are plenty from which to choose. While this chapter is focused on reading fiction, we don't want to give the impression that finding the right book implies always turning to fiction. There are great nonfiction books, including biographies and autobiographies, that shouldn't be overlooked. Early in the school year it is important to find out students' interests and match children with books. Part of the guidance you can provide is also ensuring that there are characters and settings in some of the books that are familiar to each student. Too many adults from minority cultures have reflected on childhood experiences of never being given books with characters like themselves. Once they found such a book, their interest in reading changed; seeing oneself in literature is an important starting place for many readers. With a sense of "belonging" to books, it is also important to provide students with the experience of entering new worlds and new cultures through books. Children can find a mirror to themselves as they read; they can also see through windows in literature to worlds beyond their own.

We have introduced you to several readers, in Chapter 1, typical of those found in classrooms around the country—readers with particular styles and preferences in reading. As we think of all these good readers, we know that nurturing them in the love of reading is going to take a variety of activities. Reflecting on just two of these students helps us introduce our point that a wide variety of activities will be needed. First, there is Sara. She is an avid reader who will love book discussions and shared classroom reading activities of many sorts. Book talks and teacher read-alouds feed her voracious appetite for more and more reading material. LaToya, on the other hand, prefers working alone to participating in group activities and is impatient with class book discussions. She needs more silent reading time and may work well with dialogue journals as a way to respond to her reading. As we extend our reflection to the rest of the readers described in Chapter 1 (or think of how people we know read), we can see that variations in styles of engagement, in ways of working with groups, and in preferences for topics are certainly realities we need to deal with.

Yet there are some basic components of reading that underlie each student's competencies. What is it that all these readers need to be able to do? What do they all benefit from in classroom instruction, and what do they all need to know? Even though students have preferences in how they read, we think all of them need to know how to do the following:

1. Read actively and strategically to construct meaning from texts.
2. Identify major features of narrative writing (setting, characters, plot development, and theme) and major literary elements (point of view, figurative language, etc.).
3. Connect personally with literature—make associations between themselves and the settings, problems or events, and characters in the stories they read.

4. Develop understanding of the different genre of literature—from folktales and poetry to science fiction and fantasy.
5. Select literature they will enjoy reading and identify favorite books and authors.
6. Evaluate books and know the characteristics that define high-quality books.
7. Share their responses to books they read, both in writing and orally in discussions with peers.
8. Make connections between and among texts read and other sources.

How do we develop these abilities in the classroom? The rest of this chapter (see the graphic organizer in Figure 6.1) explores ways we teachers can create opportunities for children to become readers of and responders to literature. As a prelude, we want to look at ourselves as "model readers" and at the power that comes from our activities in the classrooms. Then the following two major sections deal with classroom practice. In the first of these sections, we present a wide variety of strategies that help teachers scaffold in small groups active, engaged reading of literature. In the second, we look at a variety of ways to provide students with more independent, student-led contexts in which they can develop their abilities as participants in the literate culture, where talk about books and authors is part of the fabric of life.

Teachers as Model Readers

Reading aloud to children for 10–20 minutes a day from engaging pieces of literature can be one of the most enjoyable times of the day for both a teacher and a class. Whether it occurs when students first come into the classroom in the morning, just before or after lunch, or at the close of the day, some special time designated for the teacher's reading orally to the class sets the tone for what reading is all about. The class shares a common literary experience in this way, and all students can talk about the same characters and situations, regardless of their reading level. References to the text can then be made at any time of the day and can serve as a useful tool for the teacher. For example, a friend of ours had a class one year that seemed very passive and unwilling to solve problems. She began reading from *Dear Mr. Henshaw* (Cleary, 1983) and used Lee Botts as an example of a child who didn't let problems overcome him but learned to solve them. When her students needed to take initiative, she would ask, "What do you think Lee would do here?" And she would follow up by giving students time to think, talk, and come up with options. Lee became a part of the class, and "Lee-like action" became an ongoing goal of the class. When

FIGURE 6.1. Graphic organizer for Chapter 6.

children would get into conflicts or when something didn't work, the class would try to think like Lee.

Getting Started with Read-Alouds

If you are a new teacher, or new to your grade level, you need to think carefully about which books to read aloud. Several sources can be of help. First, and most immediate, are other teachers and school or public librarians, many of whom have a great deal of experience helping children select books and also listening to their evaluations of those books. Second, if you have the opportunity, talk to some children who are a grade beyond the level you are teaching. Find out what books they consider their favorites from the level you are teaching. These long-remembered favorites can be a good place to start. Then there are good reviews of children's books in many journals and texts. Each year the October issue of *The Reading Teacher* journal publishes a list of "Children's Choices," which are books selected by children from those published that year.

Once you have located some suggestions, take them home and read them. It is much better to read a book yourself first than to begin reading aloud a book you yourself have not read and enjoyed. Your attitude toward the book communicates more than the actual words you read! Furthermore, there may be aspects of the book that are not appropriate for your community or the class context, and unless you read the book first you may find yourself in an embarrassing situation. Previewing is a way to ensure that you have selected a book that will match your class. However, if you just don't have the time, your next best option is to select books that have been award winners or that come well recommended. Some school districts have recommended lists of books. You can enjoy these with your students and experience the joy of discovery with them.

Deciding what books to read over the year is another consideration. Do you read easy books? Do you read books above the level your children could read themselves? Do you read only or mostly fiction? Our suggestion is that you model your own desires for the kinds of reading you want students to engage in by reading from a variety of genres. Make a list for yourself of what you select to read aloud. Read some realistic fiction; read some historical fiction; read some poetry; and read some biography and informational books as well (see Chapter 5). You want your students to explore with you the range of good materials that are available to them. Perhaps you want to introduce them to some local authors or poets. This can be a lovely part of your oral reading and may lead to an author visit, or at least to writing to the author.

We also suggest that you balance reading challenging books with reading some easier ones. The first book you select may be one that you want to use to create a community around the book, as our friend did with *Dear Mr. Henshaw*. You may want to use the oral reading to introduce an author to the class and to stimulate your students to read other books by the same person. Depending on the grade level, this author could be Patricia Polacco, Tomi de Paolo, Katherine Paterson, Gary Paulsen, or Russell Freedman.

Finally, even though we are focusing here on reading full-length books with children, you want to read daily from a variety of shorter materials, too. Children need to hear you read from the newspaper and from children's and suitable adult magazines, as well as from jokes, songs, and poetry (as noted above). The power of the model set by teachers as readers is real; what you read is what your children will view as important to read, whether you say so in actual words or just through actions.

Thinking Aloud While Reading

Another powerful use of reading aloud is engaging in "thinking aloud" while you read. This means not only that you read all the words in the text but also that you share the thoughts that come to your mind as you read. For example, when reading *Snowflake Bentley* (Martin, 1998), you may pause in your reading and show children the pictures as you comment, "That really reminds me of when I was a child and we had a huge snowstorm!" If you are confused by some description or word, stop reading and say (in your own way), "Wait, I don't think this makes sense. Let's see, could the author mean . . . ? I want to reread this section to check this out." Then reread it orally and share your own way of ascribing a meaning to the term or phrase. As you read on, you can interject comments to indicate to students how you visualize some scenes and characters, how you respond emotionally, and how you enjoy some descriptions and word choices.

You can model a variety of kinds of thinking aloud with your students, to help them understand what good readers do when they engage with text. If you make a list for yourself of the kinds of thinking you want to demonstrate for your students, you can make this time very useful to your more direct teaching. Having become aware of what good readers do as thinkers through this activity, your children may be more motivated to practice such thinking later. What are some of these key behaviors you want to model? Here is a good beginning list:

1. Make predictions about what you think is going to happen.
2. Monitor your own doubts and questions.
3. Engage in "fix-ups" when things don't seem to make sense.
4. Make personal connections.
5. Express emotions.
6. Create visual images in your head, and describe these.
7. Savor particular parts of texts as you read.
8. Relish the use of good descriptions and of new words and phrases—and help students try to remember these.

Scaffolding to Develop Students' Engagement in Reading

Teachers read aloud to students to help them become emotionally involved with stories; they also read aloud and think aloud to model the active, engaged thinking that goes on in the minds of readers as they make sense of the texts authors have produced. The goal is that all students will find both the pleasure of reading and that they will read actively. Modeling your own thinking makes more accessible to novice readers the importance of their being involved in constructing meaning and connecting with the text as they read. You want them to appropriate these same behaviors when they read silently. This means that they need many opportunities to practice active, engaged reading. Some students require more support for their reading than others. As you learn to listen carefully to students talk about what they are reading, and as you react to what they write in response to reading, you can determine the depth of support they need. You also will want to establish some ways of more formally checking to see that students are growing in their ability to comprehend different texts.

Gradual Release of Responsibility

To ensure that the modeling of the teacher transfers to students, some conscious supportive activities are required. Pearson and Gallagher (1983) described this teaching process as the "gradual release of responsibility." The goal is that eventually students will internalize and employ the active engaged process of reading independently. Some students will need little support to develop their reading. Others may need considerable practice and support.

Because students are at such different places in their reading and thinking, it is good to structure time for small-group guided reading sessions. These small groups should be flexible and not have the same children in them all the time. They can be based on particular strategy needs and can also reflect the reading level of the text some children need to be working in to learn optimally. When there are only four to eight students in a group it is possible to listen to all of the students and give them time to participate orally.

Most teachers mix large-group introductory lessons with small-group interactive sessions. The large-group sessions can be done with a single text, often from the basal reading program, so all students have the opportunity to learn from the teacher. Following the whole-group lesson, students can be grouped to begin using the focus of the lesson in their own reading. While the teacher works with one group, other students may be reading in their appropriate level of text applying the same strategy perhaps using a strategy guide the teacher has developed to write their responses or while reading independently and using sticky notes to record their responses. Later the teacher can review the students' work and provide feedback. After several sessions focused on the target strategy the teacher can ask students to complete a particular activity in written form so their level of mastery can be determined. Those who are not secure can then be given more guided activities to continue their development. Mixing small-group and partner work during this stage of release of responsibility can help students, too. Some do better in a one-on-one setting, especially if they are shy, have some learning challenge, or are still learning English.

By thinking of ways to scaffold for students so they can develop competence in all aspects of their reading, teachers are differentiating instruction. Sometimes providing easier texts is a good way to differentiate. Sometimes varying the activity so students can respond visually, physically, or verbally helps. Other times students need to be in small groups with a teacher to think through their engagement. Yet, for others time with a partner preceding any small group work is most comfortable.

In the following section, we present some key strategies you can use to scaffold instruction and help students practice active reading.

Focusing on the Internal Structure of Stories

Even before they begin any reading instruction most children have already developed a sense of story, from being read to and from watching television, movies, and dramatic productions. They know that stories have characters with problems that need to be solved; they know that most stories end happily with a resolution that is satisfying. Most stories have particular settings, although some folktales are quite sparse in the description of where they take place. Very young children often can differentiate the genre of story, too. They know if a story begins, "Once upon a time . . ." it is not going to be about news of their community or even realistic fiction but will be a folktale or a fairy tale. However, there are some students who may not have had experiences that have led to their understanding of story. It is always important to listen to your students; ask them to retell an event, to restate the ideas in a story you have read in class, or to tell about a movie or TV program they have seen.

A goal of kindergarten and first-grade teachers is to help children develop a sensitivity to story genre and elements by mapping characteristics of stories after they are read. Some teachers do as Debbie Gurvitz has done. As she and her students read several versions of the basic folktale, "Stone Soup," they create a matrix comparing and contrasting versions (see Figure 6.2). As children contribute what they know about the stories, Debbie writes their contributions on the matrix. During the kindergarten year, Debbie models the way to think about the structural elements of these takes. She often asks students to retell or summarize stories she reads to them. She also asks students periodically to draw pictures of the stories they hear.

Title Author Illustrator Copyright	Stone Soup Marcia Brown 1947	Stone Soup Tony Ross 1987	Nail Soup Harve Zerrach Margot Zerrach 1964	Group Soup Barbara Brenner 1992	Stone Soup John J. Muth 2003
Characters	3 Soldiers Townspeople	1 chicken 1 wolf	Old Lady "Man with no home"	6 kid rabbits 1 mom rabbit	3 Asian monks
Setting Genre	France Folktale	Farm Fairy Tale/Fantasy	Sweden Woods Folk Tale	Rabbit's Hole Fairy Tale	China Folk Tale
Problem	The solders were very hungry & the people didn't want to shere their food. They looked even hungrier.	The wolf was going to have the chicken for dinner. How could the chicken save her life?	Man was hungry & homeless. Old Lady was afraid of him & didn't want to share her food and house. She was lonely.	Mom couldn't make dinner. Went to Grandmother Rabbit's house. Kids didn't know what to do. Little rabbit wouldn't help.	Monks enter a town of suspicious people who won't open their doors to the travelers.
Resolution	They made stone soup with 3 stones, lettuce, butter, barley, carrots, beef bones.	The chicken outsmarted the wolf. She made soup. The wolf did work. The wolf ate soup. was so full and tired that he fell asleep.	He told her to get a nail & make nail soup. They added food, danced and had fun. She let him sleep in her house.	Little Rabbit finally gave a rock. Mom was surprised by how they shared & made soup taste so good.	Monks make stone soup and invite all villagers to join them for a feast; a real celebration.

FIGURE 6.2. Chart for "Stone Soup."

The first-grade teachers on her team take this use of text structure a step further. In the fall they model attention to story elements and create story maps for the children. Later, they ask their children to compare characters in two versions of "Sleeping Beauty" as they read from different books. This activity is one that students do independently with teacher guidance. They have found that individual work seems easier than partner work for children at this stage. One child's work is shown in Figure 6.3. At the upper grades the story maps can be created by the students as a way of helping them focus on the essential elements of stories they read. (See example in Chapter 4 of the map of Cinderella.) After individual maps are drawn other children can use these visual artifacts to talk about similarities and differences in what they selected as central elements. The goal is that all students can use a sense of story structure to guide their reading and summarizing. The maps and written summaries are evidence of their success.

The Directed Reading–Thinking Activity

One of the strongest ways you can help students learn what it means to become actively engaged in the pieces of literature they are reading is to scaffold students' reading via the "directed reading–thinking activity" (DR-TA). Developed by Stauffer (1969), this activity is widely used in a variety of ways both for listening (where it is called DL-TA) and reading. The basic DR-TA involves the teacher working with a small group of students (6–12) as they read a short story or selection, pausing at teacher-selected stopping points to think and predict. The purpose of this teacher-guided reading of the text is to help students think actively and become personally engaged in the reading.

Name _Jana_ _____   Date _____

Character Comparisons

Fairy Tale #1 _snow white_ _____

    a good character _snow white_ _____

    a bad character _The qeen_ _____

Fairy Tale #2 _sleeping buety_ _____

    a good character _Briar Rose_ _____

    a bad character _the Witch_ _____

FIGURE 6.3. Character comparison.

The questions that mark the DR-TA are as follows:

- "What do you predict will happen?"
- "How were your predictions?"
- "Can you support what you thought from the story? (Can you prove or disprove your prediction?)"

At each stopping point, the teacher focuses the discussion of the story on predictions the students make. In using the DR-TA, the teacher does *not* ask specific factual questions of students. The teacher's role is to guide the students' thinking as they make predictions, and as they read to find evidence to support or challenge those predictions. The further into a story the students read, the more accurate their predictions usually become. The teacher listens and notes the students' use of the author's clues to meaning and their general knowledge of stories and genres as they discuss their ideas.

A key to successful use of the DR-TA is that no one has read the story or reads ahead of the others. Prediction is only real when everyone is engaged in speculating. If a student has read the material before, ask that student to become an observer—to make notes on the other students' predictions and the ways they verify or change their ideas, based on what is in the unfolding story.

The other essential strategy teachers want to develop with the DR-TA is the students' use of text information to either revise or confirm predictions. Many times as teachers begin this process students engage in predicting with eagerness. Asking for their reasons for their particular predictions leads them to a deeper engagement with the text. Some students have difficulty adjusting predictions to the actual content of the story they are reading. If students are not making good inferences and connecting different segments of the story the teacher may need to ask them to reread a section and locate information that will inform their evaluation of their predictions and help them move forward with the author's meaning. The teacher may say, "Before we go on to the next section of the story look again at what the author has written. I think we are overlooking some important clues to what may happen."

Preparing to Lead a DR-TA

The teacher has an important role in preparing for the guided DR-TA. Before the students begin reading, the teacher has already previewed the story and determined the length of the sections that will be read before each stop for discussion. The initial predictions may be stimulated by the use of the title, author, and pictures, or by reading the first paragraph or so of the text. Sometimes students need a combination of all of these pieces of information in order to get grounded in the ideas likely to be presented. Students should not be asked to predict if there are not sufficient clues to some plausible meaning to make the predictions a good lead-in to the actual story. For example, the title of a story like "The Surprise" is not adequate to make plausible initial predictions. However, reading the title and the first paragraph of the story may provide a much clearer idea of what is to come.

In determining how much text should be read between each stopping point, the teacher wants to be sure that there is enough information for the students to check likely predictions, and also enough new information for further predictions to be made. Some stories just don't have enough interesting content for students to make good predictions; these should not be chosen for the DR-TA. By making a story map of the events you can determine what should constitute good stopping points. Many authors use some form of foreshadowing to prepare readers for what is going to occur later in the story. Breaking the stopping points so students can discuss these hints can increase their engagement with the story content.

Another aspect of preparation is deciding if you have a story where the stopping points fall at page breaks or in sections so students aren't too tempted to read ahead. It may be useful at first to read the story aloud to the students without their having access to the printed text. This prevents looking ahead. Another way is to give students index cards and even clip the card over the section not to be read. This also makes a clear point to students that the goal is their engagement and interaction with the group.

Guidelines for Participants

The teacher begins a DR-TA lesson by explaining to students the basic rules for participation. First, students must read only the assigned sections of the story. When they have finished, they should put a finger or bookmark in the page, close their book or other text, and wait for others to finish. While waiting, they can think back on their predictions and what evidence was presented either to support their predictions or to make them want to change these. If there are great differences in students' reading rates, give the fast readers paper and pencil so they can draw ideas, jot down ideas they have, or note interesting or new vocabulary terms they want to discuss later.

Second, there are no wrong answers in this activity. Good thinking is what is required. Third, students should listen to each other's ideas, because no one knows what is really going to be the outcome. The teacher should reassure students, "If someone else contributes a prediction before you have an opportunity, don't worry." The teacher will summarize the predictions before initiating the reading time, and everyone will have a chance to commit to one of the shared predictions.

The DR-TA Cycle

There are three basic components of the DR-TA cycle. First, the teacher asks students to make predictions about what they think is coming next in the story; then students read to prove or disprove their predictions, noting information and evidence in the text; finally, at the designated stopping points, students discuss their predictions and reformulate new predictions to lead them into the reading of the next section of the text.

For you, as a teacher, listening to students discuss their ideas provides a great opportunity to evaluate their depth of reading. It is very easy to tell whether students are following the genre of the story (e.g., folk tale, fable, realistic fiction, and fantasy) by the nature of their predictions. You can also ascertain easily whether they are noticing the important information in the story—information about characters, setting, time, and problem. Sometimes the author's choice of words or phrases is what provides clues to unfolding meaning. Giving students an opportunity to return to the text to read the segments that have helped them confirm or alter their predictions adds yet another opportunity for reflection on the author's style and content. Many times, through the discussion of these chunks of text, students rethink their developing interpretations and alter their ideas. Keeping the pace of reading discussion moving so that students really enjoy the story is important. Therefore, you cannot give all the children an opportunity to discuss their own predictions at each stopping point. What is important is that two or three different predictions are elicited each time you stop for reflection and prediction. Once there is a real variety of ideas on the table, it is your role as the teacher to say,

"These are good predictions. How many of you think that _____ is most likely?"

"How many of you are more inclined to agree that _____ will happen?"

"And how many of you like _____ as the possibility?"

In this way, you keep the pace moving along and heighten interest by the presentation of alternatives. At each stopping point, involve different children in making the predictions, so that they all have an opportunity to share verbally. Also, call on different children to reflect on the question "How were our predictions?" If some children are shy about providing a prediction, asking them to respond to the evaluation of predictions may help them enter the discussion more easily. The better you know your own students, the more easily you can help scaffold for each one, so they will all learn to participate and feel comfortable sharing and thinking with the group.

An Example of the DR-TA

Before initiating the reading of a new story, *Mexicali Soup* (Hitte & Hayes, 1970; see the Appendix at the end of this chapter), the teacher reviews with the group of 12 students the process they will use. Each has a copy of the story turned face down on his or her desk, and a folded sheet of paper to cover the part of the text beyond each stopping point. The teacher suggests that students write on the paper if they want to remind themselves of a particular prediction or if they find information in the story they want to use to prove or alter a prediction. She puts on the board a list of group discussion behaviors for all to follow:

Listen to each other.
Give positive nonverbal feedback.
Raise your hand to speak.
Link your ideas to those of others.
Read only as far as you are instructed to, and when you're finished, mark
     your spot in the story and turn it over so we know you are done reading.

The teacher then writes the title of the story on the board and holds up her color copy of the initial picture, which shows a city street full of people (children playing and adults shopping at a local grocery). The buildings indicate that it is an old urban neighborhood. She asks, "Look at the title and picture for a minute. Think about this story. What do you predict the story will be about?" She gives the children an opportunity to look carefully at the picture and to think about the connection between the picture and the title. Then she asks, "Well, what do you predict will happen in this story? What kind of story do you think it is?"

During the ensuing discussion, children share their ideas. Deanna volunteers, "I think it is a realistic story, because the picture looks very normal—the people are out on the street like they live in a crowded city. Maybe someone is going to have a party and likes some special soup."

Per speaks next. "I think there is a sale at the grocery on some special concoction called 'Mexicali Soup.' Maybe it is a deli, something that creates some problem in people who eat it."

The teacher responds, "Well, we have two quite different ideas here. Does someone else want to contribute their thinking? We know at this point we are really venturing out, since we have very little information from the authors!"

Anna is eager to share. "I think it's about how people get all mixed together in the city coming from lots of different places, and somehow they will work together to solve a problem."

Then Ryan adds, "Well, I thought it was really about making soup to eat. Maybe people get together and share—maybe they eat together."

With these four ideas, the teacher summarizes the four possibilities and asks the other students to raise their hands to commit to one of these. "Do you think it is most likely to be about some celebration [she looks for hands in the air], the effect of a strange concoction [she again waits for students to raise their hands], how people from different places get mixed together [she again looks for commitment], or about how some folks really get together and make soup [she again waits for responses]?" She then focuses the students on reading. "Well, let's read the first two pages and see what happens."

After all the students indicate they are ready by closing their text pages, the teacher asks, "Well, how were our initial predictions?"

Robert begins, "Well, it *is* about making real soup! Mama used to live in the country but is going to make her favorite soup now."

Anna adds, "She says it is her family's favorite soup."

Off to the side, Greg groans. The teacher turns to him and asks, "What was that contribution, Greg?" Greg then explains, "Well, with that list of ingredients it seems like a plain old vegetable soup. Ugh!"

At this point the teacher can tell that the students have a sense of the setting and characters and are reading carefully, so she now leads them to think of the possible problem that will arise. She asks, "So what do you predict is going to happen in the story?"

Tamika volunteers, "Well, Maria is with her friend calling to Mama. I think she isn't going to want to come home for supper. Maybe now that they're living in the city, the kids won't want her food any more. They'll go with their new friends."

"Maybe she will make a really good-smelling soup and the neighbors will come to find out what it is, and then she will open a restaurant," Anna excitedly predicts next. Several students seem uncertain about what would happen, so rather than prolong the predicting, the teacher asks for commitments to these two ideas. "How many think her family won't come home? How many think she will be successful and maybe even open a restaurant?" After a chance for thinking and committing, she then guides the group to continue reading. "Go on and read the next two pages, and then think about our predictions again."

While they are reading, the students begin to make audible noises that indicate they are thinking and responding to their prediction ideas. After time for everyone to read, the discussion begins again as the teacher asks, "Well, how were our predictions?" Ryan volunteers quickly, "Well, I think the kids will still come home to eat. Maria just asks her to leave out the potatoes, but doesn't say she won't come home to eat." Tamika supports his comment. "Yeah, I agree with Ryan." "Is there any further evidence in the story that makes you agree with Ryan, Tamika?" the teacher queries.

Tamika continues, noting a paragraph in the story. "Here Antonio also says he's coming home, that he gets very hungry working at the grocery."

"Good evidence, Tamika. Thank you. Now, what about our other prediction?" the teacher continues the discussion.

"Well, it could still be that in the end they decide she makes the best soup. Maybe others will smell it. But, now it seems like there is a problem—city life is different, city tastes are different," muses Carl out loud.

"I think the kids will make their mom sad and she won't make the soup after all," predicts Kari. "It seems that each one wants something changed, and you can't do that and still have the soup."

And the teacher enters again to move the process along quickly enough for the children to sustain their interest in the story. She knows they are thinking deeply about the issues the author is raising. "Let's make our next predictions. What do you think will happen now?" And so the cycle continues as the students listen and think together. The pattern the authors have established continues as each child in the story mentions something he or she wants left out of the soup. Finally the mother storms into the kitchen to make the soup. When she emerges, she brings a nice pot of hot water to the table. Her closing line is "The new Mexicali Soup is so simple! . . . You just leave everything out of it" (Hitte & Hayes, 1970).

Summary

The DR-TA provides the teacher an opportunity to guide students to think like good readers do—anticipating, predicting, and then confirming and modifying their ideas with the story as it unfolds. Children learn that it is natural to make and then change predictions based on changing information. By listening to each other, they build an idea of how other readers use information and events in stories to shape their emerging hypotheses of events and themes. The group process also involves some readers more actively than they would otherwise be in reading alone. The goal is always that the students use the scaffold of this activity to become more active in all their reading. From the DR-TA, the teacher moves students into individual reading with the same active thinking process. Some of the activities we suggest later are helpful in this transfer.

Variations on Engaged Reading

We have begun this chapter on literature with the DR-TA because it is such a good model of active reading. We also like the DR-TA because it can be used successfully with both fiction and nonfiction. The process is somewhat different with informational or nonfiction texts, but students can be easily engaged in thinking ahead of the author in both kinds of texts. The questions with nonfiction are not "What do you think will happen?" but "What do you want and need to know next? What do you think the author will explain next?"

Many children need both the teacher's thinking aloud about his or her own engagement while reading and many experiences of working with a group to develop active reading habits. Another extension of the DR-TA is the use of bookmarks for students to have with them as they read silently. A bookmark can have on it a version of the basic DR-TA questions: "What do you predict? (What evidence makes you think that will happen?) How was your prediction confirmed?

What new prediction do you want to make?" Some teachers also have students write answers to these questions in their reading logs, so they can move around the room and engage with students individually. We like these extensions of the DR-TA, because they make clear to students that the group prediction process is a model for what they should do individually when they read on their own. Bookmarks can also be used to enhance students' engagement with other forms of thinking. See Figure 6.4 for an example of a bookmark that asks students to connect, visualize, and compare with other characters or stories. The bookmark provides a way to capture one's thinking while reading so readers can return and share ideas later.

Story Problem Solving

One of the key activities readers engage in while reading is trying to solve the problem posed in stories. This is one reason we make predictions: We want to figure out how the characters are going to resolve the conflicts they face. What will

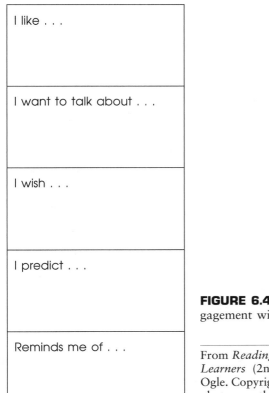

I like . . .

I want to talk about . . .

I wish . . .

I predict . . .

Reminds me of . . .

FIGURE 6.4. A bookmark to encourage students' engagement with stories.

Mama do in *Mexicali Soup* when her children all want some different ingredient left out of her special soup? One of us (Donna Ogle—the "I" in this passage) loves to read mysteries because that genre is specifically focused on the ways characters, often detectives, deal with the myriad of clues to some crime. I enjoy trying to solve the problem before the author reveals the outcome. For example, when reading a John Le Carré or Tony Hillerman mystery, I often find myself thinking about the clues when I am not reading. I want to figure out what is really happening in the mystery. Sometimes I won't pick up the book again until I think I know what will happen. Recently, the *Harry Potter* books have created that same engagement for me. I want to know how Harry and his friends are going to survive the latest evil threatening them, and I want to come to my own solutions before I read on. Regardless of genre, problem resolution is the central focus of most stories. To help students read these stories more successfully, a different kind of guidance or scaffolding can be useful, a paired problem-solving guide.

A key to solving problems is time for thinking. Many young readers haven't slowed their reading enough to permit deeper processing of ideas, which would enable them to formulate alternatives that might solve problems in stories. Given this concern in a local middle school, a literature teacher and I developed a paired problem-solving activity (Ogle, 1992) to help students engage more deeply in thinking while reading. We identified one stopping point in each of a series of short mystery stories after the characters, setting, and problem had been introduced. We knew that teams working together would make thinking more interesting for most students, so we developed a "Problem-Solving Think Sheet" for them to use to guide their thinking (see Figure 6.5a). Pairs of students followed the guide on this worksheet to think through the information that had been provided, and to come up with three possible ways the problem might be solved. After brainstorming over and writing down these possibilities, they rated which they thought was most likely to lead to a successful resolution, and they gave their reason for that choice.

As we first began to work with this strategy, we realized that some students benefited when they could draw their conception of the problem. So we added this as an optional step in their thinking about possible solutions (see Figure 6.5b, step 5). For many students, this ability to make the situation more concrete definitely helped them read with more comprehension. They were unaware of just how little they had been taking in and adding to their own mental representation of the story before trying to create a visual depiction of the situation.

In the middle school literature class, we used the problem-solving worksheet with six different mysteries the teacher regularly used with her short story unit. We found that for most students, the process of slowing their reading and focusing their thinking helped direct their attention to important information and developed their comprehension. One small group of boys, however, found the activity too slow and not interesting. They were strong readers and really wanted to move

Problem-Solving Think Sheet

Name _____

Story _____

1 What is the main problem that the characters have to solve?

_____

_____

_____

2 What information has the author given you that may be important?

_____

_____

_____

3 What else do you already know that may be helpful in solving the problem? What else does the character need to know?

_____

_____

_____

4 What do you think are the *three* most likely ways to solve this problem?

_____

_____

_____

5 Which is the best way to solve the problem and why?

_____

_____

_____

_____

FIGURE 6.5a. Problem-solving think sheet.

Problem-Solving Think Sheet

Read the first part of the story silently. Then work with your partner to see how you might solve this problem. Use this worksheet to help guide your thinking.

1. Think about the characters and the setting of this story. What is important to note about them?

2. What is the main problem that has to be solved?

3. As you think about how you might solve the problem, what information has the author given you that might be important?

    A.
    B.
    C.

4. What additional information might be useful in making a decision?

5. As you try to solve this problem, you can draw a diagram illustration of what you think are important considerations, if you want to. You may want to do your drawing on the back side of this page.

6. With all your good thinking what do you think are the three most likely ways to solve this problem?

    A.
    B.
    C.

7. Which is the best way to solve the problem, and why?

FIGURE 6.5b. A worksheet for the paired story problem-solving activity, including an optional step (step 5) to permit students to draw their conception of the problem.

more quickly through the stories. Therefore, we concluded that such guided reading is valuable for some students but that, like all forms of instruction, it needs to be adapted to learner variables.

Many teachers have adapted this problem-solving process with students in the primary grades through high school. The guided talk between the two partners seems to be a key to enhancing their attention to key information, linking their prior knowledge to the text problem, and motivating their interest in the story. The strategy works well with stories and even informational articles when the focus is on a central problem. Like the DR-TA, this strategy involves students' thinking together; however, it also involves using writing to monitor their thinking, and predicting in a deeper way than can be done when the activity is totally oral.

Story Impressions: Developing Predictions before Reading

Intermediate students can become freer about making predictions and learn the joy of trying to think ahead of the author through another involving strategy, "story impressions," developed by McGinley and Denner (1987). The whole focus of this strategy is on students' trying to predict what the story is going to be. The teacher creates a list of words that reveal key elements of the story—setting, some indication of characters, and the problem that will be developed and resolved (plot)—and creates a list of the words in the order in which they occur in the story. Working in partners or small groups, the students take this set of words and phrases and create a paragraph or two that tells a plausible story, using these words in the correct, given order. When each group is finished, its members share their constructions with the class. By the time several groups have shared, the words are certainly familiar, and the possibilities of what might occur have enlarged each child's ideas and raised more questions than would be possible from a single reader's approaching the text alone.

A set of words for a story impression for a folk tale called "The Dancing Man" is given below:

Dreary village
Poor boy
World sings
Waves dance in the sea
Silver slippers
Long journey
Danced the wind in the trees
Made sick girl smile
Grew old and weary

First, create your own story from these words. Then look at the story impression we have provided in Figure 6.6. Do you feel ready to read the folk tale now? Has this increased your motivation? As students put more of themselves into predicting and thinking of possibilities, they usually become more interested and engaged in the actual reading. Afterward, a good conversation is naturally focused on the similarities and differences between the stories the class has created and the actual story of the author. Sometimes students prefer their own stories; this is a great opportunity for them to go back, expand their pieces, and engage in real creative writing.

Drawing: Stimulating Thinking during and after Reading

An important aspect of reading is creating visual images in one's head as one reads. Many researchers have found this ongoing mental activity a hallmark of good readers. From Durrell (1956) to Gambrell and Almasi (1996) and Sadoski and Paivio (2004), attention to readers' imagery has proven valuable. When we create images from words, we are clearly engaged with the author, and the text has

---

Life in the dreary village was not pleasant for everyone. There was a poor boy who always tried to keep up everyone's hopes and spirits. He thought song and music was what made the world sing and relayed that message to the people in the village. He would saunter down to the shore at night and watch the waves dance in the sea. One night he was struck with an idea and the next day he would leave.

In his silver slippers he always wore to dance in, he set out on a long journey. His journey lead him through large jungles where he watched and listened to the music of the night. On the third day of his journey, he was awestruck as the cold came and softly danced the wind in the trees. Through the wind's song he was enlightened in where to go.

Early the next day he arrived in a village. He walked past the first four huts and stopped to knock at the fifth. Inside there was a little girl lying in a bed next to her mother with a tear-stained face. The little girl was in very grave condition. The boy was determined to sing and dance until he made the little sick girl smile. He danced for days and finally the little girl arose from her bed and smiled from ear to ear. Now the boy could return to his village and grow old and weary knowing he had made a difference in the life of that girl.

FIGURE 6.6. A student's story impression for a folk tale called "The Dancing Man."

come alive. Yet we find many students who have no idea how to visualize as they read. They have never seen the possibilities that others regularly assume as part of reading.

I (Donna Ogle) still remember an experience I had watching a group of fourth graders discuss a chapter in *Sarah, Plain and Tall* (MacLachlan, 2004) with their teacher. She asked them to put their heads on their desks and see what images came to them as she read a passage orally. It was a beautiful description of the dunes along the ocean that merited imaging. Yet, when she finished and asked the students to raise their heads and describe what they saw, one student exclaimed, "It was all dark!" Another agreed; they had formed no images at all!

Post-It Note Sketches, Collages, and Paired Drawing

Readers who don't form images are missing a valuable part of engaged reading. Simply asking students to stop periodically and create a visual representation of what they see as they read can stimulate this thinking. Give students Post-It notes to put at particular points in their novel or other selection, and have them create images of the characters, the location, or some conflict. If some have difficulty drawing, let them use stick figures or create visual diagrams. They can also use magazines to find pictures that seem to capture the characters or other elements of the story and share these with the class. In some cases, we have had students work together to create collages of story elements from magazine pictures. This takes away the burden of doing the drawing themselves if they are hesitant. The important thing is for students to begin thinking of stories visually as well as verbally.

One literature teacher (described in Ogle, 2000a) uses sketching as a means to get adolescents to read poetry deeply. He puts students with partners and asks them first to individually read and draw the key meaning of the poem, then to share their drawings, and finally to create a single revised drawing to represent their joint interpretation. This activity has stimulated a great deal of attention to, and much more enjoyment of, the poetry.

Sketch to Stretch

Developed by Short and Harste with Burke (1996), "Sketch to Stretch" is a small-group drawing activity. After reading the same story, each child draws a single image of the theme or central message of the story. These drawings are then shared one at a time in the small group. The first student holds up his or her drawing, and then each of the other group members has a chance to comment on what they see in the drawing. Finally, the artist has the closing comments, explaining what he or she intended. After listening to what the other group members have noted in the drawing, the "reader/artist" often expresses surprise at everything that was interpreted from the drawing. Each member in turn shares his or her drawing, and the others comment on what they see.

If the teacher wants to bring the activity back to the whole-class level, he or she can instruct each group to select one of its images, which will then be shared with the class. These can be put on a bulletin board later for continuing reflection and enjoyment.

Drawing: A Window to Students' Comprehension

We have found that children may have difficulty representing the theme of a story in a single image. Some tend to draw the sequence of main events. Depending on the abstractness of the story and a student's level of familiarity with it, different forms of representation may be more useful. Even if students draw the sequence of events, this provides an opportunity to discuss what each child finds most central in the story. It also helps students develop the habit of imaging as they read. The drawings open up thinking in a new way.

Teachers can use these drawings and the discussions around them as a good form of evaluation. In one middle school classroom, the teacher permitted students individually to represent the text as they wished. In doing so, she was able to learn that students held quite different images of the characters—and had created different meanings for the text—than she held. In one case, after reading "Thank You, Ma'm" by Langston Hughes (1997), students drew what they thought was meaningful about the short story of a black boy caught stealing an older woman's purse. One student represented the woman as white with blond hair and the boy as black with curly hair (see Figure 6.7). Although Hughes had written about two black characters, this student had interpreted the text in another way. Only when the drawings were shown could the class discuss the social implications of the text more fully, having understood this particular student's interpretation. Understanding how students think when they read is difficult; drawing provides a window on the thinking and meaning construction that may not be available from other, more verbal activities. It certainly helps students become more aware of the power available in texts to create images of the inner and external worlds of literature.

Say Something and Save the Last Word for Me: Reflecting on Text

As students reach the middle grades, two other activities can help them make personal connections to the texts they are reading, especially when they are quite complex. The first of these is called "Say Something" or "Think–Pair–Share." The other is called "Save the Last Word for Me" (see Short et al., 1996). In the first strategy, students read the same text together. When they have read (silently or orally) a designated section of the text, they think about their ideas, may write something on paper, then turn to each other and say something about what they

FIGURE 6.7. A student's Sketch to Stretch drawing for "Thank You, Ma'm" by Langston Hughes.

read. They may summarize what they think is most important; they may connect with a character; or they may even raise a question for their partner. The key is that each student talks about what they both have just read to the partner and then listens as the partner also says something. This is a very simple strategy, but it establishes clearly the need for personal engagement and commitment when reading.

The other strategy, "Save the Last Word for Me," has been used at both the middle and secondary levels. In this strategy students are given 3 × 5 cards and told that when they finish reading they should find quotations (three to five) from the text that they particularly like. They write each quotation on one side of a card, and tell on the other side why they chose it. Then when the group is finished reading, the students share their quotations, one at a time. Each member of the group can comment on each quotation. Then when all others are done, the writer of the card reads what he or she put on the back as the reason for the choice. Each person shares one of his or her cards until all have had a turn. Depending on the size of the class, this activity can be conducted in small groups or with the whole class. Teachers can use the cards students have created as a form of evaluation.

Journal Writing

Responding to what we read in written form encourages reflection and the making of personal connections to literature. Some teachers have had real success in getting students to respond to what they read by having students record their responses in journals. These journals can be individual, can be shared with a partner who writes back, or can even be created jointly by a small group. Journal entries can take the form not only of reflections on the reading but of imaginative extensions of it (see Figure 6.8 for a good example, in which a student reading a story of life in a sod house on the Great Plains in the 19th century imagined living in such a house).

One second-grade teacher we know has made individualized reading and journal writing major components of her literacy program. Each child has his or her own journal and writes in it two to three times a week to tell the teacher about what is being read. Sometimes the entries are summaries; sometimes they highlight special parts and exciting plot events; and sometimes they are connections triggered by the reading. The teacher responds each week to the students, too (see Figure 6.9). In this way there is a real sense of "conversation" about the books the children choose to read, and all children can develop their own interests and preferences.

A variant on this idea is to have students write to and with each other. Especially as they get older, students can write a great deal, and sometimes it is hard for teachers to keep up regular responses. In the intermediate grades, other teachers have had success encouraging student response to reading by putting a "buddy journal" program in place. Each student reads a story and then writes about it for a "buddy," another student in the class the teacher has helped the student select as a partner. Periodically, the buddies share their writing and respond to each other. In this way, the children build expectations that there is an audience for their ideas—and a dialogue ensues. Many times teachers need to model this process carefully before it becomes fully useful. Students need to learn how to think and

---

April 9, 1816

Living in a soddy is never my first choice but sometimes it can be really cozy and nice. John thought that I would not like a sod home, but I actually don't mind it.

Except for just a couple faults . . . Well, for starters dirt falls from the roof top and sprinkles on our food at dinner time! The children sometimes cover therir food or eat quickly. Frequently, snakes or gophers dig holes into our house. Just the other day Ethan screamed. I ran over to him from the stove and there was a gopher sticking his head up from his hole. I assured Ethan that a little gopher could not hurt him.

FIGURE 6.8. A student's imaginative extension, in a journal entry, of a story about living in a sod house on the Great Plains.

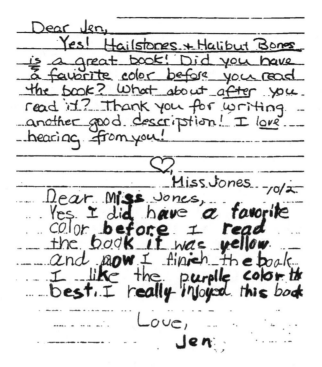

FIGURE 6.9. Two entries in a "dialogue journal" from a second-grade class (one entry by the teacher and one by the student).

write about texts. But the record of the growth in responses is evidence enough for the value of this kind of activity.

We work with many students who feel very uncomfortable about their writing ability. Teachers can group such students in clusters of three or four to create "journaling teams," whose members work together in creating written responses to what they read. One member with better writing skills serves as scribe while all contribute their ideas. Another member can be the illustrator for the group, creating some visuals to represent their thinking. Some children are good with rap and have turned many a story into their own living rap, to the delight of their classmates. These variations in journaling help meet students where they are and involve them in the enjoyment of stories.

Readers' Theater and Choral Reading

Stories can come to life for children as they read them orally. Both Readers' Theater and choral reading engage students in reading without the movement that acting out a play requires. They are much more manageable and can be done quickly.

In Readers' Theater, the text is divided into parts for different readers. Some parts are reserved for the narrator, but as much of the text as possible is turned into dialogue for the characters. Intermediate- and middle-grade students can create their own Readers' Theater scripts, but there are many already commercially available, and some children's magazines have play scripts in them. In performing a story using Readers' Theater, the students select parts, practice these (using different tones and inflections to communicate each character's part), and then present the full text to an audience—usually other members of the class first, and then another class. Some minimal prompts can be used to communicate aspects of character (hats, scarves, or small tools and books). Usually the students sit on stools or chairs as they read their parts. This form of oral reading deepens students' understanding of characters' emotions and personalities and helps them learn to communicate to an audience. It is also excellent for less confident readers because it provides a strong motivation for them to practice rereading text until they become fluent reading it.

Choral reading is another group oral reading form that works well across grade levels. In choral reading the group reads a text together, reserving some parts for individual voices and small groups. Poetry works well for this dramatic form. The class can take a narrative poem and decide which parts or verses should be read by everyone and which should be for solo voices or small groups. Then all students practice rereading the text individually before they determine where special inflections should be placed. These can be marked on copies of the text and then practiced orally. Finally, after some rehearsal, the text is produced by the whole group. Humorous poems like "I Saw an Old Woman Who Swallowed a Fly" can introduce children to this pleasurable activity. More profound poetry can also be used nicely in this format. For example, *Harriet and the Promised Land* (Lawrence, 1968), a long poem about Harriet Tubman, makes a wonderful choral performance. Paul Fleischman's (1988, 1985) collections of poems about insects and birds, *Joyful Noises: Poems for Two Voices* and *I Am Phoenix*, also work beautifully for choral reading.

We have found that for students who speak dialects of English or who are second-language English speakers, participating in both choral reading and Readers' Theater helps build their familiarity with standard English pronunciation and makes learning this school dialect more enjoyable. Even attention to aspects of grammar comes more naturally through these activities.

Pantomime

Read a selection from a text and try to put your body into a posture that captures the meaning of the ideas or images. This variation on the art of pantomime—mimicking without words—can help students deepen their involvement with text and can become yet another exciting way for students to respond as they read. To keep this a manageable activity, draw names or randomly select students to stand up at intervals and transform the story being read by the group into a physical image. Some teachers have had success using a small-group process with pantomime. The class first reads a section of the story; then each small group meets and creates its own pantomime of that section. These bodily interpretations are then shared one at a time with the whole class. Finally, the teacher asks each group to create a prediction for what will happen in the next part of the story. This can be pantomimed by the groups again if the text has enough substance to encourage such forward thinking.

Active boys, who often feel marginalized in the seatwork of school, come alive when they can move their bodies. Taking this energy and turning it over to the construction of story meaning can provide real joy and relief to fidgeting students. Research in Chicago by the Whirlwind Arts Partnership, now named Reading in Motion (accessible at *readinginmotion.org*), showed that the use of similar physical portrayals of stories by young readers led to greater comprehension both on school tasks and on standardized tests.

As a variant on this activity, some teachers have also had success asking students to pantomime vocabulary words as a way of helping them retain new words. Children love to engage in such creative learning activities.

Developing the Joy of Literature Discussion

Reading instruction has been dominated too much in the past by teachers asking questions of students after they read stories. Recently, there have been several experiments having students in small groups learn to discuss stories, some with teachers as facilitators and some with students conducting their own discussions. Research has shown that having students talk about what they read does lead to higher levels of comprehension. And some of the research suggests that when the talk is led by peers, better discussion and deeper learning occur than when the teacher is in charge. Many suggestions have been made about formats for book discussions with intermediate- and middle-grade students. If you read about just one model, you may not find what best suits you and your students. We have seen teachers use a variety of ways to move students into the joy of talking together about what they have read. Think about discussion groups you have been part of, if you have had this experience, or the groups friends have told you of. Have you watched *Oprah* and observed Oprah Winfrey's book club? There are many ways we as adults share our reading experiences.

Our suggestion is that you read through these options and think about your own teaching. Begin using discussion groups with a format that seems most natural and comfortable to you. Then explore some of the other ways so you can expand your own comfort zone. In the process, involve your students in reflecting on what works best for them, too. They can become "researchers" and "evaluators" with you.

As you read about the different forms of discussion, think about these questions:

1. What is the teacher's role?
2. What preparation is asked of the students?
3. What is the format for the discussion?
4. What materials do students read? (Is it the same text they discuss? How much do they read prior to discussion?)
5. What is the goal of the discussion?

Great Books Shared Inquiry

One of the first programs for involving children in deep discussions of literature was developed by staff members of the Great Books Foundation (Plecha, 1992). They have modeled their student program on the adult Great Books shared inquiry program. The basis of the adult model is an ongoing discussion group with two volunteer leaders. The group selects the book to be read each month (or periodically), and the leaders develop a series of questions that will guide the discussion. These questions follow a particular format. Two or three rich interpretive questions for which there is no clear answer are the keys. Once the group leaders determine what they think will provoke the best discussion, they then develop a set of follow-up questions for each of the two or three more general questions. Each member agrees to read the book to be talked about prior to coming to the group. During the actual discussion time, leaders call on participants to respond to the guiding questions. All answers need to be grounded in the text itself, not in other readings, deeper knowledge of the author or situation, or the speakers' own experience.

The first use of the Great Books model for schools involved parent volunteers leading the groups. Soon, however, the value of the model of interpretive questioning for classroom teachers led to the inclusion of teachers in the in-service training program. More recently, the Great Books Foundation has developed a whole literature program for classroom use, with selections representing high-quality literature appropriate at the different grade levels (*www.greatbooks.org*). They also provide professionl development sessions for language arts and content-area teachers to learn to make the questioning format of shared inquiry an ongoing part of classroom discourse. Currently the Foundation is also exploring ways to use new technology to expand communications. First graders in Arlington, Virginia, used their Palm Handheld computers to record their own questions about an African folktale they had read. They also used software to draw pictures and create audio voiceovers of poems and turned their efforts into a podcast (Palmer, 2006).

This approach to literature discussion has the teacher leading the discussion around a set of carefully prepared questions. All participants read the same text and come prepared for discussion. Teachers begin by asking an interpretive question. Students think about the question and then *write* their responses individually. This variation on the adult model helps students construct their own ideas, so that they can then listen actively and contribute fully to the discussion. Once the writing time is over, the teacher convenes the group for the discussion.

The teacher keeps a record of the discussion flow by making a seating chart with each student's name and location on it. As students speak, the teacher notes their contributions to the discussion and ensures that all have a turn. After the discussion, the teacher can reflect on the discussion by reviewing his or her notes.

Grand Conversations

As teachers, we want students to discuss with each other what they have read for a variety of reasons. For all of us (teachers and students alike), discussion can deepen our enjoyment and understanding of a text; it can open us to understanding that one text can be interpreted in a variety of ways; and it can help us learn to listen to each other more deeply. Just the process of listening to someone explain an aspect of a story that we had missed often motivates us to reread and rethink something we had skimmed through when reading only for our initial purpose.

When most adults talk about books, there are no real leaders—just a group of peers talking. Therefore, some teachers have chosen to model this more unstructured form of conversation about a text. Some have had real success putting students right into peer-led groups with the purpose of talking about a shared reading experience. With students in the leadership role they can more easily explore their own feelings, interpretations, and questions. The teacher usually is part of the group and serves as a facilitator to keep the group focused. However, we have found that for these "talking groups" to be successful in most classrooms, there need to be some ground rules and some guidance in the kinds of questions that are asked. For children who have never talked with a group about their reading and responses, scaffolding can be very useful.

Short and Klassen (1995) report success with student-led discussion groups. They find that if the teacher is in the group, the discussions are not nearly as deep or personal as when the students engage with their peers alone. Several activities support these discussions, too. Before the group time, students can construct Save the Last Word for Me cards to bring to the group (see the earlier description of Save the Last Word for Me). When they come to the discussion group, the students take turns discussing the quotations on their cards.

Book Clubs

Intermediate-grade students in projects led by Raphael and McMahon (1994) have formed "book clubs" as part of their literary instruction. Raphael and McMahon's program involves students making reading choices from a number of selections on a general theme. The teacher selects three or four books representing a variety of interest and reading levels within the theme units that the class is exploring over some weeks of time. The students preview the books and then write down their top choices. The teacher then divides the class into "clubs" based on the books the children selected. The students also learn a variety of activities for engaging more fully with the novels they are reading. These activities are listed in the covers of the reading logs the students keep; the lists provide a reminder of good ways to engage with text while and after reading.

Periodically, the children come together in their book club groups to discuss their novels. The activities they do in their logs provide the substance for their individual contributions to the discussion. These activities reflect the realization that

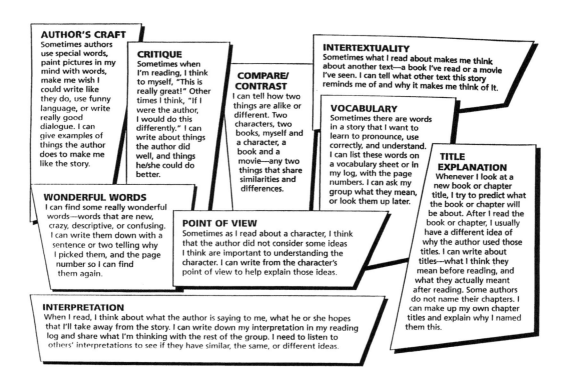

FIGURE 6.10. A set of activities for students to do in their reading logs prior to engaging in book club discussions. From Raphael and McMahon (1994). Copyright 1994 by the International Reading Association. Used by permission of the authors and publisher.

different books and different children call for particular types of responses. Figure 6.10 depicts the activities. In this format for discussion, the choices of books are constrained by the unit of study and the teacher-selected options. All children in a particular group read the same text and talk about it together. The teacher is generally a member of the discussion group, guiding students to think about the text. The format for the discussion is based on the log entries the students have made.

Literature Circles

Good readers engage in a variety of activities as they read. Just as the book club program models different ways of responding to text in the reading logs, so the "literature circles" program developed by Daniels (1996) and Daniels and Bizar (1999) specifically recognizes the different ways people talk about books together. Rather than asking students to shift roles during a discussion, each child in a literature circle is assigned one role for each discussion period. Each child uses a guiding worksheet to prepare for this role. The major roles for each discussion team (the groups stay together for one novel) include Questioner (see Figure 6.11a), Passage Master (see Figure 6.11b), Word Wizard (see Figure 6.11c), and Artful Artist (see Figure 6.11d). However, roles can change, depending on the book and the level of the students. And students take different roles for different discussion days, so all learn to look for vocabulary, all learn to develop questions and serve as Discussion Director, and so forth.

In this form of discussion, students all read the same book and share their responses to it. There is no teacher in a leadership role; the teacher can observe and make notes on the group's success and on questions that arise. Students know they have a responsibility to the whole group and need to be prepared to make their contribution.

An advantage of this program is that students learn about different ways they can contribute to group discussions and different ways they can also engage when they are reading (thinking of vocabulary, images, characters, etc.). The liability is that by only taking on one role at a time, some students think of fulfilling a "task" rather than of reading to engage fully with a text. Sensitivity to how the focus on roles is introduced and to how long roles are maintained can overcome this limitation.

Readers' Workshop

Based on a model of workshops for sharing writing, some teachers have developed a Readers' Workshop format for sharing reading. In this format, all students read different books of their own choosing on a regular basis. As they read, they keep written responses to their readings; these can be both very personal reactions and also responses to particular foci the teacher is interested in developing. Stems such

Questioner

Name _____

Group _____

Book _____

Assignment p. _____ – p. _____

Readers tend to think and wonder and ask themselves questions as they read. What questions went through your mind while you were reading this? What did you find yourself wondering about, wanting to talk over with another reader, or wishing you could ask the author? Your job is simply to jot down some questions or topics about today's reading that the people in your group might enjoy discussing when you meet next. Your group will probably be interested in "fat" questions—the big, rich, open-ended questions that people can say a lot about, debate, and even disagree about—rather than those "skinny" yes–no or factual recall questions.

QUESTIONS FOR GROUP DISCUSSION

1.

2.

3.

4.

SAMPLE QUESTIONS

Why did the author have this happen?
If I could talk to the author I'd ask . . .
How is this part of the book connected to earlier parts?
What was going through your mind when you read this?
Why did the character behave this way?
How did you feel when reading this part of the book?
Did anything in this part of the book surprise you?
What do you think will happen next?
Did this section seem realistic?
What do you think is the author's point or theme?

FIGURE 6.11a. Guiding worksheets for roles taken by students during literature circle discussions: (a) Questioner, (b) Passage Master, (c) Word Wizard, and (d) Artful Artist. (a) From Daniels (1994). (b, c, and d) From Daniels and Bizar (1999, pp. 81–84). Copyright 1994 and 1999 by Harvey Daniels and Marilyn Bizar. Used by permission of the authors.

Passage Master

Name _____

Group _____

Book _____

Assignment p. ____ – p. ____

You are the **Passage Master**. Your job is to pick parts of the story that you want to read aloud to your group. These can be:

—a good part	—an interesting part
—a funny part	—some good writing
—a scary part	—a good description

Be sure to mark the parts you want to share with a Post-It note or bookmark. Or you can write on this sheet the parts you want to share.

Parts to read out loud:

Page	Paragraph	Why I liked it
____	_____	_____
____	_____	_____
____	_____	_____
____	_____	_____
____	_____	_____

FIGURE 6.11b. Passage Master.

as "I like this section because . . ." or "This character reminds me of . . ." can help students think of ways to respond in writing to their stories. Periodically, groups of students gather to share their written responses in small groups.

Nanci Atwell (1987), one of the first to write about this form of literature sharing, explains that what she wants to achieve is the intimacy and naturalness of the discussions that take place around a family's dining room table as they discuss what they are reading. She combines the group sharing with minilessons (where she introduces literary concepts and helps students read more deeply) and with individual conferencing. She begins her class periods with a minilesson, followed by time for silent reading, during which she confers with individual students. Students respond in writing as they read, and later have time to share with each other.

This form of literature reading and responding permits the most individual choice of materials for reading and response, while still providing for teaching and some sharing. What is missing is the shared reading, so students who listen to each other have little basis for engaging in a real discussion. They may or may not have read the same text. There is little chance for readers to challenge or extend each other's interpretations, as each one may be in a different text. The format does in-

Word Wizard

Name _____

Group _____

Book _____

Assignment p. ____ – p. ____

You are the **Word Wizard.** Your job is to look for special words in the story. Words that are:

—new	—strange	—interesting	—hard
—different	—funny	—important	

When you find a word that you want to talk about, mark it with a Post-It Note or write it down here.

Word	Page	Why I liked it
_____	_____	_____
		_____
_____	_____	_____
		_____
_____	_____	_____
		_____
_____	_____	_____
		_____
_____	_____	_____
		_____

When your group meets, help your friends talk about the words you have chosen. Things you can discuss:

How does this word fit in the story?
Does anyone know what this word means?
Shall we look it up in the dictionary?
What does this word make you feel?
Can you draw the word?

FIGURE 6.11c. Word Wizard.

troduce students to a wider range of books than is ever possible when groups of students read the same book. After listening to a classmate discuss an exciting or moving book, others are often drawn to reading that same recommended book—a much more inviting suggestion than if a teacher of middle-grade students makes the same recommendation. Students also learn how to summarize ideas in the books they read, because others are not likely to have much foundation for understanding their remarks otherwise. They also may become more persuasive in shar-

Artful Artist

Name _____

Group _____

Book _____

Assignment p. ____ – p. ____

You are the **Artful Artist**. Your job is to draw anything about the story that you liked:

—a character
—the setting
—a problem
—an exciting part
—a surprise
—a prediction of what will happen next
—anything else

Draw on the back of this page or on a bigger piece of paper if you need it. Do any kind of drawing or picture you like.

When your group meets, don't tell what your drawing is. Let them guess and talk about it first. Then you can tell about it.

FIGURE 6.11d. Artful Artist.

ing their responses, as their peers depend on them for input about the book and author.

Nonfiction Literature and Informational Materials

We need to make clear that while much of what is called "literature" is fiction, it is not limited to fiction. Great literature comes in many genres. Some of the best of the great books are histories and biographies. Our current era is particularly marked by an increase in informational writing of high quality. (We have devoted Chapter 5 to making this clear, but it is worth repeating here.) The Pulitzer Prize for biography, the yearly awards for the best essays, and the listings of best-sellers by genre reflect the range of materials available for good discussion. The National Council of Teachers of English now gives the Orbus Pictus award for the best non-fiction book each year, and the names of the winners provide another good source for reading and discussion.

Informational books may also be some of the best for discussion. Leal (1992; Leal & Moss, 1999) has researched the quality and quantity of children's discussions with three genres of books—realistic fiction, narrative nonfiction, and expository nonfiction. The intermediate students she observed and tested did best with narrative nonfiction for discussions and seemed to learn most from this format. There was more content to talk about, and the purpose of discussion was more apparent—they wanted to learn from each other. Therefore, as we think about teaching students to enjoy literature and engage fully with it, we need to keep our definitions broad. Poetry, fiction, and various forms of informational nonfiction, especially narrative nonfiction, all need to be included in our classrooms.

Putting It All Together

In this chapter, we have introduced several options for guiding students' reading of literature, particularly fiction. Yet we hope it is clear that students need to develop certain underlying strategies so they can participate successfully in any and all of these activities. As teachers, we need to include strong components of both modeling and guided reading, so that these strategies are not left to students individually to figure out. Rather, it is our responsibility to see that all students become active, strategic readers and know what they need to do to be successful and enjoy the process. This means listening to students as they read and respond to literature and determining their strategies for reading. Then we must establish a classroom schedule ensuring that all students have opportunities to learn those strategies that they do not use or know. Beginning with teacher modeling and guided practice, over time students should build their own independent use of active reading strategies and should learn to participate in group discussions and activities that bring literature alive.

Some of the strategies we have explained in this chapter—the DR-TA and its variants, problem solving, story impressions, some of the art activities, and the various strategies teachers model in their own reading—are all best developed under teacher guidance. Most students won't understand the nature of individual interpretation if they don't hear other students respond to the same text but with a different sense of the meaning. Therefore, rich teacher-guided lessons are important to ensuring that all students develop into good readers. These guided lessons can also stimulate students to listen to each other and to begin to talk together about what they read.

A major goal of reading instruction is to develop readers who learn to respond to literature in a variety of ways and know how to discuss it with their peers. In fact, Almasi's (1995) research demonstrated that generally children have deeper discussions when teachers are not present. Therefore, time needs to be devoted to student-to-student exchanges. Learning to talk together about books does not come naturally to many students. They need to develop respect for each other, learn to take turns, listen actively, and respond appropriately. There are many options you can try until you find the structures that work best for you and help you develop your students as strong readers. Sketch to Stretch, Say Something, and literature discussions of a variety of types all build students' independence and confidence in their construction of meaning and their ability to think deeply about what they read.

Finally, we need to remember that students are not all alike. Although some will be like us in their enjoyment of talking with others about what they read, we will have many students who find such verbal exchanges less than compelling. For those students, we need to provide many opportunities to draw, write, participate in oral-language activities, and demonstrate their response to literature in other ways. Some of our students will want to spend most of their time responding individually, while others will need to be energized by group activities. It is our challenge and privilege to create classrooms that nurture all of our students, and in the process to learn from the insights and depth children bring to literacy activities.

Appendix

"Mama! Yoo-hoo, Mama!"

There was the fine new school building where Juan and Manuel and Maria went to school, and there was Maria with her new city friend, waving and calling.

216

"Wait a minute, Mama!" Maria came running to put her schoolbooks in the stroller with Juanita.

"Mama, may I play a while at Marjorie's house? Please?"

"Very well," Mama said. "A while. But do not be late for supper, Maria. I am making my special soup tonight."

"Mmmm-mmm, Mexicali Soup!" Maria said. Then she looked thoughtful. Then she frowned.

"But—Mama?"

"Yes, Maria?"

"Mama, there are such a lot of potatoes in your Mexicali Soup."

"Of course," Mama said, smiling.

"Marjorie doesn't eat potatoes. Her mother doesn't eat them. Her sister doesn't eat them. Potatoes are too fattening. Mama. They are too fattening for many people in the city. I think we should do what others do here. We are no longer in the mountains of the West, Mama, where everyone eats potatoes. We are in the city now. So would you—Mama, would you please leave out the potatoes?"

"No potatoes," Mama said thoughtfully. She looked at Maria's anxious face. She shrugged. "Well, there are plenty of good things in the Mexicali Soup without potatoes. I will add more of everything else. It will still make good soup."

Anxious means worried.

Shrugged (line 25) means raised the shoulders.

217

Maria kissed Mama's cheek. "Of course it will, Mama. You make the best soup in the world."

Mama went on with Juanita to the markets, to the street of little markets, thinking aloud as she went. "Tomatoes, onions, celery. Red peppers, chili peppers, good and hot. And garlic. But no potatoes."

Mama went to Mr. Santini's little market for the best tomatoes and celery. She went to Mr. Vierra's little market for the best onions and garlic. "And the peppers," she said to Juanita. "We will buy the peppers from Antonio. Our own Antonio, at the market of Mr. Fernandez. Here is the place. Ah! What beautiful peppers!"

Antonio came hurrying out of the store to the little stand on the sidewalk. "Let me help you, Mama! I hope you want something very good for our supper tonight. I get very hungry working here," Antonio said.

"Ah, si!" Mama said. "Yes, Antonio. For to-night—something special!" She reached for the hot red peppers strung above her head. "Mexicali Soup."

"Hey! That's great," Antonio exclaimed. Then he looked thoughtful. Then he frowned. "But—Mama—"

Santini /sän·tē´·nē/.
Vierra /vär´·rä/.

Fernandez /fär·nän´·das/.

"Yes?" Mama said, putting some peppers on the scale.

"Well—Mama, you use a lot of hot peppers in your soup."

"Of course," Mama said, smiling.

"A lot," Antonio repeated. "Too many, Mama. People here don't do that. They don't cook that way. They don't eat the way we did in the mountains of the West. I know, Mama. I have worked here for weeks now, after school and Saturdays. And in all that time, Mama, I have not sold as many hot peppers to other ladies as you use in a week.

Mamacita
/mä·mä·sē′·tä/ is a
Spanish word for
mother.

"Mamacita," Antonio said. "Please don't put hot peppers in the soup."

"No peppers," Mama said thoughtfully. She looked at Antonio's anxious face. "Well—" Mama shrugged. "There are plenty of good things in the soup without peppers. I will add more of something else. It will still make good soup."

Antonio took the peppers out of the scale and put them back on the stand. "Of course it will, Mama." He kissed her cheek. "Everyone knows you make the best soup in the world."

Mama went on with Juanita toward home. "Tomatoes, onions, garlic, celery," she said to herself. "Yes. I can still make a good soup with those." She hummed softly to herself as she crossed a

street blocked off from traffic, a street that was only for play.

"Hey, Mama! Mamacita!"

Juan and Manuel left the game of stickball in the play street. They raced each other to the spot where Mama stood.

"Oh, boy! Food!" said Juan when he saw the bags in the stroller. He opened one of the bags. "Tomatoes and celery—I know what that means."

"Me, too," said Manuel. He peeked into the other bag. "Onions and garlic. Mexicali Soup! Right, Mama?" Manuel rubbed his stomach and grinned. Then he looked thoughtful. Then he frowned. "But, Mama—listen, Mama."

"I am listening," Mama said.

"Well, I think we use an awful lot of onions," Manuel said. "They don't use so many onions in the lunchroom at school, or at the Boy's Club picnics. You know, Mama, they have different ways of doing things here, different from the ways of our town on the side of the mountain. I think we should try new ways. I think we shouldn't use so many onions. Mamacita, please make the Mexicali Soup without onions."

"Manuel is right!" Juan said. "My teacher said only today there is nothing that cannot be changed, and there is nothing so good that it cannot be made better, if we will only try. I think there may be better ways of making soup than our old way. Make the soup tonight without tomatoes, Mama!"

"No tomatoes?" Mama said. "And no onions? In Mexicali Soup?" Mama looked at the anxious faces of Juan and Manuel. Then she shrugged. She closed the two bags of groceries carefully. She pushed the stroller away from the play street. She shrugged again.

Voices came after her. Juan's voice said, "We will be hungry for your soup tonight, Mama!" Manuel's voice called, "Mamacita! You make the best soup in the world!"

In the big kitchen at home, Mama put the groceries on the table by the stove. She hummed a little soft tune that only Mama could hear. She stood looking at the groceries. No potatoes. No peppers. Tomatoes—Mama pushed the tomatoes aside. Onions—she pushed the onions aside.

Mama sat down and looked at what was left.

The front door clicked open and shut. Rosie came into the kitchen. Rosita, the young lady of the family.

Rosita /rō·sē′·tä/.

"Hi, Mama. Oh, Mama—I hope I'm in time! I heard you were making—" Rosie stopped to catch her breath. She frowned at the groceries on the table. "All the way home I heard it. The boys and Maria—they all told me—and Mama! I want to ask you—please! No garlic."

Mama stopped humming.

Rosie turned up her nose and spread out her hands. "No garlic. Please. Listen, Mama. Last night, when my friend took me to dinner, I had such a fine soup! Delicious! The place was so elegant, Mama—so refined. So expensive. And no garlic at all in the soup!"

Rosie bent over and kissed Mama's cheek. "Just leave out the garlic, *Mamacita*. You make the best soup in the world."

A deep voice and many other voices called all at once, and the front door shut with a bang. "Mama! We are home, Mama!" Then all of them, Juan and Manuel and Antonio, with Maria pulling Papa by the hand—all of them came to stand in the kitchen doorway.

Papa reached for the baby, the little Juanita, and swung her onto his shoulders. "I have heard of something special," Papa said. "I have heard we are having Mexicali Soup tonight."

Mama said nothing. But Mama's eyes flashed fire. She waited.

"Your soup, Mama—" Papa said. "It is simply the best soup in the world!"

224

225

173

"Ah, *sí!* But you want me to leave out something?" Mama's voice rose high. "The celery, perhaps? You want me to make my Mexicali Soup without the celery?"

Papa raised his eyebrows. "Celery?" Papa opened his hands wide and shrugged. "What is celery? It is a little nothing! Put it in or leave it out, *Mamacita*—it does not matter. The soup will be just as—"

"Enough!" Mama said. "Out of my kitchen—all of you!" Mama waved her arms wide in the air. The fire in Mama's eyes flashed again. "I am busy! I am busy getting your supper. I will call you. Go."

"But, Mama," said Rosie, "we always help you with—"

"No!" Mama said. "Out!"

Rosie and Juan and Manuel, Antonio and Maria, and Papa with the baby, tiptoed away to the living room.

There was only silence coming from the kitchen. Then, the sound of a quiet humming. Soon the humming mixed with the clatter of plates and spoons, the good sounds of the table being set for supper.

The humming turned into singing. Mama was singing a happy song from the old home in the mountains. Juan and Manuel, Antonio and Maria, Rosie and Papa, looked at one another and smiled and nodded. Mama was singing.

Ask the children to think about what Mama is doing and why she starts humming.

226

Then from the kitchen Mama's voice called to them. "The soup is finished. Your supper is ready. Come and eat now."

"Ah! That is what I like to hear," said Papa, jumping up with Juanita. "The soup is ready before I have even begun to smell it cooking."

"Mmm-mmm!" said Juan and Manuel, racing for the big kitchen table.

"Mmm-mmm!" said Maria and Antonio and Rosie when they saw the steaming bowls on the table. "Mama makes the best soup in the world!"

But what was the matter?

"This doesn't look like Mexicali Soup," said Maria, staring at the bowl before her.

"It doesn't smell like Mexicali Soup," said Antonio, sniffing the steam that rose from his bowl.

"It doesn't taste like Mexicali Soup," said Juan and Manuel, sipping a sip from their spoons.

"This is not Mexicali Soup," said Rosie, setting her spoon down hard with a clang. "This is nothing but hot water!"

Everyone looked at Mama.

Mama smiled and hummed the old tune from the mountains.

"You have forgotten to bring the soup, Mamacita?" suggested Papa.

"No," Mama said, still smiling. "The soup is in your bowls. And it is just what you wanted. I made the soup the way my family asked me to make it.

"I left out the potatoes that Maria does not want. I left out the peppers that Antonio does not want. I left out the tomatoes that Juan does not want. I left out the onions that Manuel does not want. For Rosita, I left out the garlic. And for Papa, I left out the celery, the little nothing that does not matter.

"The new Mexicali Soup! It is so simple! So quick! So easy to make," Mama said. "You just leave everything out of it."

After the class has completed the story, have volunteers try to read Mama's last speech as she would have said it. Tell them to remember how satisfied Mama must feel with the trick she has played on her family.

CHAPTER 7

Strategies for Vocabulary Development

Look and listen in any classroom on any given day and you will find teachers and students doing a multitude of things with vocabulary (see this chapter's graphic organizer, Figure 7.1). For example, on a Wednesday preceding Martin Luther King Day, we asked one teacher to keep track of everything she did that she would label "vocabulary instruction." Here's what she listed in her notes:

Provided quick synonyms for words with familiar concepts (actual example: "diadem" in a fairy tale).

Helped bilingual students remember high-frequency words that were well established in their native language (e.g., notebook = *quaderno*).

Introduced the concept of "democracy" to fifth graders beginning to study the American Revolution.

Got a group of students to consider synonyms for overused words (e.g., "said") in their writing.

Led students to appreciate the connotative words of the author Roald Dahl as he described adults unfavorably in *Matilda*.

Helped students in a cooperative group use the context and a dictionary to unravel the meanings of some new words.

Helped students locate the exact word they were looking for but couldn't remember in a thesaurus.

Assisted students in understanding the figurative language and the literary and biblical allusions in speeches of Martin Luther King, so that they could present the speeches with full understanding in a district speech contest.

176

Resource Locator—Strategies and Resources Discussed in Chapter 7

FIGURE 7.1. Graphic organizer for Chapter 7.

Just a quick look at this list points out some of the difficulty in making any simple, all-encompassing statements about "vocabulary instruction." All of these teacher–pupil encounters involved vocabulary, but each was different in the purpose of the instruction, the depth of word knowledge required for the task, and the type of instruction or facilitation that might be most suitable. Also, as any teacher knows, entry-level knowledge can vary wildly from student to student.

Vocabulary learning is really a "special case" of comprehension. Our vocabularies are the clearest examples of social construction in action; most of our vocabulary learning takes place in encounters with others, through firsthand experience, through talk, and through reading (Nagy & Anderson, 1984; Cunningham & Stanovich, 1998). Vocabulary is a reflection of our knowledge and experience and of our social interactions; building a personal vocabulary is a highly constructive process. This model of vocabulary learning relates very directly to the model of comprehension we outlined in Chapter 2. Because comprehension has an individual dimension, students need to become "word aware"—to develop personally meaningful vocabularies, and to become attuned to the richness and diversity of language. Because of comprehension's social dimension, students need to be engaged in learning words relevant to the cultural literacy we all share; typically, in schools, this is content vocabulary. Finally, as comprehension is a process, the learning of constructive and metacognitive strategies for word learning is also critical. Thus our first task in this chapter is to ask, "What do we want to see in our students with respect to vocabulary development?"

Starting with Students: Vocabulary for Many Purposes

Think back to Maria and Nikki, whom we met in Chapters 1 and 2. What happened to their vocabularies as they undertook their exploration of butterflies? First, they developed an interest in new words; that is, they developed "word awareness" when it came to new butterfly terms. Maria illustrated her new list of terms, and Nikki kept a notebook, as both girls took pride in their ever-expanding vocabularies.

The girls' interest in butterflies also led them to develop ways of organizing and adding to their specialized content vocabulary. After recording her first new words, Nikki realized that one category of new vocabulary was "butterfly types," so she began a page with that heading; later she followed with a page on "butterfly wing shapes." Then Maria drew diagrams that were headed "parts of the butterfly." With content vocabulary, unlike vocabulary from stories and other narratives, the structure of the content helps the reader organize, understand, and retain meanings.

Along with their growing content vocabularies, Maria and Nikki's wide reading improved their general vocabularies. Repeated exposure in reading to the most frequent words ("a," "an," "the"), connector words ("therefore," "furthermore," etc.), and adjectives ("beautiful," "shimmering," etc.) improved their general reading vocabularies and helped their fluency.

Finally, the girls developed strategies for new word learning. For instance, they began to use generative word parts—such as the root "migrate" to understand terms such as "migration" and "migratory," and the root "lepi-" both to decode and to understand several new words. They also began to use dictionaries to answer questions (e.g., "Is a lepidopterist a person who studies butterflies or kills butterflies?") and to gain more information about terms they partially knew.

In all this learning, their teacher, Susan, was there to teach, coach, support, and provide direction. Now let's look at vocabulary learning from the teacher's perspective. What can we do to help students become word aware, to develop broader general vocabularies, to learn crucial content vocabulary, and to develop independent word-learning strategies? Teachers can address vocabulary in the classroom in several ways.

Developing Word Awareness

First, teachers need to structure classrooms that develop "word-aware" learners. We put this first because we know, as all teachers do, that motivation is an essential prerequisite for all learning. Also, research suggests (Beck, Perfetti, & McKeown, 1982) that even strategies as simple as a "word of the day" activity, or having posterboard "Word Wizard Walls" (on which students enter new words) hanging in our classrooms, can heighten students' receptivity for learning new words incidentally. The more playful and humorous vocabulary activities can be, the more learning is likely to take place. In one study of middle school student's vocabulary learning, the researcher (Haggard, 1985) was surprised to see how many of the students knew the highly infrequent word "behooves." This is certainly not a word that most of us come across with regularity. Interviewing teachers and students about this perplexing finding, the researcher found that it stemmed from the principal's announcing over the school intercom, "It behooves each and every one of you to clean out your locker before the break. Anything left in the lockers will be thrown out." The students thought this was the funniest-sounding word they had ever heard. For the rest of the week before vacation, they directed each other, "It behooves you to give me back my pencil," or "It behooves you to get your feet off my desk." The humor, the group enjoyment, the practice, and the heightened awareness all added up to word learning without lots of instructional effort.

Building General Vocabulary

Besides creating a lively, word-rich, word-aware environment, teachers need to help students build general vocabularies through wider reading. Unlike reading textbooks, in which the new words are new for almost all the students, reading fiction results in some general word learning but also differs from student to student. Where one child may not know "sword" in the *Castle in the Attic* (Winthrop, 2000), five others will. Three of these may know "armor" but not "mace"; the other two may know "mace" but not "halberd." In another book, some students will know what "the pot calling the kettle black" implies, but others will not. Thus, beyond the key concept words of a story or chapter, there is a high degree of individual difference in learning that teachers must accommodate.

Developing Content Vocabulary

In content learning, it is more important for teachers to ensure that a core vocabulary of content words is learned by all students. In general vocabulary learning, a student can easily infer the meaning of a new word like "pallet" in the sentence "He lay on his pallet and went to sleep." It is easy to infer that it is some type of bed, and to go on from there. It's not as easy to determine the meaning of a more complex, content-specific word, such as "photosynthesis." Content domain vocabulary is also additive; in a content area like math, it is hard to imagine a student getting very far in geometry if the terms and concepts "circle" and "diameter" have not been well and specifically established several grades earlier. So, in content learning, more formal methods of building and retaining shared vocabulary are typical.

Encouraging Strategies for Independence

Across all types of vocabulary learning, understanding that there are strategies that can be applied for word learning and that there are generative units within words (prefixes, suffixes, and roots) helps students become independent. Students need knowledge of these generative parts, of references, and of learning and study strategies to implement strategies for all those learning situations the teacher we consulted saw in a single day. They also need to know when to apply this knowledge and how to do it. In this way, learning vocabulary and developing strategies to do so independently are metacognitive acts.

Figure 7.2 graphically represents our model of vocabulary instruction. In this chapter, we'll ask the following questions: How can we teachers build "word awareness" in our classrooms? How do we help students develop general vocabulary knowledge? How can we stimulate the learning of vocabulary in content areas? How do we build independent word-learning strategies? Because one chapter can only just skim the surface of these topics, interested readers may want to con-

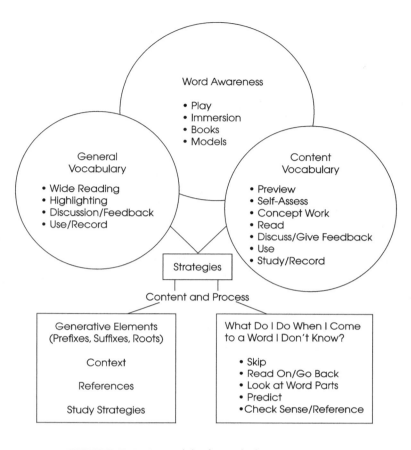

Word Awareness

- Play
- Immersion
- Books
- Models

General Vocabulary

- Wide Reading
- Highlighting
- Discussion/Feedback
- Use/Record

Content Vocabulary

- Preview
- Self-Assess
- Concept Work
- Read
- Discuss/Give Feedback
- Use
- Study/Record

Strategies

Content and Process

Generative Elements (Prefixes, Suffixes, Roots)

Context

References

Study Strategies

What Do I Do When I Come to a Word I Don't Know?

- Skip
- Read On/Go Back
- Look at Word Parts
- Predict
- Check Sense/Reference

FIGURE 7.2. A model of vocabulary instruction.

sult more specific resources on vocabulary instruction to flesh out this picture (Blachowicz & Fisher, 1996; Stahl, 1999; Nagy, 1988; Dale & O'Rourke, 1981).

Developing Word Awareness

The Importance of Talk

Wide exposure to new words is a powerful force for word learning, particularly when attention is paid to making the exposure motivating and pleasurable. For students of all ages, particularly students who are not secure in English, having lots of time for classroom talk is an essential aspect of encouraging informal word learning. Along with "show and tell" activities at the lower levels, and "current events" discussions and cooperative groupings for older students, word-aware classrooms maximize students' opportunities to hear and use language. Repeated story and poetry readings are excellent stimuli for word learning. Connecting new vocabulary to rich illustrations and engaging story lines helps to make it comprehensible and memorable (Freeman & Freeman, 2000). As with all things happening in classrooms, some judicious attention and planning by the teacher can maximize student learning (Elley, 1988).

Because the language in books is so much richer than the language in everyday talk (Cunningham & Stanovich, 1998), read-alouds are an important part of exposure. Teachers in word-aware classrooms can do the following:

- Use illustrations to express, label, and clarify meanings. For example, in the delightful book *King Bidgood's in the Bathtub* (Wood, 1985), words such as "battle," "trout," "masquerade," "feast," and "plug" are clarified by the superb illustrations.
- Use illustrations as a template for retelling using story vocabulary. Students who are not yet able to write elaborate summaries can use illustrations to retell to their teachers and classmates. Jesse, a first-grade teacher at the Academy of St. Benedict the African in Chicago, read her students the chapter book "The BFG" by Roald Dahl (1982) and asked students to draw and retell a favorite scene. Her student, Michael, used his drawing (see Figure 7.3) to describe the scene where the BFG (the Big Friendly Giant) and Sophie are in the room with the door *blocked* by the *circular boulder*. Michael retold the BFG's dream of *riding an elephant to pick*

FIGURE 7.3. "BFG" picture for retelling.

fruit (in the bubble) in a room full of *dreams caught in bottles by the dream catching net*. Meanwhile, Sophie was getting more and more *confused* (the question mark) which was all seen by the lurking Bone Crushing Giant. Using his picture as a mnemonic, Michael was able to organize his thinking show his understanding of and ability to use the underlined words which he could not yet write.

• Use new words in questions: "If you were going to be in a 'battle,' what would you take?" Such questions involve students in meaningful, thoughtful responses to new words, and they tend to use these words in their responses: "Well, for the battle, I'd take . . ." This also gives teachers a chance to clarify meanings when students have misconceptions.

• Involve students in creating images for new words to cement their meanings in a personal way. For example, drawing and labeling can bring home the meaning of new words.

• Read and reread favorite books, and recommend that these be taken home to be read for and by parents. Research indicates that students learn more about a word's meaning each time it is used in a meaningful way (Eller, Pappas, & Brown, 1988).

• For English as a Second Language (ESL) students, create word lists and personal dictionaries and notebooks that use words in their native language as well as in English.

Use of good literature, repeated exposure to new words, use of new words in discussion and image making, and relation of words in English to ESL students' first languages are all ways vocabulary from a read-aloud situation can find its way into students' oral vocabularies.

Vocabulary Visits

A strong oral vocabulary allows students to later develop strong reading vocabularies. Listening to books and discussing them is one rich avenue for oral vocabulary development. Further significant new research on young students and their learning suggests that the primary curriculum is ripe for content learning and that there now exist many more resources for content reading for young children (Duke, Bennett-Armistead, & Roberts, 2003). One strategy of using content-area trade books to build vocabulary is "Vocabulary Visits" (Blachowicz & Obrochta, 2005, 2007). "Vocabulary Visits" are virtual field trips in which vivid visuals and books are used to develop concepts and vocabulary for primary grade students.

Teachers assemble thematic text sets which, because of their nature, have a repeated conceptually related vocabulary (e.g., *weather—storms, hurricane, thunder, lightning, damp*). They locate or create an engaging visual, blown up to chart-size, to stimulate discussion of what can be seen, heard, smelled, tasted, and felt—the senses that students use on an actual field trip. For example, *What do you see?* (lightning, flash, storm); *What do you hear?* (crash, boom, thunder); *What can*

FIGURE 7.4. Example of a dual-language chart from a Vocabulary Visit.

you feel? (wet, rain, damp, soggy). These can be constructed as dual-language charts to scaffold the learning of ELLs in the group (see Figure 7.4).

The process involves students in brainstorming to activate what they already know, and then active listening to content books. The teacher works with students to make a chart where conceptually related words are displayed. These labeled charts are used for "active listening" where students are called on to signal "thumbs up" when they hear some of the new words. They also add to the chart as they are read the other books in the text set. Students also take part in semantic sorting and writing activities. "Vocabulary Visits" are motivating and develop concepts and both oral and written vocabulary for young students.

Classroom Labeling

Besides read-aloud sharing, classroom labeling is a good way to teach new vocabulary. The objects and situations in the classroom provide natural contexts for learning. A large-type label maker for young students, and a smaller size for older students, can be used to produce a vocabulary set that is contextualized by the classroom. This process can also assist the students in spelling for writing when they want to describe the classroom aquarium or write about mealworms in science class. Students in advanced classes can use a professional label maker to label new equipment in a science lab. Gym class students can label the bins for storing sports gear. Labeled pictures also provide useful, contextualized information, particularly for older students, ESL students, or limited English proficiency (LEP) students. Richard Scarry's illustrated volumes can be useful in advanced classrooms when basic vocabulary is needed. Scarry has also produced a series of books in many languages, so that terms can be compared across languages and used by all students.

Wide Reading

Wide reading is also a powerful determinant of vocabulary growth. Sustained silent reading, the process of including independent reading in each day's instructional program, ensures that students receive a regular inflow of new words and see these words repeated. Experiments such as the "book flood," which involved students in a large volume of independent-level reading (Anderson, Wilson, & Fielding, 1988), have indicated that wide reading means wide vocabulary growth. Also, such "low-workload" techniques as keeping a word wall or bulletin board of interesting words that are discussed as they are added have proved to be productive tools for informal word learning.

Using Technology

Capitalize on students' love of technology by utilizing technology that can teach. When TV and videos are used for instruction, consider using programs and videos with closed captioning. These are not only useful for students with hearing impairments; they have also been found to make new vocabulary more comprehensible, especially for ESL students. Newscasts, presidential addresses, and other topical events are often captioned. Taping them for use in discussions of current events can help students hear and see new words at the same time.

Electronic materials and CD-ROMs, as well as computer word-processing programs, can also be useful for providing multiple inputs to word meaning. Many computer-based reading materials allow students to hear the story at the same time they see the words. Several versions, such as those by Discis Books, also allow readers to highlight words to hear them pronounced again and defined. Some word-processing programs (such as Kids Works 2 and Wiggleworks) print in primary or regular type, have a file of vocabulary rebuses, and use synthesized speech to read back to students what they have written.

Uses of these tools may require adult mediation. One study of videodisc technology where students could access mediation in the form of definitions and illustrative sentences indicated that they knew when to ask for help but were not able to judge whether or not definitions or illustrative sentences would be most helpful in expanding their word knowledge (Gildea, Miller, & Wurtenberg, 1990). Students tended to ask for definitions which helped them less than illustrative sentences or accessing information-rich pictures, which were more facilitative of learning. The researchers suggest, as these were older students, that looking for directions was a result of prior instruction and students need to be instructed on how to use the various capabilities of electronic texts.

One important aspect of technological teaching tools is activity on the part of the learner. Koren (1999), working with second-language learners, found that facilitation which called for active inferencing on the part of the learner was one key to word learning from electronic text. Students learned more from tasks that required inferencing than they did from glossed texts. Pawling's (1999) case studies of high school students found that metacognitive reflection was an important part of learning and that the students welcomed working on and responding to electronic text where "no one was there to make fun of your answers." The ability of media to build prior knowledge is also important. A study by Xin and Reith (2001) with students with learning disabilities found that using video to anchor text by presenting a prior-knowledge video that highlighted new vocabulary words which were then mediated by instructional sentence comprehension and cloze tasks, resulted in greater learning for all but most of all for students with learning disabilities.

Many websites can provide motivating word learning information and activities for students. We like the following websites:

A.Word.A.Day (*www.wordsmith.org/awad*)
SearchEngineWatch.com (*searchenginewatch.com*)
SuperVocab.com: Your Vocabulary Builder (*supervoca.com/index.php*)
Word Confusion (*www.funbrain.com/words.html*)
Vocabulary University (*www.vocabulary.com*)

Music can also provide another entryway for new vocabulary. CD-ROM music videos often provide words to match the music, and students also enjoy karaoke singing, which involves reading lyrics to match the music. Technology has a motivational factor that will frequently interest students who would be reluctant to learn in other ways. Put a computer mouse or an iPod in a kid's hand, and you have instant motivation.

Using Humor and Word Play

Word awareness can be stimulated by having students read and share books about words and books in which word play, and plays on words, is an important part of the book's humor. Books by Fred Gwynne (1970), such as *The King Who Rained*, provide simple, single-phrase examples of confusing homophones (words like "rained–reigned," which sound alike but have different meanings and spellings) and words with more than one meaning. For example, having a "mole" on your nose can be interpreted in two ways. To encourage interpretation and to share the fun, you might want to try having students share these funny misconceptions in Readers' Workshop, act them out dramatically, or show two interpretations in art to explain the mix-ups.

Because we all have stories like these in our backgrounds, students might like to make a collection of their own misconceptions, with illustrations. One fourth-grade class collected its own book of examples of linguistic misconceptions (see Figure 7.5 for one page from this book). Interviewing parents and adults on their misconceptions can provide more examples and more laughs.

Besides using books that exemplify word play, include books on words and word play in your classroom library. Riddle, joke, and pun books abound for all ages (see "Using Riddles, Jokes, and Puns," below), and there are many enjoyable books that deal with etymologies and interesting word forms that students will read independently. Including books on words in your classroom collection; read-

Jake

I remember being really confused when I first heard the term "hot dog." I wondered what I was being offered to eat.

FIGURE 7.5. A page from a fourth-grade classroom's book of humorous linguistic misconceptions.

ing excellent examples to the class; and having students use the ideas in art, drama, and their own writing provides models for word play and develops word awareness. You can also use such books as references to investigate different types of "word genres"—interesting categories of words, the most familiar of which are synonyms and antonyms.

Investigating Word Genres

Books on words can also be used as resources for developing curiosity about different types of words. Most school curricula deal with common word categories or genres, such as synonyms, antonyms, similes, and metaphors. But what about acronyms, portmanteau words, imported words, slang, collective words, and other creative categories of words? Include these in your investigation of words.

Portmanteau Words

When you pack a suitcase, or "portmanteau," sometimes you scrunch things together to make room. For example, you might put your socks in your shoes. A "portmanteau word" is a "packed" word formed by merging a portion of one word with a portion of another. For example, "smog" is a common portmanteau word based on a combination of "smoke" and "fog." English has a rich history of creating new words in this way—a tendency readily picked up by advertisers, journalists, comic book writers, and even scientists. Advertising has given us the "motel" ("motor" + "hotel"); cartoons have provided "zap" ("zip" + "slap"); science has created the "beefalo" ("beef" + "buffalo"); and political journalism has given birth to such words as "insinuendo" ("insinuation" + "innuendo") (McKenna, 1978).

Other Word Genres

Students enjoy compiling sets of these creative genres, making bulletin boards, doing crosswords, solving word search puzzles, and playing other games with these interesting types of words. Espy (1975), an author of many books on words, suggests investigating some of the following:

> **Acronym:** A word formed from the initial letters of other words (e.g., "scuba" = "self-contained underwater breathing apparatus").
> **Anagram:** A word or phrase formed by scrambling the letters of a word (e.g., "dear–read").
> **Borrowed words:** Words used in English that originated in other languages (e.g., "cafe," "lariat," and "pretzel").
> **Collective words:** Words that label a group, typically of animals (e.g., a "gaggle" of geese, and a "pride" of lions).

Lipogram: A word or phrase lacking a certain letter or letters (e.g., "Pete wed Helen when he met her"; all vowels are missing except "e").

Malapropism: Use of an incorrect word for a similar-sounding one (e.g., "That's an interesting faucet of his personality").

Mixed metaphor: A confusing or incongruous mixing of two parts of other well-known metaphors (e.g., "A stitch in time waits for no man").

Onomatopoeia: A word whose sound relates to its meaning (e.g., "buzz" and "gulp").

Oxymoron: A phrase composed of words that seem contradictory (e.g., plastic silverware).

Palindrome: A word or phrase that reads the same forward or backward (e.g., "mom," "dad," and "Able was I ere I saw Elba").

Spoonerism: An unintentional transposition of sounds (e.g., "Please pass the salt and shecker papers").

You might have your students research the origins of the words "malapropism" and "spoonerism," which refer to people or characters.

Using Riddles, Jokes, and Puns

Students become interested in riddles and jokes in the early grades, and "pun-o-mania" hits in the middle grades. As noted above, riddle, joke, and pun books abound and quickly circulate in most classrooms. Creating riddles, jokes, and puns is one way to stimulate exploration of words and to build interest and flexibility in word learning.

Word Riddles

Mike Thaler (1988), a prolific author and conference speaker, has collected many ideas for riddle and joke making. One way to make "word riddles," questions with pun-like responses, involves choosing a subject and generating a list of related terms. For example, if your subject is "pig," your list might contain such words as these:

ham	pork
pen	grunt
hog	oink

You take the first letters off one of the words and then make a list of words beginning with that letter pattern. If you choose "ham," you make a list of words that begin with "am," such as these:

*am*bulance
*am*nesia
*am*phibian
*Am*erica

Then you put back the missing letter—

*ham*bulance
*ham*nesia
*ham*phibian
*Ham*erica

—and make up riddles for the words:

RIDDLE: How do you take a pig to a hospital?

ANSWER: In a hambulance!

RIDDLE: What do you call it when a pig loses its memory?

ANSWER: Hamnesia!

Name Riddles

Thaler (1988) also suggests name riddles. Look for names with the related word part, as in this further example in the "pig" mode:

RIDDLE: What pig discovered the theory of relativity?

ANSWER: Albert Swinestein!

Tom Swifties

"Tom Swifties" are created by writing a quotation, followed by a descriptive adjective or verb that has some semantic relationship to the quotation. They get their name from the frequent occurrence of such sentences in the old *Tom Swift* adventure books for boys. Examples of Tom Swifties include the following:

"Let's hurry," said Tom swiftly.
"Your sewing is extremely sloppy," she needled.
"Catch that stray dog!" he barked at the bystanders.

Students enjoy creating and explaining Tom Swifties.

Hink Pink

Hink Pink asks students to come up with a pair of rhyming words to match a defining phrase. Each word in the pair has the same number of syllables. The person who creates the phrase cues the guesser with the term "Hink Pink" (two one-syllable words), "Hinky Pinky" (two two-syllable words), "Hinkety Pinkety" (two three-syllable words), and so forth. Here are some examples:

> CLUE: Hink Pink—an angry father.
>
> ANSWER: Mad dad.
>
> CLUE: Hinkety Pinkety—an evil clergyman.
>
> ANSWER: Sinister minister.

These are lots of fun, and often students can come up with more than one answer for a clue. Any meaningful answer is acceptable.

Using Word Games for Practice

Word awareness can be encouraged by using both homemade and commercial games focusing on words and word play. To select games to make, use, and adapt, consider these guidelines:

1. Games should be simple to use without teacher intervention.
2. Vocabulary level should be appropriate.
3. Play should call on students to use the words in some meaningful way.
4. Games should utilize outside resources (e.g., dictionary, class notebook) for self-checking.
5. Games should limit the number of players so that all players are involved.

Many class-constructed games follow one of six models: matching card games (like Rummy or Fish), race-and-chase board games (like Parcheesi), memory games (such as Concentration), Bingo, pencil-and-paper games, and guessing games.

Card Games

Card games work on the pairing principle. A pair is made when a word is matched with one of the following: a synonym, a definition, an antonym, a cloze sentence in which it makes sense, a picture symbolizing its meaning, an English translation, or some other match appropriate to your class. Prepare a deck of at least 40 word cards with pair cards, such as the ones in Figure 7.6, constructed by students from

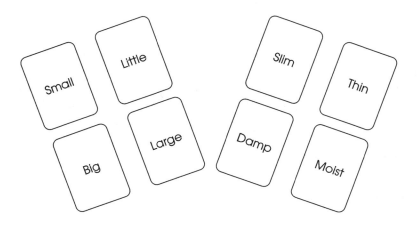

FIGURE 7.6. Pairs of cards representing words and their synonyms or definitions, constructed by students from words across their weekly curriculum.

words across their curriculum for the week. Their deck made pairs of words and synonyms or definitions. Cards are shuffled, and seven cards are dealt to each player. Each player can choose a card and discard one card in turn. Pairs may be placed on the table. The first player to pair all cards wins. Two popular card games are the following:

• *Fish*. For Fish, all the cards are dealt, and players pick one card from the player on their left in turn. Pairs may be placed on the table. The first player to pair all cards wins.
• *Old Teacher*. Old Teacher is a variation of Old Maid. An extra card is prepared with a drawing of the teacher (or some generic teacher). This is played like Fish. The person who is left with this card is the "Old Teacher."

In all card games, students must read their pairs. A student can be challenged by another student if the challenger does not agree with a pair. The dictionary settles such disputes. If the challenger is correct, he or she may take an extra turn. If the challenger is incorrect, the player gets an extra turn.

Race-and-Chase Board Games

Race-and-chase games require a posterboard game board and pieces for moving around the board. Many teachers like to construct "generic" race-and-chase boards that can be used with many sets of cards. If the card space fits the cards from the card games, cards prepared for one purpose can be used for many others.

A 2 × 3 index card cut into halves or thirds is an excellent size for word cards. Moving pieces can be commercially purchased at teacher stores or taken from old games bought at garage sales. In addition, dice or spinners are useful.

One of the easiest race-and-chase formats is Synonym Match. The stack of word cards is placed in the center of the board, and the synonym cards are arranged, face up, next to the board (see Figure 7.7). Each student in turn rolls a die (or spins a spinner) and picks up a word card. If the student can correctly locate the synonym match, he or she can move the number of spaces indicated on the die or spinner. The dictionary again serves as the authority. Harder versions of this game involve using the words in original sentences.

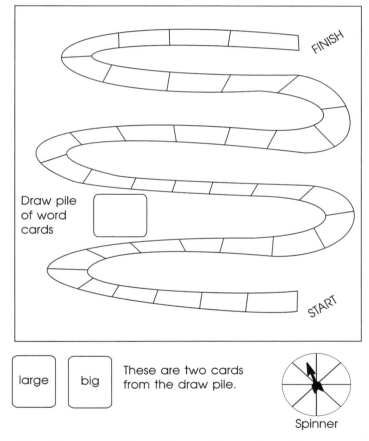

FIGURE 7.7. Game board and cards for the race-and-chase game of Synonym Match.

Memory Games

Like commercial memory games, word memory games involve finding matches and remembering cards. Play the game of Concentration with a maximum of 25 cards—12 word cards, 12 match cards, and 1 wild card. All the cards are shuffled and placed face down in a 5 × 5 grid. At each turn, a student turns two cards face up and reads them. If the cards are a match, the student takes the cards. If they are not a match, they are turned back over and left in the same place. Play continues in turn until only a single card remains. Students may use the wild card only if they can supply a suitable match orally. This can be checked at the end of the game by looking at the remaining card. The student with the most cards wins.

Bingo

A variant of the popular game of Bingo can be played by any size group. Students each have sets of word cards from which they construct a 5 × 5 grid. They lay out their cards in any manner they choose, placing a "free" card in the space of their choice. The caller chooses definitions from the definition pile and reads them out. Students can place markers on the words that match. The first student to mark an entire row, column, or diagonal wins. Students check by reading the words and definitions. The cards are then reshuffled, new cards are composed, and the winner becomes the caller for the next game.

Pencil-and-Paper Games

Categories. One of the most popular pencil-and-paper games is Categories. Students draw a grid of suitable size (2 × 2 for younger students, 5 × 5 for older ones, or some size in between) and label each vertical row with a category (or the teacher may provide categories). Then one student flips through a book and chooses a word whose number of letters matches the number of columns. For example, students in a ninth-grade study hall working on World War II constructed the grid shown in Figure 7.8.

Players are given a designated time limit to fill in as many squares as they can (a kitchen timer is useful). At the end of the time limit, points are totaled. Players get 5 points for every category square they fill in that no other player has filled in; 2 points for every category square filled in that others have filled in, but with other words; and 1 point for every category square filled in where someone else has the same term. Inappropriate entries may be challenged and carry no point totals if they are not suitable. Categories can be related to content and thematic units, though using a few "fun" or "silly" categories in each grid adds spice and laughter.

World War II

	People	Places	Terminology
M	*Montgomery*	*Munich*	*mount an offensive*
E	*Eisenhower*	*Europe*	*escalate*
N	*Nazi*	*Normandy*	*negotiate*

FIGURE 7.8. A 3 × 3 grid for a game of Categories, constructed by ninth-grade pupils studying World War II.

Word Challenge. Word Challenge is another category game in which the categories are preset to think about particular characteristics of words (Abromitis, 1992). For example, common categories might include "synonym/similar," "antonym/different," "example," and "related word." This is played the same way as Categories (see above).

Guessing Games

Twenty Questions. Twenty Questions is an excellent verbal game that can be adapted to help students think about words they are learning. The student who is "it" selects a word card from a prepared stack. Other students can ask questions in turn, using only ones that require a yes-or-no answer. The "asking" team gets 20 questions. A turn ends with a "no." If one student correctly guesses the word, that player becomes "it" for the next round. If no one guesses the word, "it" gets another turn.

Word of the Day. Many teachers do the venerable "word of the day" activity in a guessing-game format. In some classrooms, each day a set of clues is prepared and put on the board. An envelope is taped below for guesses, and these are discussed at the end of the day. Another teacher chooses a word that she uses throughout the day. For example, in the morning, she may say, "Oh, I had such a bad headache this morning I had to medicate myself. I took two aspirin." Later in the day, discussing the death of Lincoln and its aftermath, she may say, "I wonder what Dr. Mudd used to medicate John Wilkes Booth? I don't think they had aspirin then." At the end of the day, she asks students whether they can identify the word of the day and tell what it means. Students become keen listeners for new words when this approach is used.

Developing General Vocabulary Knowledge

Wide reading is a major developer of our general vocabularies, and this growth starts right in the preschool years. Students from homes where regular read-alouds are the norm come to school with many thousands more words in their vocabularies than children from homes where "lap reading" does not take place. The vocabulary of even simple children's books is more complex than everyday conversation, even that of college-educated adults (Cunningham & Stanovich, 1998). Also, words are repeated in reading in differing contexts, allowing the reader to add more meaning to the word with each encounter. The use of cooperative groupings in reading helps students learn how to think and talk about literature, especially when the teacher attends to mentoring and modeling the group processes (Evans, 1966). One of the basic roles in literature discussion groups is that of "vocabulary researcher," the group participant responsible for picking words for discussion. Some teachers use log sheets or personal dictionaries to record vocabulary chosen and discussion.

When teachers choose words for students, there is always a chance that some words are already known by some students. Our own research indicates that when students make their own selections, they choose words at or above their grade level a majority of the time (Blachowicz, Fisher, Costa, & Pozzi, 1993). Some teachers prefer to have each student choose his or her own words and then share these in the class; from these are picked some "class" words (words everyone will study) and words for individual study. The teacher can contribute to the class words if a significant word needs discussion.

Logs

Logging is a way for students to personalize the words they have chosen for study. A log entry can be traditional (a word with its definition and a personal sentence) or nontraditional. Nontraditional log entries using pictures (see Figure 7.9 for some examples) give students two ways to code and remember their vocabulary. Having them label each drawing makes it more personal and clear and allows the teacher to look for misconceptions.

Peer Teaching

For vocabulary practice, students can do peer teaching. In peer teaching, each student selects one word to teach to the other students in the group and makes sure he or she knows the meaning (from context, from a reference, or from consulta-

Vocabulary from *The Witches*		
Word	Page	Interpretation and sentence
bedazzled	*18*	 *goofy with wonder* *Sammy Sosa bedazzled me* *with his homers*
spooked	*23*	 *scared; made* *me feel spooky* *The dark hallway spooked me*
drowsy	*42*	 *The warm room made me drowsy*

FIGURE 7.9. Some examples of nontraditional entries (including graphics) in a vocabulary log.

tion with the teacher). Each student's chosen word is written on three index cards. The students meet in groups of three, and a word at a time is shared. The teacher gives a word card to each student and asks for possible meanings. Students come to consensus on the word's meaning, with the word's chooser acting as arbiter. The meanings are written on a card, along with personal comments and a picture or word cue selected by each student. Each writes a personal sentence, and the teacher monitors these to see how groups are progressing and to clarify usage. The cards become a part of each student's word box.

Sharing of Personal Words

There are many ways the teacher can structure sharing of personal words with the larger class; these include sharing with graphics, word maps, pictures, and computer programs. The more words individual students know, the more chances there are for incidental learning for all students. Letting students use their own words for "word of the day" activities, having new word charts, webbing similar words (see below), and using a hypercard word stack are all ways for students to build a large and flexible general vocabulary.

Developing Content and Academic Vocabulary

"What does 'matrimony' mean?" 7-year-old Cathy asked her teacher a week after her sister's wedding.

"Oh, that's just another word for 'marriage,' " her teacher answered.

"Well, what does 'consummate' mean?" asked Cathy.

The ease with which Cathy's teacher answered the first question, and the teacher's difficulty with the second, are good examples of differences in word learning (not to mention teacher–student relationships)! The first question is an example of learning a new meaning for a concept that is already established. The second exemplifies the harder task of teaching a new word and a new concept at the same time. Other issues concern helping students develop specialized content-focused vocabularies, in which words that they may think they know are used in special ways—for instance, "charge" in a unit on electricity versus "charge" in a unit on consumer education. Also, students need to learn the academic vocabulary used in describing and completing school tasks. Words such as "punctuate," "evaluate," and "outline" themselves form the vocabulary of academic life. Let's look at how we as teachers can help students' vocabularies grow in all these ways.

Learning New Words for Already Known Concepts

Developing a fund of synonyms for known concepts is an important part of vocabulary growth. Teachers can teach students, or groups or classes, how to create "synonym webs." To do this, start with a base word and brainstorm synonyms and use a thesaurus to generate others. Through talk and group discussing, words that are "alike" are placed in clusters. The words are then placed on a web to show their relationship (see Figure 7.10). To clarify differences in synonymous terms, a synonym web can also be created to help with clarification of connotations and denotations or particularities of usage.

Learning New Words for New Concepts

Learning new words and new concepts at the same time requires deep and rich concept-oriented vocabulary instruction. Mapping and webbing are strategies most teachers know; these help students see major concepts and other related concepts, ideas, and terms. For example, a concept map for the word "guitar" is shown in Figure 7.11.

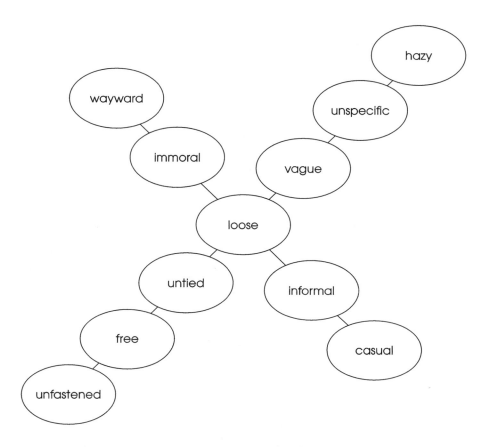

FIGURE 7.10. A synonym web for the word "loose."

Most strategies that we know work for good comprehension also develop related vocabulary. For example, a K-W-L lesson (Ogle, 1986; see Chapter 5) can be started with vocabulary. Before reading the *Ranger Rick* selection "Twiga's First Days" (1976), the teacher placed some vocabulary on the board and asked students to look at the vocabulary to make some predictions about what they were going to read. When the students generated a number of predictions, the teacher puts these on the board under the vocabulary list (see Figure 7.12). Then these vocabulary-generated predictions directed the rest of the K-W-L process.

Building and Retaining Content-Specific Vocabularies

Developing content-specific vocabularies is a major goal of the vocabulary curriculum (Hiebert & Kamil, 2005). Other tasks of content vocabulary teaching and learning include building content-specific vocabulary sets. Different content areas have their own specialized uses of vocabulary; "character," for example, means

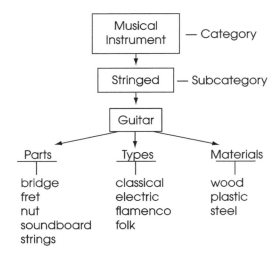

FIGURE 7.11. A concept map for the word "guitar."

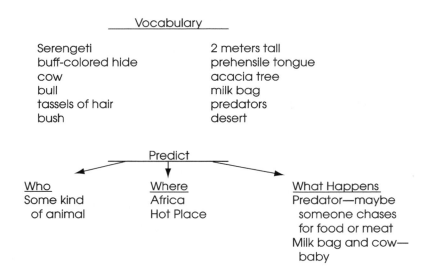

FIGURE 7.12. Vocabulary from an article about giraffes, and predictions generated from the vocabulary in a K-W-L process.

different things in drama class and in calligraphy class. Personal dictionaries and word books can help. Students can also keep logs in a vocabulary square format (Readence, Bean, & Baldwin, 1995). A square for each word is divided into four quadrants; students enter the word, its meaning, an association or synonym, and a graphic aid for remembering the word in the respective quadrants (see Figure 7.13). Maps and webs, as noted above, can also help students organize vocabulary in relational sets.

Marzano proposes a six-step approach to teaching content vocabulary, which he refers to as academic vocabulary. The steps are:

- Step 1: Explain—Provide a student-friendly description, explanation, or example of the new term.
- Step 2: Restate—Ask students to restate the description, explanation, or example in their own words.
- Step 3: Show—Ask students to construct a picture, symbol, or graphic representation of the term.
- Step 4: Discuss—Engage students periodically in structured vocabulary discussions that help them add to their knowledge of the terms in their vocabulary notebooks.
- Step 5: Refine and reflect—Periodically ask students to return to their notebooks to discuss and refine entries.
- Step 6: Apply in Learning Games—Involve students periodically in games that allow them to play with terms.

The Tennessee Department of Education has developed a resource site for teachers with application games that are quite useful for the classroom. They can be accessed at *www.jc-schools.net/tutorials/vocab*.

dissect	cut carefully
Word	Synonym/association
to cut in two	cut $\overline{\text{planaria}}$
Meaning	Picture and labels

FIGURE 7.13. A vocabulary square format for log entries.

Learning Textbook Vocabulary

Textbooks frequently print words in boldface for study or place words for study at the beginning or end of a chapter. Students can use one of the following strategies to guide their own learning of these words.

Knowledge Rating

"Knowledge Rating" (Blachowicz & Fisher, 1996) is a good way for students to highlight and keep track of their own vocabulary learning in textbooks. A student places the highlighted words from the chapter on a simple grid like the one in Figure 7.14. Then the student rates his or her level of knowledge of the words: Which words are known fairly well, which has he or she heard of but doesn't really know, and which are not really known at all? Below the grid, the student attempts to predict:

Knowledge Rating

Word	I know . . .	I have seen . . .	I don't know . . .
tar		✓	
skyscraper	✓		
girder		✓	
quilt	✓		
picnic	✓		
ascend			✓
rooftop	✓		

FIGURE 7.14. A grid for Knowledge Rating.

What is the topic of this chapter?

What do I know about this topic or these ideas?

Then, while reading, whenever the word is encountered, the student enters the page number so the context can be examined after reading. After reading, the student enters a meaning which may be supplied in the chapter or may have to be gotten from the textbook's glossary or a dictionary.

Semantic Mapping or Webbing

Students can also take the words highlighted in the text and place them in relationship to the topic on a semantic map or web before reading. During or after reading, students can refine, revise, or add to the map.

Vocab-o-Gram

A Vocab-o-Gram is a classification chart showing the categories of story structure which can be used to help organize concepts and vocabulary from a story (Blachowicz & Fisher, 2006). This graphic organizer provides information regarding the student's knowledge about the key words and how they are used within the story. It can also be used to assess the depth of vocabulary knowledge; whether learners understand the relationships among words is crucial for instruction of a narrative. The teacher selects words reflecting the important aspects of a selection and has students work in teams to classify them. Class discussion of the proposed classification before reading sets some predictions; discussion after reading clarifies the predications and refines students' knowledge of the words. The completed Vocab-o-Gram can be used by students as an aid to summarizing and response. (See Figure 7.15 for an example of a Vocab-o-Gram template.)

Developing Independent Strategies

The What, How, and When of Word Learning

Being an independent word learner is really a metacognitive process. Students need to have a certain amount of knowledge about words and how they work as a backdrop for strategy use. For example, the notion that words have generative parts—roots, prefixes, and suffixes—that provide an "internal context" to a word's meaning is an important concept to be understood. Standing behind the concept is knowledge of some of these familiar generative parts that can be keys to meaning. Knowing that "sub-" means "below" and that "-marine" is related to *mare*, the Latin word for "sea," can help students unravel "submarine." Besides knowledge of word parts and inflectional endings, students need a knowledge of

Vocab-o-Gram Template

Use vocabulary to make predictions about . . .	
The setting	What will the setting be like?
The characters	Any ideas about the characters?
The problem or goal	What might it be?
The actions	What might happen?
The resolution	How might it end?
What question(s) do you have?	
Mystery words:	

FIGURE 7.15. Example of a Vocab-o-Gram Template.

references, such as the dictionary, that can help them when they need questions answered about a word's meaning.

But just having this knowledge *about* words (sometimes called declarative knowledge) is not enough. Reading a book to learn about a car doesn't mean that you can go out and drive one. Students need to know how to employ strategies to learn new words ("procedural knowledge") and when to use these strategies ("conditional knowledge"). Let's look first at some of the knowledge base on generative word parts and references, and then at the strategies for using words in context.

Word Parts

What Students Need to Know about Word Parts

It makes sense to start with prefixes when teaching about generative word parts. There are fewer prefixes than roots or suffixes; their meanings are generally the same from word to word; and their spellings are relatively stable from word to word (Graves & Hammond, 1980). Also, four prefixes, "un-," "re-," "in-" (and its other spelling forms), and "dis-," account for more than 50% of the affixed words in school English (White, Sowell, & Yanagihara, 1989). Similarly, though suffixes change their spelling more frequently when added to roots, there are only a few that account for many words in English. Inflectional endings for nouns ("-s," "-es"), verbs ("-ed," "-en," "-ing"), and adjectives ("-er," "-est") account for most of the suffixed words in English. Others can be useful not only for understanding a word's meaning but to help students recognize the word's root—the prime key to meaning after the suffixes are stripped away.

Root words can be complex and confusing. Nagy and Anderson (1984) suggest that so many roots are so far from their meaning that they are often not illuminating. The form "mort-" meaning "death," is helpful for "mortal" but not so helpful for "mortify," which has strayed far from its original meaning of "put to death" to a much softer, though still painful, meaning ("humiliate"). Nevertheless, there are many root forms that are quite generative, particularly in the content areas. Templeton (1983) suggests starting with Greek roots, which have the most stable spelling. The idea is to start with a word students know, such as "transport," and build a set of related words.

But as well as knowing the contents of words (the prefixes, suffixes, and roots), students must know how to use these.

A Process for Teaching about Generative Word Parts

A process for teaching about generative word parts (based on work by Graves & Hammond, 1980) moves from the known to the unknown.

1. Start with a known word, if possible (e.g., "tricycle").
2. Identify a part and give definitional information on this on part (e.g., "tri-" means "three").
3. Collect other examples of words that include this part (e.g., "triceratops," "triglyceride," "tripartite," and "triangle").
4. Define these words, focusing on the shared part.
5. Sort examples from nonexamples, if relevant (e.g., "trip"—the "tri" here is not a combining prefix.
6. Create a visual or verbal reminder—for example, a list such as the one shown in Figure 7.16.

Students can also be encouraged to make up new words by combining parts. Using illustrations can make this more fun, as in the case of the word "sub-Nintendo" (see Figure 7.17).

An excellent resource for lists of word families and meaning clusters is provided by Marzano and Marzano (1988) along with other excellent teaching ideas. A reminder is in order, however: In all cases, knowledge from internal context needs to be checked in the larger context. The word "run" has over 40 entries in most dictionaries. Only the context can focus students on the right meaning or help in choosing an appropriate combining part.

Dictionary Use

Like all other word learning, using a dictionary strategically is a metacognitive activity. Students need knowledge about dictionaries: They need to know that dictionaries are organized alphabetically, and that multiple meanings for one word are located under a single entry, whereas homographs (words that are spelled the same but are completely different) are listed with superscripts, and so forth. But they also need to know when and how to use a dictionary.

Knowing about Dictionaries

Most good school dictionaries contain elegant and informative sections for teaching about dictionaries. Besides straightforward instruction, examining different dictionaries, making a class chart of the "extras" in various dictionaries (e.g.,

tricycle
triceratops
triglyceride
tripartite   **FIGURE 7.16.** A list serving as a reminder of the prefix shared
triangle   by a number of words.

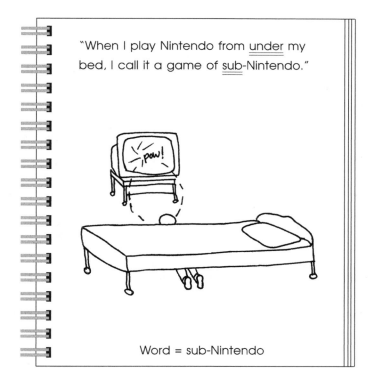

FIGURE 7.17. An illustrated example of the creation of a new word from generative word parts.

"Mary's dictionary has a pronouncing gazetteer"), and examining different types of dictionaries (sports dictionaries, tool dictionaries, etc.) can build interest and awareness. Of special use to all classrooms are the "learner dictionaries." These dictionaries, often meant for students who are just learning English, provide accessible, easy-to-understand definitions of common vocabulary words. Check *www.longman.com/ae/dictionaries/content.html* for some excellent examples of these useful classroom tools.

Knowing When and How to Use Dictionaries

Work by Nist and Olejnik (1995) suggests that students are most successful in using dictionaries after they have encountered a word in its context. This encounter narrows down the syntactic and semantic range of what they are looking for, and in the best cases raises a particular idea or question ("Hmmmmm, 'springbok'— that might be some kind of animal"). Then going to the dictionary has a particular purpose—to gain information about the idea or to answer the question.

At this point, the how becomes important. For many students, finding the right definition results in choosing the first one (there is something magic about that first one) or the shortest one (there is an efficiency motive here). What many students don't know is that definitions provide certain categories of information about most words. Definitions typically place the word in a category (a springbok is a gazelle), describe appropriate attributes (horns), and relate the word to other concepts—sometimes subordinate, sometimes related (a relative of the eland), sometimes synonymous, sometimes featural attributes (found in the Serengeti).

To help students understand what a definition has to offer, you might want to try "definition frames" with them. Schwartz and Raphael (1985) outline a four-step program to help students become more aware of what they call a "concept of definition."

1. Introduce a definition frame (see Figure 7.18) on an overhead projector.
2. Do several examples with different words.
3. Use the frame to generate a definition: A [word] is a [category] much like a [synonym] or related to [relational terms], which is [defining attributes].
4. Model the use of the frame to predict and collect definitional information on new words where a dictionary is used to come to the meaning.

Figuring Out New Words from Context

Besides ensuring that students are surrounded by words in contextual settings, teachers also want to help students hone their abilities to figure out new words from context. This process involves several stages of active problem solving (McKeown, 1985) as well as ongoing reflection. The strategic process of context use can be envisioned as having three components:

1. Students must know why and when to use context. Studies of at-risk readers frequently reveal great cognitive confusion about the potential uses of strategies (Downing & Leong, 1982). Controlling the why and the when involves awareness of both the limitations and contributions of context to word learning. Sometimes the context is quite explicit about word meanings; at other times, the clues given by the author merely suggest an attribute or relationship. Students need to see and discuss various levels of context explicitness to develop sensitivity to the different levels of help context can provide.

2. Students must have a general idea of what kinds of clues may be provided by the context. The following subsection on teaching about context amplifies these characteristics.

3. Most important, students must know how to look for and use these clues. Several strategy sequences have been suggested, including looking at the word and

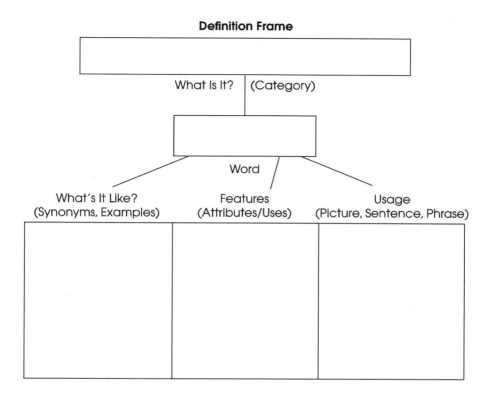

FIGURE 7.18. A definition frame.

around the word (Herman & Dole, 1988), and proposing and verifying meanings (Blachowicz & Zabroske, 1990; Buikema & Graves, 1993).

Teaching about Context

To sensitize students to the types of information context can supply, try to have them examine and collect different types of context clues authors provide. This type of instruction is typically included in school curricula and commercial instructional materials in the middle grades. Instead of worksheets focused on using single paragraphs, consider minilessons built around selections from anthologies or periodicals. Introduce examples of context use in minilessons and have students examine and discuss them. Then make wall charts with examples they discover in their own reading. For example, one class discovered that context can do the following:

1. Provide a direct definition or synonym. ("The farrier, the man who makes shoes for the horses, had to carry his heavy tools in a wheelbarrow.")
2. Indicate what a word's referent is like/not like. ("Unlike the peacock, the mudhen is not colorful.")
3. Tell something about location or settings. ("The shaman entered the Hopi roundhouse and sat facing the mountains.")
4. Tell something about use or function. ("He used the spade to dig up the garden.")
5. Indicate what kind of thing or action a word signifies. ("Swiveling his hips, waggling the club, and aiming for the pin, he drove his first four golf balls into the water.")
6. Tell how something is done. ("He expectorated the gob of tobacco juice neatly into the spittoon.")
7. Provide general topics or ideas related to the word. ("The dancing bears, the musicians, and the cooks carrying huge plates of food all came to the church for the fiesta.")

Students can collect, explain, and display their new words, so that concrete examples of the ways in which context provides guidance to words' meanings can be gathered from their own reading. These will also provide models for writing, and their own creations can also be displayed.

Metacognitive Context Instruction

Once students have a basic sensitivity to the some of the ways context reveals meanings, structure some group lessons that help them build and test hypotheses about word meaning. Direct students to do these things:

Look—before, at, and after the word.
Reason—connect what you know with what the author tells you.
Predict—a possible meaning.
Resolve or redo—decide whether you know enough, should try again, or should consult an expert or reference.

After students become familiar with using a contextual process, student teams can lead the lessons. Working with the teacher, they can choose two words a week they think will be unfamiliar to the group and can model the process with the first word and lead the discussion on the second. Students also like to play "Mystery

Word," in which photocopied pages (from newspapers, magazines, etc.) are posted on the chalkboard daily, with one or two words designated "mystery words." Students note on index cards what clues they have picked up about each word, indicate where these clues are located, and formulate hypotheses about the word's meaning. The cards are placed in an envelope tacked below each selection. At the end of the day, the student team that has posted the words reviews the cards and discusses the words. If needed, a dictionary is consulted to see whether the students' reasoning about the word clues and the words is consistent with established definitions. When context isn't helpful, students often rewrite sections of text to make the surrounding text more explanatory or provide a synonym version for later study. Many of these versions have been collected and kept for later use by future students dealing with the same textbooks.

Beck, McKeown and Kucan's (2002) strategy of Questioning the Author can be also be used to question the author's use of vocabulary within the context of a larger text. Teachers and/or students pose questions generated about new words from reading a text and then use the process of text examination and discussion to answer their own questions or to posit more for discussion.

Using the Cloze Procedure

The cloze procedure, which we introduced as an assessment technique in Chapter 4, can also be used to help students learn to use context to infer word meanings. It is a particularly useful strategy in individualized instruction, such as in a tutoring program. When done with an overhead projector, the cloze procedure can be effective with a small group as well. Whereas cloze passages for assessment typically remove every fifth word, cloze for instruction can be used selectively and flexibly.

Oral Cloze. Oral cloze, with rich discussion around the choices, can be used for emergent readers or for any students who need practice with oral expression. Selected content words are can be deleted from a high-interest, natural-language, or predictable selection. For example, *Alexander and the Terrible, Horrible, No Good, Very Bad Day* (Viorst, 1972) is popular with both younger and older students because of its humorous content, predictable refrain, clear and captivating illustrations, and familiar experiences. In using it for oral cloze, the teacher first shares the illustrations (clearly showing a bedroom with a skateboard, etc.) and then reads aloud, substituting a pause for each of the words in brackets:

> I went to sleep with gum in my [mouth] and now there's gum in my [hair] and when I got out of [bed] this morning I tripped on the [skateboard] and by mistake I dropped my [sweater] in the sink while the [water] was running and I could tell it was going to be a terrible, horrible, no good, very [bad] day. (Viorst, 1972, pp. 1–2)

As the story is read by the teacher, the students supply possibilities for the words omitted. Student enthusiasm for the story makes the "contribution rate" high and provides many alternatives for discussion of possible vocabulary and contextual appropriateness.

After the story or segment has been read and a number of suggestions offered, students often like to tape-record different versions, in order to keep oral records of "Alexander's different terrible days." The goal is not to limit choices to the author's vocabulary but to generate a range of words that will fit the context. This develops sets of synonyms and a sense of flexibility in vocabulary choice.

Zip Cloze. One problem that readers sometime encounter when using context is a total loss of the sense of the selection at some place in the passage. Where more sophisticated readers might push on and attempt to recapture the meaning, less flexible readers often become frustrated and give up. The "zip" procedure (so named by a second-grade class with an innate sense of onomatopoeia) supplies constant feedback to such readers to "keep them going" in the context.

The story to be used can be an ordinary book, big book, or wall chart, but the most effective format involves putting the story or passage on an overhead transparency. Masking tape is used to block out the words that have been chosen for deletion. The children first skim for gist, then supply the masked words one at a time. As each possibility is predicted and discussed, the tape is pulled (or "zipped") so that the readers receive immediate feedback from the text, as well as being given more of the context from which to make further predictions. The zip procedure can be used in individual books by rubberbanding a sheet protector over the page and using a marking pen to blank out words. Children enjoy preparing zip selections for other students and can work on individual goals to increase their own awareness of certain word classes (tape over the nouns) or sentence elements (tape over the words or phrases that describe something).

Maze Cloze. For students who need more support or practice in distinguishing between related words, the maze cloze procedure can be used. Rather than deleting words from a passage, students are provided with several choices at each contextual point. First exercises of this type should provide clear, unambiguous choices, as in this example:

                                         house.

The boy on the hill lived in a yellow   cat.   The house

                                       umbrella.

                  very.

had seven stars.

           rooms.

Synonym Cloze. Synonym cloze passages support students in using context by providing students with a support system. As in a regular cloze passage, words are deleted, but further cues are provided by placing a synonym or synonym phrase under the space. Here is an example:

> The boy petted his [puppy]   before going [outside]
>   little dog   outdoors.

The access to additional cues in this type of exercise is especially useful for students who need to broaden their vocabularies by building stores of synonyms.

Putting It All Together

In this chapter, we have attempted to describe instructional strategies for at least four different goals of vocabulary instruction: to build word awareness; to develop a broad general vocabulary; to develop strategies for learning and retaining specific content vocabulary; and to develop independent word-learning strategies. We have also dealt briefly with issues of differentiation for students whose first language is not English. These instructional strategies primarily model and provide guided practice. The challenge for the teacher is to find meaningful independent practice and appropriate evaluation for students. Practice modes need to be carefully chosen to match the goal of instruction. For building word awareness, student participation and the building of personal word dictionaries may be suitable bases for evaluation. For building general vocabularies, students' writing and ability to deal with more complex material can provide insight into growth. For content learning, content-sensitive measures (e.g., writing and speaking about topics using new words, labeling figures, and drawing diagrams) can measure vocabulary learning relevant to a domain. For independent word learning, measures of student strategies and vocabulary problem solving may be appropriate. For all word learning, measures of words in use can provide the best assessment tools.

CHAPTER 8

Strategies for Engaging
in Research

Our understanding of the term "reading" keeps expanding. For many of us who love to read fiction and want children to love stories, the increasing attention to reading for the purpose of conducting research may at first not seem particularly exciting or inviting. Yet this use of reading is certainly important, and children need to become confident in conducting research through their use of reading. We as teachers will communicate our own attitudes pretty quickly to our students, so it will help if we develop a real interest and a positive stance ourselves.

Remember, research can be fun. It is particularly enjoyable when we are researching topics of high interest to us. Many of us engage in research as we plan for vacations and trips. In Chapter 5, one of us (Donna Ogle—the "I" there and here) shared some of the reading done in preparation for a trip to Russia. In fact, I was engaging in research. I just didn't need to carry my efforts to the final phase of writing a report or giving an oral presentation to others. My audience was myself, yet I was researching. Think, too, of the students we have introduced in this book. Recall Maria's expanding interest in butterflies that started with her watching a television documentary (see Chapter 2). If we can think of the excitement that comes to children who know how to use multiple texts to answer questions and then report their learning to others, our role as teachers can take on both further importance and an additional sense of purpose. There are many kinds of research we engage in; what we want to do is to have children begin experiencing purposeful and engaging research early, and to teach them the skills necessary for them to be successful and thoughtful researchers. Our purpose in this chapter is to provide guidance in how to do this (see the graphic organizer in Figure 8.1).

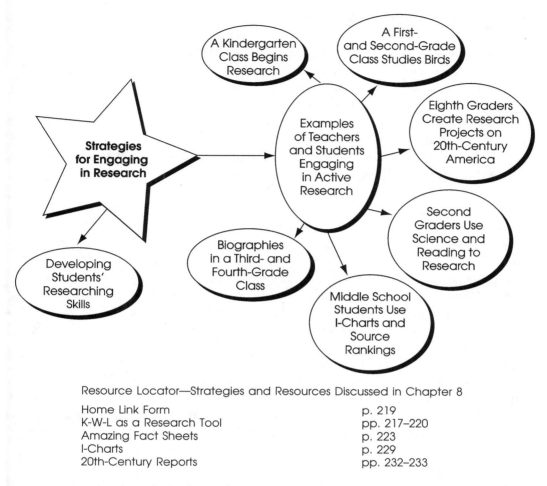

Resource Locator—Strategies and Resources Discussed in Chapter 8

Home Link Form	p. 219
K-W-L as a Research Tool	pp. 217–220
Amazing Fact Sheets	p. 223
I-Charts	p. 229
20th-Century Reports	pp. 232–233

FIGURE 8.1. Graphic organizer for Chapter 8.

Recent attention to content and learning standards has highlighted the importance of the ability to engage in research. This ability is now included as part of what is expected of students. The foci vary from state to state and district to district, but a common thread certainly runs through many of the standards. These statements of what students should know and be able to do provide guidance for all classroom teachers and show the evolving sophistication of research. Figure 1.3 in Chapter 1, which presents the Illinois state goal and standards pertaining to research skills, provides a particularly clear and detailed example of what students at all levels are currently expected to be able to accomplish in this area.

How can the common thread in the state and district standards for research skills be summarized? We feel that students need to learn how to do the following:

- Formulate good questions (identify key terms to access the topic).
- Identify possible resources and check their authenticity.
- Use text aids to access information (glossary, table of contents, index).
- Locate specific information and make notes.
- Combine information from multiple sources.
- Organize and synthesize information meaningfully.
- Evaluate sources and specific content.
- Use technological resources.
- Create presentations or reports, using graphic and technological tools.
- Monitor oneself throughout the process.

Let us discuss each of these skills in turn. To conduct research from written texts, it is first essential that students possess the ability to formulate good questions on topics that interest them. Then they need to collect resource materials that are most likely to provide the information they seek. A critical sense is needed, so that the authority of the sources can be checked; there are often disagreements among "authorities," and ways to verify authenticity and currency are needed. From there, young researchers need to be able to locate specific information in texts. They certainly don't want to read completely through long documents; rather, they need to know how to quickly locate the section that is pertinent to their own inquiry. Therefore, the ability to use a book's table of contents and index, as well as the various graphic and boxed pieces of information, is important. It is also essential for students to use information from more than one source to collect the data needed; this implies skill both in taking or making notes and in synthesizing information. Using multiple sources also requires the ability to critically evaluate what constitutes accurate and timely information. Often children find different information as they seek answers to questions, and they need to develop criteria for evaluating which sources are most believable. Given the "unedited" nature of information on the Internet, checking for accuracy of source information has become even more essential than it was 10 years ago, when published materials constituted most of what students used in conducting their own research.

Research generally also includes the ability to prepare reports from the information search efforts. The question of what kinds of data reporting students should be asked to do needs to be considered. Traditionally, we were satisfied if students could use correct paragraphs and maintain coherence in writing reports. Now we are often asking that students also use different forms of graphic representations in their reporting—tables, graphs, charts, pictures, and other visual organizers. Students also need to use the resources available on their computers to create finished looking reports and may need to also create power point presentations.

As we developed our standards in Illinois (see Figure 1.3), our team felt that we would do students a disservice in preparing them for their futures if they did not learn to use a variety of media, including computer graphics, in preparing reports. Therefore, despite some concerns about the availability of technology in all schools (and the state's concern for its own responsibility in making such resources available), it was decided that this skill was so important that it would be included in the state standards. Considering the kinds of research and reporting students should be able to do, we considered another question, too: How many and what combinations of types of sources should be included?

Children need to learn to use the Internet to find information; they also need to learn to use other technological tools, such as CD-ROMs and audio and video recordings. We also know that primary research (either interviewing people or doing experiments) needs to be combined with other reading-based research as children collect the kinds of information that make for good research. In establishing the goals we want our students to meet and the kinds of research products we want to have them create, making expectations clear from the start is important. Then it is possible to outline the skills and abilities children need in order to achieve the expected standards, and teachers can provide the supportive instruction needed so students can meet them.

It is also important to think carefully about what is specific to reading for research; how does reading to conduct research differ from other forms of reading? Can we develop these skills as we work with other reading activities? To extend our thinking, some examples of what elementary teachers are doing now in classrooms around the United States are presented in the next section. Keep asking these questions: "What should I expect of my students? What do they need to know to be successful readers? What standards and expectations does my community and state hold?"

We also need to involve our students in thinking about the ways they can engage in research activities. One third-grade student who was interviewed recently about how he completed his piece of research reported, "Well, you first have to decide on your questions. Then you need to know how to look for the information you need in books—you use the index and other help in the books." If third-grade students can be this confident and knowledgeable about their own research skills, intermediate-grade teachers can extend them quite easily. Providing such children with engaging projects and units of study seems a must. What has already been gained in the primary years should not be lost subsequently.

Examples of Teachers and Students Engaging in Active Research

A Kindergarten Class Begins Research

As Debbie, an outstanding kindergarten teacher, puts it, "The first task of the teacher is to build a sense of community and a sense of respect for the children. Then you can do almost anything." And she does. She wants her students to be active, confident learners. One of her basic goals is to nurture and help them answer the enormous numbers of questions they have as they first come to school. Rather than see those questions stifled with a "too-full" curriculum, Debbie helps her children use their questions and curiosity as the foundation for the evolving curriculum. Because most of the children don't know how to read well, she enlists older students (often third graders become mentors to the kindergartners); she involves the school librarian; and she invites parents to work with their own children at home and to come to the classroom and assist in the classroom day.

Debbie has established themes for each month—one related to literature and another to content learning. Each month she introduces an activity that parents engage in with their children at home, and then the children bring the results back to school. In September the class gets acquainted as they focus on favorite books. Debbie sends parents her first "home link" form, in which they are instructed to discuss favorite books with their children. When a parent and child have selected a child's favorite book, the child draws a picture illustrating why he or she likes that book, and the parent writes that name and author on the home link form. When the children bring the forms back to school, each child has an opportunity to "read" this information to the class. Children learn that they are important, that what they contribute is valued, and that they can help create "written pieces" to share with others in the class.

In November, the activity turns to a study of Native Americans. Debbie plans for the class to study many aspects of Native American life and contributions. As they begin the unit, Debbie and her students use the K-W-L framework (see Chapter 5) and brainstorm what they know about Native Americans. Debbie makes a list of all this information as the students share their ideas. This large list is part of the classroom environment for the month. Next, and as a part of the process of discussing what they know, the children begin to frame questions about what they don't know. Soon they have generated a substantial list of questions. Then each child chooses one question he or she wants to do research on with a parent. That question is printed on the home link form for this unit (see Figure 8.2), and in a few days each child has brought back the form with his or her question "researched." These forms are then shared and become a major part of the learning experience on this topic.

Debbie has developed this process over a few years. She says that at first, the parents did all the work for the children. Then she learned to write explicit directions to the parents so they would engage with their children in finding information about their topic (see the directions in Figure 8.2). When she made the directions very explicit, parents learned to involve their children collaboratively in learning. For example, as a result of the class discussion and their subsequent listing of questions, one child selected the question he most wanted to learn about: What weapons did Native Americans use? With a parent's assistance, the child ex-

Home Link Form for November

The kindergarten students have been studying Native Americans. As part of our study, the children have completed the first two steps of our Native American K-W-L:

K—what we know, W—what we want to know, L—what we learned.

First, we listed all the facts we *know* about Native Americans.

Second, we listed all of the things that we *want* to know about Native Americans.

Now, we plan to complete our K-W-L. Your child has chosen one question to research.

Please follow the directions below and complete the assignment with your child.

Directions for K-W-L	Research Question:
1. Discuss the question together.	
2. Discuss with your child ways in which you could complete your research.	**I Learned That:**
3. Research *together*.	
4. Once you locate the information, discuss your answer *together*.	
5. Have your child retell the answer in his or her own words.	
6. Have your child write his or her response, if your child can write, or you may print his or her response.	
7. Have your child illustrate his or her answer.	
8. Return the completed K-W-L to school on Monday, November ____ Thank you.	Researchers: Child: _____ Parent: _____

FIGURE 8.2. The home link form used for the kindergartners' unit on Native Americans in November. Used by permission of Debra Gurvitz.

amined books from the school library. They looked at the pictures of Native Americans long ago and discussed what they had used as weapons. The parent helped the child use the words "hatchet," "bow," and "arrow." After looking at three books and finding some specific help in the text and pictures of each one, the parent and child completed their reporting. The child drew pictures of three weapons, and the parent wrote sentences to go with the drawings. When this was brought back to the class, the child was able to tell what he had learned and to make a real contribution to the class knowledge. The home link forms were displayed on the bulletin board, so the children began to understand that their research and what they learned could be recorded and preserved for others to look at and "read."

Throughout the year, the monthly content themes provide opportunities for children to engage actively in research. Each content theme begins with the K-W-L process and usually culminates in some project or book composed of contributions from all members of the class.

A First- and Second-Grade Class Researches Birds

Caitlin is another teacher who has taught us much about what primary-school children are actually capable of learning. She has a unit organization for science and social studies, and is committed to a constructivist approach to learning through an integration of reading and writing with content. She knows that her children are curious about the world around them and will do much on their own if she establishes an open-ended environment for their learning.

When her class began a study of birds early in the spring, Caitlin filled her room with books for the children's reading and review. Some books were too difficult for the first graders actually to read but had great pictures and captioned information. Some were fiction, some were poetry, and others were good informational texts for young children. Caitlin, like Debbie, used the K-W-L framework for her unit. She divided her large back bulletin board into three sections. The first was labeled "What We Know about Birds," the second was labeled "What We Want to Know about Birds," and the third was labeled "What We Learn." As they began the unit, the children volunteered lots of facts they knew about birds. Caitlin recorded these on strips of paper and wrote each child's name beneath his or her contribution. Later she pinned these statements to the board. During the discussion of what they knew about birds, the children began to ask questions. Caitlin also wrote these on strips of paper and added them to the bulletin board, this time in the center column. As the children continued to learn about birds, she added new questions that arose in their study to this board.

The children had "center times" during the day when they could work on their research about birds. They knew that if they found something in a book that was difficult but that helped them answer their questions, the teacher would photocopy a section for them. These photocopied pieces often became part of their research information pinned to the third section of their bulletin board, "What We Learn." With guidance children also used Internet resources to find good illustrations and basic information. Some of these were printed with the citation noted and also added to the board. Other questions that were answered were written on $5'' \times 8''$ index cards or sheets of paper and pinned up for all to see. The bulletin board made the whole learning process visible to the class, and the students could see how research is an ongoing process of learning. When they learned that some of the "facts" they had posted on the first section of the board as "known" were not accurate or only partially so, they either crossed out those statements or modified them with carets and added information. In this way, the children also learned the process of editing and modifying knowledge. It is so much easier at this level, when children are all learning together, to keep an openness about their own ideas and to modify them without any negativity associated with the process. Sometimes the second graders could help the younger first graders with their reading and writing. In this way, all shared at the level they were capable of, and students helped each other.

Caitlin also wanted to help the children begin to think of categories of information. She periodically asked them to find groups of facts that fit together from the large board sections. One of the first groupings the children noticed was "Kinds of Birds." Once they had identified four statements that all dealt with different kinds of birds, she helped the children take these cards and regroup them together on the board. At the end of the unit, Caitlin and her students put all their process together in a big book with three sections. When it was time to construct the book, each category had a page with a title, so the children could make much more sense of all the individual pieces of information they had gathered.

Caitlin used the whole group as a unit in creating a research project. Each child had a part to play throughout the time the class was working on birds, and each could contribute in his or her own way. Some children were good at drawing and would create illustrations of the different birds—their body parts, the kinds of nests they made, and where they lived. Others were better at doing the research by reading in the books. They would find interesting ideas and read these orally when there was class "sharing time." Some children became good bird watchers and would bring in reports of birds they had seen in the schoolyard or at home. All children read, wrote, and drew, but some concentrated more of their energies on particular parts of the project. Because there were small pieces of paper on which children could write "research notes," they were not intimidated by the process. And because the content was always before them on the bulletin board, children could browse the material and build confidence in what they knew and could also read independently. Caitlin did not tax any of the children by insisting on individual projects but created an environment in which learners at all levels could flour-ish.

Second Graders Use Science and Reading in Research

Judy, a second-grade teacher who loves science, often uses scientific topics as a centering for her learning activities (McKee & Ogle, 2005). She likes to begin with actual hands-on activities to stimulate students' curiosity about the topic, and then to extend the learning through the use of books, magazines, and visual materials. One unit on the rain forest begins with the children's visiting the zoo and experi-encing the animals of the rain forest. Judy has told the children she wants them to look carefully at what they see and remember as much as they can, so they can make their own journal entries. When they return from the outing, the children take out their journals and write about what they saw and experienced. Many in-clude quite detailed drawings. Then as they talk about their experience, using their journals as reference points, the students deepen their thinking as they listen to each other. From this discussion, questions come naturally. Judy explains that each child is to keep his or her own science journal throughout the unit, and that the children can draw pictures and label them as part of their exploration of the topic. Judy often models creating good journal entries for the students and uses their own drawings or some found in the extensive classroom book collection she pro-vides for each unit to create visual enhancements. In science, diagrams are an im-portant part of most topics so Judy encourages sketching and drawing.

As students get involved in the science topics their questions become much deeper. One interesting tool Judy has developed to help her students deal with the enormous amount of interesting information they encounter as they read independ-ently is the "amazing fact sheet" (see Figure 8.3). She keeps a box of these lined sheets on the top of a bookcase, so children can take one any time they find a fact they want to record and later share. The child simply writes down the fact, his or her own name, and the title and author of the book in which the fact was found. When "sharing time" comes, Judy will take the box and give children time to read their special facts. When they share what they have written, they also tell the source from which it came. Thus, early in second grade these children are already making research "note cards"—something usually reserved for sixth to eighth graders. They are also learning to cite references and to share the excitement of knowledge with each other.

At an appropriate time in the unit, Judy asks the students to take several of the amazing fact sheets and group them into categories that make sense. From these groupings, the students can then each write a summary paragraph of the facts they have learned. Judy guides them into constructing a sentence stating the main idea; then the specific pieces of information can provide elaboration on the

An amazing fact about _____

is _____

_____

found by _____

in the book _____ by _____

An intriguing fact about _____

is _____

_____

found by _____

in the book _____ by _____

A fascinating fact about _____

is _____

_____

found by _____

in the book _____ by _____

FIGURE 8.3. The "amazing fact sheet" developed for use in a second-grade classroom. Used by permission of Judy McKee.

theme. This helps students think of how to collect similar information, and it makes the writing of summaries much easier than would otherwise be the case.

Biographies in a Third- and Fourth-Grade Class

The middle of the school year—during February and March, when we celebrate Presidents' Day, Martin Luther King Day, Black History Month, and Women's History Month—seems to be the time when many teachers ask students to write reports on famous Americans. What teachers do to introduce this assigned research makes a tremendous difference in the quality of the produces that will be created. Simply assigning the task is not enough!

Peter, a teacher with a combined class of third and fourth graders, loves history and has taken on the use of biography as a special focus in his instruction. He wants his students to understand that there are some basic components in a biography of a famous person, and he wants his students to use these in seeking information and later in writing their reports. He also wants his students to be able to compare different people in terms of their contributions and the kinds of obstacles they had to overcome. So he uses each student's individual research as a part of a class "matrix," which fills a whole wall and permits anyone entering the classroom to gain a clear idea of who the people are and what has been learned. This visual matrix helps students organize ideas and information, and is the first step in helping them synthesize the pieces of their research. Reading across the matrix permits comparisons of these great Americans from different periods of time; this is a real form of critical thinking.

The unit begins as Peter puts the name of a famous American familiar to his children on the blackboard. One year he used Michael Jordan and another year Abraham Lincoln. He began by asking his students to tell what they knew about Jordan and to give reasons for his fame. As the children made contributions, he clustered their remarks. Comments about Jordan's achievements in basketball, he grouped together in one area; comments about Jordan's family of origin, his childhood, and his difficulty making the high school basketball team, he clustered in another part of the board; and comments about Jordan's current life and contributions, he put in a third area. After Peter felt the discussion had generated enough information, he asked the students to look at what he had written on the board and see whether they could tell why he placed the information in the groups that he did. The students could see quite easily that he had put similar comments together. Some dealt with Jordan's youth, some with his adult personal life, and some with his accomplishments. This discussion provided a good entry into the idea he wanted the students to think about: They needed to approach thinking about famous people by considering certain aspects of their lives. Because Jordan had not suffered as many difficulties as some "heroes," this category did not emerge as dominant in the initial brainstorming. Peter noted that he would need to try one other person, to be sure his students also thought about "obstacles" as a major category in many biographies.

The next day, he put the name of Martin Luther King, Jr., on the board. As students volunteered what they knew (which was very little), he asked them whether they recalled the three categories of information they had known about Jordan. When "accomplishments," "early life," and "adult life" were recalled, he listed them on the board and then gave the students copies of a short encyclopedia article on King. He asked the students to identify the major topics about King. As the students read the article, several seemed puzzled. What would they do? This biography was different from the one they had read just the day before. It talked about how hard it was for King and other black Americans to live freely. Churches, schools, and even travel in trains and buses were segregated. King fought to get equal rights for all blacks. After the students read the article, Peter asked them to work in pairs and use a spider map to record specific key pieces of information they had learned about King. They should group the information into categories, and then they should give a label to each category. (Figure 8.4 shows a map with all the categories that the class eventually developed.) In the discussion of King that followed, Peter helped the students see that "problems," "obstacles," or "hardships" could all be used to describe one component of his biography. At the end of the lesson, he put the basic categories together on the board and asked the students to write them in their notebooks also. The next day, each would read a short biography and see whether these same categories would be useful in making notes about the famous person. (Peter knew that still another category, "interesting or unusual attributes," would soon be added to their maps. He also knew he would use a website for biography to extend students' understanding of these components and to help them research and write their own reports.)

By the time each student had selected a person to research for his or her biography, the students had a good sense of some basic categories to use for framing questions and for organizing their information as they gathered it. They all decided to include information about early life, adult life, and the accomplishments of their person. For extra credit, they suggested a new category of "the times" or context in which the person lived. A few wanted to be sure that any obstacles the person had to overcome were included. This created a heated discussion, as some students thought their famous person might not have had to overcome real obstacles. Finally the class decided that this, too, would be an optional category; however, it would not count as extra credit but would be a central part of the project. If there were obstacles, they must be described.

Peter, as teacher, set the requirement that students read from at least three sources—one an online encyclopedia, one a biography, and one from some other source (a magazine article, a video, a TV program, etc.). These would be brought to class and shared as part of the report, which would be both written and orally presented. He encouraged the students to dress in a way that would reflect their famous persons, and even to use some musical background that would be appropriate for each person and time frame. Adding such concrete touches has worked for him over the years in helping the children make the project personal and engaging.

Middle School Students Use I-Charts and Source Ranking

One of the most frequent complaints about students' research efforts is that they often seem to become good copying activities, with little individual synthesis of content. Many (1996) reported on her observations of seventh-grade Scottish children during a research project in which each chose some aspect of World War II. Their lack of skill in knowing how to go about research proved to be a dramatic impediment to their learning and critical thinking. This same lack of strategy characterizes many American students, too, unless they receive good support and instruction on how to engage in researching topics.

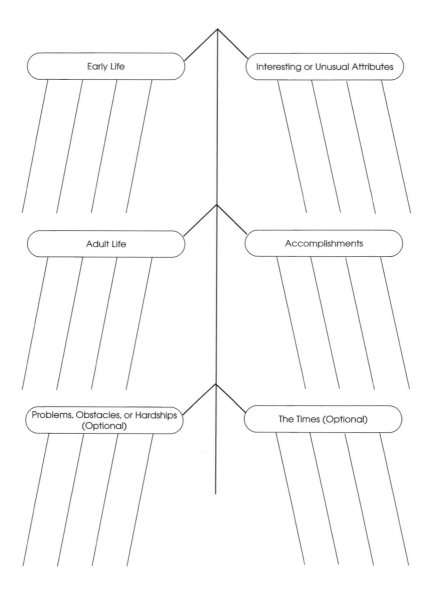

FIGURE 8.4. The graphic organizer/spider map that was developed over time in one third- and fourth-grade classroom for recording biographical facts in various categories.

Sandra, a middle school language arts teacher, wanted to develop better research skills in her students, so she began the fall with a unit on conducting research and had the whole class work on the same topic, the flier or aviatrix, Amelia Earhart. The students first talked about what kinds of questions should be addressed in learning about a famous person. Sandra found out that the class had little awareness of Amelia Earhart after she had the class do a K-W-L. Her next step was to go to the media center where she got a videotape on Earhart and showed it to the class. She also showed the class the Internet site, The Earhart Project, which made the search for Earhart real, because there is a whole organization devoted to the mystery of her disappearance. This also hooked some of the students as there are still unanswered questions about what had happened. From that extensive introduction the students were able to generate some of the basic framework they needed from which to explore Earhart's life more fully.

Because Sandra wanted to focus on the importance of multiple sources of information she next had the students read two short biographical sketches of Earhart from older encyclopedias (see Figure 8.5). As the students worked with partners they created venn diagrams showing what information was the same and what was discrete in each piece. When they had shared their diagrams the teacher then led them in a discussion of why there were such differences. She posed the questions, "Who do you think the author of this piece was?" and "Why do you think the author started the piece in this particular way?" Comparing these simple pieces of text helped the students understand the importance of the author in what gets included in informational text.

By the time the students had discussed these texts they had many questions. Sandra then introduced the I-chart and led the class in selecting three key questions they wanted to pursue further. With these questions in mind she determined resources to make available. She and the librarian collected some print books and magazine articles and then Sandra searched the World Wide Web for some other appropriate sources which she then printed. With these resources Sandra then determined which would be most accessible in terms of difficulty and which addressed the specific interests different groups of students had and distributed them to the small working groups. The students then used the materials to determine how each author answered their questions. Each small group of students had an I-chart on which they summarized the different authors' perspectives. They then used those perspectives to assess how they wanted to answer the questions in the summary column. One group's work is shown in Figure 8.6.

With this activity Sandra was able to help students realize both the importance of reading multiple sources of information to find answers to research questions and a systematic way they could make use of various texts in researching. The students had great fun arguing with each other and with the texts; in fact, throughout the year students continued to bring in articles and information about Earhart.

EARHART, Amelia (1897–1937). One of the most intriguing mysteries of the 20th century is: What happened to Amelia Earhart? In June 1937 she and her copilot, Lieutenant Commander Fred J. Noonan, left Miami, Fla., on an around-the-world flight attempt in a twin-engine Lockheed aircraft. On July 2 the plane vanished near Howland Island in the South Pacific. The world waited with fascination as search teams from the United States Army and Navy, along with the Japanese Navy, converged on the scene. But not she, Noonan, or the plane was ever found. As time went on, questions were raised about the flight. Was it simply an around-the-world adventure, or was she perhaps sent to spy on Japanese war preparations for the United States government? Historians have claimed that she was almost certainly forced down and killed by the Japanese.

Amelia Earhart was born on July 24, 1897, in Atchison, Kan. During World War I she worked as a military nurse in Canada, and for several years she was a social worker in Boston. She first gained fame in 1928 when she was the first woman to fly across the Atlantic Ocean—even though only as a passenger. Four years later, in May 1932, she made a solo flight across the Atlantic, followed by several solo long-distance flights in the United States. She was greatly interested in the development of commercial aviation and took an active role in opening the field to women. For a time Earhart served as an officer of the Luddington line, which operated one of the first regular passenger services between New York City and Washington, D.C. In January 1935 she made a solo flight from Hawaii to California.

In 1931 Earhart had married publisher George P. Putnam. After her disappearance he wrote her biography, "Soaring Wings," which was published in 1939.

—Compton's Encyclopedia and Fact Index (1988).
Chicago: Encyclopedia Brittanica.—

EARHART, Amelia (1897-c. 1937) Many women took part in the history of aviation (see AVIATION, HISTORY OF). One of these was the United States pilot Amelia Earhart, the first woman to fly alone across the Atlantic.

Amelia Earhart was born in Atchison, Kansas. During World War I she worked as an army nurse in Canada and was afterwards employed as a social worker in Boston, Massachusetts. She became very interested in the rapid developments in aircraft travel that took place during the 1920s. In 1928 she made history by becoming the first woman to fly across the Atlantic as a passenger. She was keen to continue her aviation activities even after her marriage in 1931 to a publisher, George P. Putnam. On 20-21 May 1932, she flew the Atlantic alone from Newfoundland to Ireland. She made many flights within the United States and in January 1935 she became the first person to fly solo from Hawaii to California, a distance much longer than that from Newfoundland to Ireland. In 1937 she began a round-the-world flight, piloting a twin-engine Lockheed Electra, with an American colleague, Fred Noonan, as her navigator. After completing two-thirds of this flight, her aircraft disappeared in the central Pacific, shortly after taking off from New Guinea. Amelia Earhart was never seen again, and the circumstances of her disappearance remain unknown.

—Children's Brittanica (1981).
Chicago: Encyclopedia Brittanica.—

FIGURE 8.5. Comparing nonfiction sources.

| Topic
Amelia Earhart | What We Know | Source 1
The Earhart Project (www.tighar.org/ Projects/Earhart/ AEdeser.html) | Source 2
"5,000 Meters Deep" by Stephen Manning (2004) (www.cdnn.info/ industry) | Source 3
Amelia Earhart by Elgen M. Long (2000); Finding Amelia by Ric Gillespie (2006) | Summary |
|---|---|---|---|---|---|
| What happened to her? | She disappeared in 1937. | She and Fred Noonan vanished near Howland Island (South Pacific). | Landed on Nikumaroro. Died from lack of water. | No one is sure, but three theories: the Japanese got her, her plane crashed in the water, or she died on the island. | No one is sure about what happened to her yet. |
| What evidence have they found? | Nothing was found. | She may have been spying on Japanese. Japanese may have killed her. | Richard Gillespie found a plane fragment, shoe sole, and medicine bottle cap. | Gillespie and Long have both searched but can't find the plane. | No evidence can prove anything yet. |
| What kind of airplanes did she fly? | Old-fashioned airplanes. | Twin-engine Lockheed aircraft. | Lockheed 10-E Electra. | Biplane: Kinner Canary; Fokker trimotor: "The Friendship"; auto-giro, Lockheed Vega. | Biplanes, Lockheeds, WWI-style. |
| Interesting Facts | First famous woman pilot. Flew solo across the Atlantic in 1932. | She was interested in commercial aviation. Married George Putnam. | The U.S. Navy didn't see her. Many don't believe this theory. | She was an adventurer's child. Her father was an alcoholic. She wore pants. | She opened the way for other women pioneers. |
| New Questions | Did she have a family? Who searched for her? | Are they still trying to find clues? | Will they find any bones? | What happened to her husband? | What was her relationship with Noonan? |

Guiding Questions

FIGURE 8.6. The I-chart completed by one middle school class studying Amelia Earhart. The I-chart form is adapted from Hoffman (1992). Copyright 1992 by National Council of Teachers of English. Used by permission of the author.

229

Teachers who use the I-chart frequently find it very useful. It provides a graphic tool for students to help move them from dependence on one source of information to a more confident approach to forming conclusions based on a variety of perspectives. It is most useful where there are issues on which all sources do not agree, such as the fate of Amelia Earhart (see the filled-in I-chart in Figure 8.6, which was created by one of our classes). The I-chart combines both the need to reduce dependence on the writing in Internet and published texts and the recognition that sources often provide different information that the student must reconcile for themselves.

A friend of ours, Roger Passman, has extended this strategy by adding a tool to evaluate sources. Together, he and his sixth and seventh graders considered what criteria should be used in evaluating conflicting information. They came to a decision on two criteria. Roger put these in a chart (see Figure 8.7), and his students used the chart to evaluate materials they were consulting for their Chicago Metro History Fair projects. This process of reflection is worth doing with any group of students about to engage in research.

Eighth Graders Create Research Projects on 20th-Century America

Kathleen (mentioned in Chapter 3) wants her eighth graders to have the opportunity to engage in an in-depth individual research project. Students entering her

Rank as a place to begin	Available source	Rank as to overall value
4	Encyclopedia	3
4	Class textbook	2
2	Historian	4
1	Relative of the famous person being studied	1
5	Library	4
4	Computer data base	4
2	Internet site	2

FIGURE 8.7. A chart ranking information sources for their value on two criteria. Used by permission of Roger Passman.

class know that this is one of the highlights of the year, and one of the most important pieces of work they will do as eighth graders. The basic goal is that each student select his or her own topic of interest—something that will help the class understand 20th-century America. (Students interested in music and the arts, for example, have chosen to research such topics as dance in the 20th century, the development of the electric guitar, and rock-and-roll music.) Kathleen knows that as the students select their own topics, they will be exploring the broader context of America and American experiences. As they listen to and learn with each other during the process and then share their final research projects, the students develop a depth of understanding of the culture that is not possible from textbook reading alone.

Steps in the research process are carefully outlined for the students and are also taught. Kathleen knows that many students don't know how to make good research note cards. Therefore, she provides a minilesson on how to synthesize information on cards and how to label the cards for future sorting into categories.

The project involves much independent work for students, and Kathleen tries to help them learn to pace their research and writing activities so they will be able to produce a finished product they will be proud to share. (See Figure 8.8a for the specification sheet she provides to guide their work, and Figure 8.8b for her outline of the process for creating reports.) The students must use a minimum of five sources, one of which must be electronic. They must show their note cards and their outline of the research project, and they must include illustrations in their final product. The list of points for each aspect of the project is clear (see Figure 8.8a) and students know what is expected. During the weeks they are working on the project, Kathleen confers with each student individually, makes notes on their progress, and provides more structure and support as necessary.

The final projects are individually presented in bound notebooks, many beautifully illustrated. The students also give oral reports of what they have learned, so that all students gain from the process. A special touch is that a large hall bulletin board of the 20th century has been created by several years of students. Each new class adds a picture or illustration of each of the topics they have researched in the appropriate decades. The board has thus become a running visual record of what interests the students and what they consider important about modern America.

Developing Students' Researching Skills

The examples of teachers and students engaging in research efforts that we have just presented illustrate (we hope) ways teachers can naturally capitalize on chil-

Rubrics for 20th-Century Report

1. Notes: Classified according to questions? Bibliographical symbol? Thorough? Orderly enough to use for outline? Legible to you? Include quotes? Apparent use of all five resources?   20 pts.

2. Questions: Thorough? Probing? Helpful to direct research? Accurately but concisely written?   10 pts.

3. Interview: Pertinence to topic? Prepared beforehand? Written out on paper or on note cards? Usable quote? Helpful to answer one or all questions?   10 pts.

4. Media piece: Pertinence to topic? Well thought out? Thoroughly prepared? Presented to class in complete manner?   10 pts.

5. Outline: Created from notes? Thorough? Appropriately speaks to and answers three questions?   10 pts.

6. Report: Introduction   5
             Three questions answered   5
             Thoughtful development of ideas   5
             Use of quotes   5
             Use of interview material   5
             Apparent use of all resources   5
             Appropriate graphics   5
             Conclusion   5
             Bibliography   5
             Style   5
             Editing   5
             Overall presentation   5
             Clear connection to 20th-century   25   85 pts.
                 American history

7. Class presentation: 5-minute concise overview/summary of topic, including its connection to 20th-century American history. (This will be graded by peers.)   20 pts.

8. Process journal: Twice-weekly synopsis of what and how student is learning about her- or himself as a researcher.   10 pts.

   Total possible points   155

FIGURE 8.8a. (a) Specification sheet for eighth graders' 20th-century reports, including number of points that can be earned for each part of the project. (b) Outline of the process for creating these reports. Both used by permission of Kathleen McKenna.

Process for Creating 20th-Century Reports

1. Choose topic; narrow it.

2. Begin keeping process journal.

3. Write three research questions; refine, redefine, and narrow them down.

4. Teacher or librarian gives research lessons.

5. Set up organizational system.

6. Weeks of note taking and additional research.

7. Find someone to interview; write request letter; prepare questions that will "fill in" research; do interview; write thank-you note; write up interview ASAP.

8. Find or create a media piece; present it to class; put it on hallway time line if appropriate.

9. Create outline or web.

10. Write first draft; have peer edit; self-edit; have teacher edit.

11. Write number of drafts necessary before final submission.

12. Complete and turn in process journal.

13. Plan for school presentations.

14. Create classroom time line every 2 weeks throughout the process.

Minilessons on each phase (e.g., letter writing, bibliographical and other writing formats, outline, peer editing, etc.) are given or reinforced throughout process. Learning centers are around the room to support each step without immediate teacher feedback or explanation.

FIGURE 8.8b.

dren's curiosity and interest in the world around them, and at the same time can build a good foundation for the kinds of skills students can use throughout their lifetimes for all sorts of research.

Most basic is the need for curiosity so that good questions can be formulated. Teachers can help students explore topics in many ways—through firsthand experiences; by reading interesting, well-illustrated books aloud to children; by engaging in discussion; and in many other ways. Students develop questions from these initial activities, and they shape these questions until they select some key ones for further inquiry. At the middle school level, one township's school system provides a guide to research for all students. After explaining what a research paper is and giving steps for writing a paper, the guide moves to a section on "Narrowing a Topic." It states it well:

The topic for a research paper should be a narrow one. To limit your topic, consider how much information is available and how long the paper will be. For example, "The Viet Nam War" would be too broad, whereas "The Effects of Agent Orange on US Vietnam Veterans and Their Families" would be a suitable topic for research. "The Chicago Fire" would be too broad, but "Causes of the Chicago Fire" would be acceptable. (Northfield Township Public Schools, 1999)

Another important aspect of conducting effective research is knowing how to select from among sources of information. In the earlier example of Sandra's middle school students, they developed an understanding of the importance of checking the authority and currency of sources. By reading biographies from different sources the students began to realize how different informational texts could be; they learned to look for basic categories of information that were included (e.g., early life, education, hardships, accomplishments, and family life). In comparing texts they saw that one author would focus on Amelia Earhart's early life or personal life while another focused on her accomplishments. Some stressed her role in helping women advance in aviation. When it came to the end of her life and the mystery surrounding her death the different sources provided quite different interpretations. This led the students to want to search even further for information and to be careful about the sources of their information.

Once students realize that authors vary in their interpretations and in the factual information they include students can more easily understand how important it is to check "authorship" on the Internet. It is important to help students distinguish books and magazine articles that have been through a thorough review process before being printed and sources on the Internet which go through no review. Teaching students to carefully examine Internet sites is important because it is so tempting to just go online and search by topic. We suggest that there are three basic questions students need to address:

1. Who is sponsoring this site? (For example, if it is a *.gov*, or *.edu* site it is more likely to be reputable than a *.com*, or *.org* site. What do they say their purpose is? Read the information about the site to get more information about their point of view.
2. When was the site last updated?
3. Is the information similar to what is in my textbook or informational book?

Because it is difficult sometimes to determine the accuracy of information included in some sites, teachers can create a Web-quest or enlist the help of the school media specialist or librarian to bookmark some special sites for the projects students do. Some services now also collect appropriate sites for school-age students so inappropriate sources are not accessible. Guiding students' use of the

Internet is a serious requirement of teachers now with so many students using Internet-based information.

Making notes while doing research is another essential skill that needs to be taught and practiced. If students read material they want to remember and use later, then we need to help then develop strategies to highlight key ideas and make notes for future reference. When teachers in primary grades begin having students collect information on "amazing fact sheets," the job of upper-level teachers is easier. Sometimes individual cards are valuable and help students later organize the cards in a variety of ways until the structure of a paper becomes clear. It is still very common for teachers to require eighth-grade students to write note cards as part of the research process. However, students need more than one form of note taking/note making. In the intermediate grades, students can learn to record information in learning logs or personal learning notebooks. Sometimes a notebook makes retaining the information easier than individual cards do. If students not only keep notes in their logs but also label the main topic of each set of notes, then these can be returned to later and information on common topics can be chunked together. Sometimes a graphic organizer with key topics listed on spokes of a spider map can serve as a framework for notes taken from different sources.

We also find that the use of the I-chart helps students move away even from single note cards that can be compiled to answer key research questions. The I-chart also ensures that students don't just download information and cut and paste different paragraphs into reports. Putting ideas into one's own words and then writing summaries of the key questions asked models the process of reading across sites, comparing information, and coming to one's own conclusions. However, some teachers who like students to complete note cards as they read sources have used this same technique by having students place note cards on a large matrix, as a way to ensure that they collect similar information from more than one source. This provides a check on authenticity and guides students to look for discrepancies that might prove important.

Organizing and synthesizing material are not easy for children. Many of the strategies we have described earlier in this chapter help children develop these skills. From kindergarten on, children can learn to group items they brainstorm on their K-W-L charts and to anticipate how authors can organize information. Categorizing "amazing facts" helps students do the same kind of category formation. Writing paragraphs for each set of facts begins a real "reporting" process. The I-chart itself is a form of organization and includes a column for summarizing answers to the questions asked. The biography units also begin by identifying a few key categories about people and providing a frame for research and writing. All of these activities help students think about organization and synthesis of information. The computer can be used in the same way if students create reports or research papers with category files.

Teaming with the School Librarian/
Media Specialist

In many schools the school library/media specialist can be an important partner in helping students learn to conduct research. Librarians use the term "informational literacy" (Bush, 2003) to describe the skills needed to engage in searching for information. The librarian may be available to help teach your students how to use the Internet and other media sources to locate important information. Before initiating a unit where students will engage in independent inquiry, contact the library/media person in your school and see if you can't collaborate on this effort. The librarian may help develop a set of Internet sites and resources for the students to use. It is helpful in planning to focus students' research around a common theme or a few areas. For example, when a fourth- and fifth-grade team we work with models the research process in the fall the students either do research on states of the United States or do mammals. While each student has a particular topic, they are all similar and teachers can guide them more easily in the research process. This focus also helps the librarian know how she can be most useful. Students learn to ask important questions, use appropriate search terms, navigate to find the areas on the sites that are useful to them, and save information they need. Having a second adult working with the students is an added benefit. As they begin research, students have many questions and need guidance.

Putting It All Together

All of the teachers we have described in this chapter have helped their students engage in the research process. We have not focused on the forms in which the students' final projects are presented, because these can vary substantially. However, it has been made clear that when students see the structure and organization that can underlie any topic, they can use those to organize their writing or presentation. It is also clear that students benefit from careful instruction in all aspects of engaging in research. Research begins when students develop interest in a topic and frame good questions to guide inquiry. Then they must have tools to locate sources, find the pertinent information in those sources, compare and contrast information, and come to some conclusions about what they think is important and true. The more they understand about the nature and structure of informational writing, the easier it is for them to create their own research reports.

As teachers, we need to begin by identifying the research skills our students already possess. The bulleted list on page 216 can be used to identify which skills our students have in their repertoires and which they need to acquire. Once we check their knowledge of each of these parts of the research process, we can then structure the more directed instructional activities the students need to be successful in each aspect of researching. Giving students a global assignment ("Do a research project") just doesn't work. There are so many specific parts of research that we need to guide students carefully, so they can take joy in their skills and find success from their efforts. Enough time to make researching successful and productive should be allocated. If these steps are made visible in the classroom so students know what to do, they also can become confident as researchers. Parents can easily help in these efforts, too, when they know what students are being guided in learning.

Teachers and elementary schools that regularly engage students in research on interesting topics will be able to take pride in what they can help children accomplish before the demands of research become more abstract in high school. Students so prepared are able to navigate secondary education and life beyond school with confidence. They will even know how to research before buying a new computer or CD player, or before selecting the school for their advanced study.

CHAPTER 9

Strategies for Performing Tasks, Studying, and Taking Tests

This is a book on reading comprehension. If you looked through older books on the same topic, you would probably not find a section on reading procedural texts to perform tasks. Many books on elementary reading don't focus on studying and test taking, either. These fairly new additions to what comprehension means have become more important for several reasons. And there is much we as teachers can do to help students function well in these types of reading situations (see the graphic organizer for this chapter in Figure 9.1). The first section of this chapter looks carefully at reading to perform tasks. The second explores in some depth the skills students need to retain what they read and to do well on examinations.

Reading to Perform Tasks

Reading to perform tasks has recently received much attention. New standardized reading tests and many state assessments now include items related to completion of specific tasks. Some of the reasons this type of reading has gained in importance are clear. First, with a focus on the uses of reading both in and out of school, the frequency of reading so that we can produce something else or perform a task is highlighted. We all often read for these kinds of purposes. In the field of adult literacy, this kind of reading has been termed "functional reading," as it has very practical uses. On-the-job skills are often based on being able to do what written instructions require, whether in a factory, a law office, or a McDonald's. In ele-

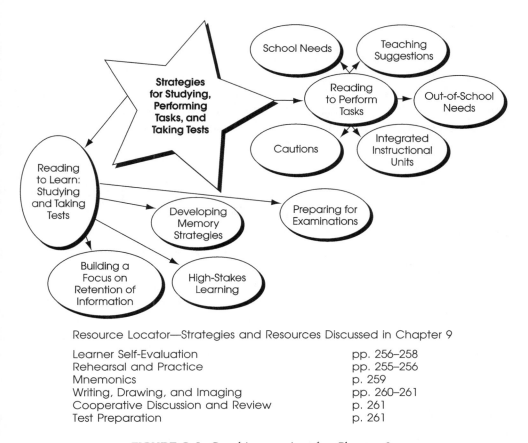

FIGURE 9.1. Graphic organizer for Chapter 9.

Resource Locator—Strategies and Resources Discussed in Chapter 9

mentary teaching, there has been an ongoing interest in students' being able to read to "follow direction" whether that be in science or math or in reading maps and charts to build understanding of larger concepts. Reading schedules to find programs on TV or bus routes is another functional task that students need to perform. These very concrete kinds of reading are part of what is meant by reading procedural texts to perform a task, the newer term being used both in the National Assessment of Educational Progress (NAEP) and in many state standards and assessment programs.

Out-of-School Needs

Think of the numbers of times each day we must all read for very practical purposes and follow directions carefully. As adults, we read in this way when we follow a recipe to cook something good; when we install a new component to a VCR or computer; and when we need to fill out our income tax forms. Many of us also read to perform a task when we want to improve our swing in golf or our serve in tennis. If we are taking medicines or are on some restricted diets, we need to read the directions closely and follow them precisely. If we have a flat tire, we need to read the manual carefully even to figure out how to remove the jack from the trunk of the car. Then we must keep reading closely to find out how to raise the car with the jack, how to remove the tire, and finally how to replace it. There are so many areas in which this kind of reading is practiced daily!

Children, too, often read to perform a variety of tasks out of school. As children take part in Boy and Girl Scouts and other clubs, they regularly have to do projects, construct objects, tie knots, make menus for camping, and so forth. All of the books that lead children through the levels of these clubs require that they be able to read to perform specified tasks.

Outside school, children also often play games and must read directions carefully to play by the rules. Look at the directions on favorite game boxes if you are not familiar with how often young people (and older ones) need to follow directions carefully even when relaxing. In another area, for both relaxation and work, computer use demands that we carefully read and follow instructions in order to install programs and later to use them successfully. (If only we could find easier instructions!) Using the World Wide Web and taking advantage of electronic games require some sophisticated reading to achieve our goals.

School Needs

In school, there are many areas in which reading to perform tasks is essential. Both mathematics and science come immediately to mind. As teachers of units that link reading and science content know, much of science depends on reading to perform a task. Each experiment children are asked to do to test theories or principles requires such reading (see the examples in Figure 9.2). The same is true in mathematics; over and over again, directions are given that require some very practical applications of what is explained (see the examples in Figure 9.3). Even in social studies and language arts, there are often projects that involve students in this form of careful reading. With the increasing use of rubrics to guide students' performance it becomes important that they carefully attend to each area delineated on the matrix.

Teaching Suggestions

How do we teachers help children develop their abilities to comprehend and execute directions? There are some basic guidelines that we need to follow. First, we need to provide many opportunities for children to read such materials—and we

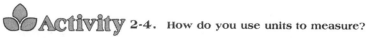

Activity 2-4. How do you use units to measure?

Materials

10 leaves
metric ruler
meter stick
balance
graduated cylinder
paper cup
water
ice cubes
Celsius thermometer
stirring rod

Procedure

1. Measure the length and width of each leaf. (Use the longest and widest parts of the leaf.)
2. Using the meter stick, measure your height.
3. Fill the paper cup half way with water. Using a balance, measure the mass of the cup of water.
4. Pour the water into a graduated cylinder. Measure the volume of the water.
5. Return the water to the cup. Using a Celsius thermometer, measure the temperature of the water.
6. Add ice cubes to the water. Stir until the temperature stops falling. Measure the new temperature.

FIGURE 2-12.

Data and Observations

1. Record the measurements of each leaf. (If the leaf is 5 and 4/10 centimeters wide, you would write 5.4 cm.)
2. Record your height in meters.
3. Record the mass of the cup of water in grams.
4. Record the volume of the water in the cup in milliliters.
5. Record the starting temperature of the water.
6. Record the temperature of the water after adding the ice.

Questions and Conclusions

1. What is the name of the unit of measurement on the metric ruler represented by the lines between the centimeter marks?
2. What are the measurements of each leaf in millimeters?
3. What is your height in centimeters?
4. What is your height in millimeters?
5. How many grams are in a kilogram?
6. What temperature change occurred after you added ice to the water? How many degrees did it change?

FIGURE 9.2. Examples of reading to perform tasks in a science textbook. From *Focus on Life Science* (p. 35) by C. H. Heimler, L. Daniel, and J. D. Lockard. Copyright 1984 by Charles E. Merrill, Inc. Used by permission of Glencoe/McGraw-Hill.

15. *Problem Solving* A 6-foot tall section of a northern red oak tree trunk has the cross section shown at the right. Find the volume of the bark. Explain how you solved the problem.

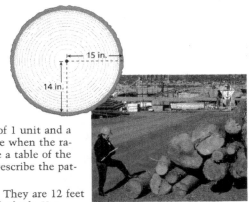

16. *Think about It* Find the dimensions of two cylinders so that one has the greater volume and the other has the greater surface area.

17. *Finding a Pattern* A cylinder has a height of 1 unit and a radius of 1 unit. What happens to its volume when the radius is doubled? Tripled? Quadrupled? Make a table of the dimensions and volumes of the cylinders. Describe the pattern of the volumes.

18. You are painting walls in an office building. They are 12 feet by 18 feet and the coat of paint is 0.001 inch thick. You have a cylindrical container of paint that is 8.1 in. high and has a radius of 3.3 in. How many walls can you paint?

This lumber company in Arizona is owned by the White Mountain Apache tribe.

Integrated Review   *Making Connections within Mathematics*

In Exercises 19–22, find the missing measures of the similar figures.

19.

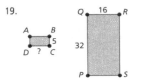

20.

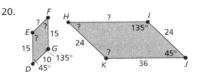

21.

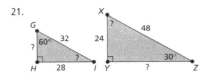

22.

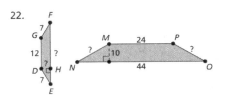

Exploration and Extension

23. *Building Your Chapter Project* Build a model slide for your park. Four posts will support the slide. The diameter of the model posts is $\frac{1}{4}$ in. Two are to be 5 inches high and two are to be $\frac{1}{2}$ inch high. Find the total volume of the model posts. How much concrete would you need to build the actual posts? The scale is 1 inch : 1 foot.

FIGURE 9.3. Examples of reading to perform tasks in a mathematics textbook. From *Heath Passport to Mathematics, Book 2* (p. 429) by Roland E. Larson, Laurie Boswell, and Lee Stiff. Copyright 1997 by D. C. Heath and Company. All rights reserved. Reprinted by permission of McDougal Littell Inc.

need to read some of these to and with them. Children's magazines often have articles that require reading to perform tasks. If you don't have many materials of this sort in your classroom make sure that you add to your supply. Bring in Boy and Girl Scouts manuals, too, so children can see the relevance of this careful reading outside school as well as in.

Second, provide opportunities on a regular basis for children to read and create some products. Make it a priority to involve children in actually reading to perform tasks when you do holiday projects. Don't read it all and explain the steps orally; engage the children with you in the reading. Let children follow the directions to create Thanksgiving turkeys, Valentines, and winter holiday (Christmas, Kwanzaa, and Hanukkah) decorations. Origami is a natural way to show students the value of careful reading; make use of it when you study Japan or when you want to have an interesting art project.

We as teachers need to model how we read to perform tasks, too. Thinking aloud when we read text that requires following the reading with actions helps students understand the relationship between reading and actions. Bring in a recipe book and tell students about some interesting cooking adventure. Then read the recipe and show them with your thinking aloud how you use reading to cook. Or bring in a book or article about how to create a piece of woodwork, if you find this more natural. Think aloud so that students see that this kind of reading is careful and requires much reader input.

We teachers also need to show students the steps they can use to make reading to perform a task successful for them. After some modeling and thinking aloud with your class, they may be able to come up with their own steps in this reading process. You may also want to provide them with the following steps and see whether these are useful to them:

1. Read through all the steps given in the directions.
2. Note any specialized vocabulary.
3. Look at any diagrams and connect them to specific steps.
4. Visualize the process as if you are doing it. Create drawings of the process if adequate ones are not provided.
5. Check to see that you have the needed equipment or resources.
6. Clarify any steps that don't make sense to you by rereading, talking it over with someone else, checking the glossary (if there is one), or scanning the diagrams carefully.
7. Begin the process and reread after each step to ensure your accuracy.

Some Cautions

Working with third- and fourth-grade elementary children as they tried to follow the steps in creating origami Valentines one year, we were struck by how difficult such reading is for them. First, many of them had no idea they should connect the diagrams to the steps in the directions. We ended up asking the children to draw a line from each step to the diagram that was an illustration of it. That was not easy for many. In some cases the text and diagrams were confusing, too. One step had two diagrams associated with it, and another had none. The children had to read carefully to make the correct associations between words and illustrations.

Second, the children were not familiar with the idea of matching their own actions with the steps in the process. They would read through the steps, then seem to put them aside while they tried to create the Valentine. The idea of reading one step and performing that part of the action was new to them. Therefore, we as teachers had to model this step-by-step action for them before they began to see how the text and their own activity had to be interrelated one step at a time.

Third, they had trouble with the words that had precise expectations associated with them. "Fold diagonally to the corner" did not seem to indicate to the children the need to match the corner exactly. It took some added modeling of the precision required in this task before some children learned to complete the steps more carefully.

As you begin to involve students in reading to perform tasks, watch them carefully and talk with them about the requirements of your particular activity. Linking text and diagrams, reading each step over carefully, following directions step by step, and completing the tasks precisely are areas that children need to learn. One of the great benefits of this form of reading, however, is that there is a product or some outcome directly associated with the reading. The rewards are clear!

Integrated Instructional Units

Natural places to help children learn to read to perform tasks are integrated units of instruction. If you take the time to write out careful directions and descriptions of the projects and products you want the children to develop in such a unit, you can give them the written directions and scaffold their independent use of them. It is great practice for students, and they will learn to rely on their reading comprehension rather than on you as the oral source of information.

In Maryland, one state assessment required students to work in cooperative teams on performance tasks that took a week to complete. The students need to follow several levels of instructions to be successful in these tasks. Therefore, teachers are becoming more aware of just how important it is for students to be able to handle these reading tasks without their teachers' mediation. And they know that it takes much practice before students can confidently accomplish this goal. Teachers now prepare more carefully for the assessment, so students have regular opportunities to engage in tasks where the steps are written for them rather than presented orally. Figure 9.4 presents the guidelines and one set of ac-

INTEGRATING MATH AND SOCIAL STUDIES

THE 3 R's
Reading, 'Rithmetic & the Revolution

OBJECTIVES

Participants will work in small cooperative groups to:

- Experience sample workstations integrating math and social studies by

  - Reading for information
  - Comparing/contrasting
  - Reading to perform a task

- Note and discuss key points for scoring tasks

- View student work samples

FIGURE 9.4a. Examples of reading to perform tasks in an integrated instructional unit: (a) Cover page and objectives from The 3 R's unit. (b) The "Geometry & George" activities from The 3 R's unit. Used by permission of Jane C. Hobbs, Charles County (Maryland) Public Schools.

tivities in a unit integrating math and social studies ("The 3 R's: Reading, 'Rithmetic & the Revolution"), which was developed by teachers in Charles County, Maryland. This unit helped students become more familiar with the format of such task descriptions.

A Coda

Many of us adults have not learned to read carefully to perform the tasks that are required of us on a regular, ongoing basis. If we begin early with our children, we can produce more careful readers who will be successful in this practical and much-needed form of reading. Presenting our own instructions in written form is a simple way to begin. Then adding reading to perform tasks to our own set of priorities can make it more real as part of our curriculum and expectations. We can be more consciously aware of what we do with children, and we can give them more guidance and support in their efforts. In the long run, this reading adds real practical value to our instruction and is generally a lot of fun.

GEOMETRY & GEORGE
Measurement

Using compasses & protractors with circles, angles and quilt design.

In your research on George Washington, you found that he was a surveyor. This means that he needed to have a basic understanding of geometry and measurement. You also have this basic understanding.

You will practice your geometry skills, and then make a quilt square by *reading to perform a task*. The quilt square will be assembled with the others from your group to form a design. Then the squares will be sewn together to form a large class quilt.

Working with circles and compasses
Activity 1
On separate paper, make at least five circles. Each circle must have a radius of at least 1 cm. and may not exceed a diameter of 8 cm. Be sure to label your circles.

Working with patterns and geometric shapes
Activity 1
On separate paper, make a pattern that demonstrates your understanding of geometry. Make a pattern that uses polygons and triangles. The pattern should form a border around the paper. Your pattern must include at least two polygons with five or more sides, and at least three acute triangles. DO NOT label the figures—instead, provide a key that identifies correctly each geometric figure used.

QUILT SQUARE
Activity 1
Now that you have practiced with the compasses and protractors, read and follow the directions to make a quilt square.

A. On separate paper, make a square that measures 18 cm on each side.

 For the next steps, you will use the lower left-hand corner of the square as the vertex or the center point.

B. Set your compass for a radius of 4 cm., and draw part of the circle in the square.

C. Set your compass for a radius of 9 cm., and draw part of the circle in the square.

 Both *A and B* should look like an arc of ¼ of a circle.

 Now, you will use your protractor to draw five angles. Each angle line should extend to the end of the square. The pattern should then resemble a sunburst.

D. Draw an angle that measures 15°.

(continued)

FIGURE 9.4b.

E.   Draw an angle that measures 300°.

F.   Draw an angle that measures 45°.

G.   Draw an angle that measures 60°.

H.   Draw an angle that measures 75°.

I.   Outline your lines, and color your design.

Activity 2
With your group, measure a square of colored construction paper to be 18" × 18".
Put your squares together to form a sunburst. Glue them to the paper.

FIGURE 9.4b. *(cont.)*

Reading to Learn: Studying and Test Taking

How often has someone asked you, "Did you read this book?," and you know you have read it, but you have no memory of its contents? Almost all of us get caught in this situation periodically, and we feel frustrated that we are not able to recall what we have actually experienced. It is even more frustrating when we check out a video and realize as we begin the show, "Oh, I have seen this before!" These experiences are related to memory—and to our failure to store experiences in such a way that they can be retrieved.

On the more positive side, one of us (Donna Ogle—the "I" here) has recently found ways to become more successful in learning the Russian language. This is in major part because I have consciously *tried* to remember what I am learning. I use numerous strategies to retain the language—including listening to audiotapes over and over, writing out cards with words and phrases I am memorizing, saying the words over and over, creating key word images for specific words, and memorizing poems and songs to give me meaningful anchors for the language.

As teachers of reading comprehension, we need not only to help students make their reading immediately interesting and meaningful but to help them retain what they read so it can be useful to them later. This is the extension of comprehension to *learning.* Think for a minute about what you do to retain ideas that you learn. What strategies do you use? How do you remember new words, names of people you meet, the plots of movies you see, and the content of material you read? What works best for you in studying for various courses you take?

In surveys of this issue with secondary students, the most frequently mentioned strategies seem to be rereading (Tierney, Schallert, & LaZansky, 1982) and rote memorization (Vacca & Vacca, 1999). Was either on your list? Do you also underline and make marginal notes as you read and use them for studying? In addition, do you use some strategies that involve active reconstruction of ideas? Do you sometimes create summaries of sections of text, either orally or in written form? Do you create graphic organizers of chapters or sections of materials? Do you have a variety of note-making options available to you—such as two-column notes, T-notes, or some variation of notes from others, and/or your own representations of key ideas and responses? Look at your list again and see whether you have also included drawing and imaging as part of your strategies. Studies confirm that visualizing is a valuable tool in memory (Pressley & Woloshyn, 1995; Hyerle, 2000). Do you have special ways to learn new vocabulary items? Do you write out word cards or make semantic maps? Is the use of key word associations and other mnemonics on your list? (These devices are often used to help remember items that don't have particular semantic associations in themselves.) Finally, have you included some strategies for studying that are geared specifically to the kinds of tests you will take—some for essay exams, and others for multiple-choice or short-answer tests?

Now think about how you learned these strategies. Did teachers help you develop a repertoire of strategies? Did this occur in elementary or secondary school, or at the university level? We still find many adults who have never learned a range of strategies and don't feel confident about their ability to learn. A niece admitted to one of us that she dropped Spanish because she didn't know how to memorize all the vocabulary and rules. When she was asked what strategies she used, she replied that she simply reread words, and tried to cover words and then guess at what they were. Asked what else she did, Annie was at a loss. She really didn't have strategies that might have made her language learning much more enjoyable and successful. Annie, and all our students, deserve to learn strategies that can help them learn well and efficiently.

In this section, we explore ways that we as teachers can help students develop a strong set of strategies to help them learn. These strategies can be taught in the elementary grades and need to be; then they need to be amplified and expanded in middle school and high school. At every level, we need to help students learn both to read and to retain the important concepts and ideas they encounter and the meanings they construct.

As teachers, it is important that we help children engage actively in reading and then apply strategies to learning new material so it will stay with them over the long term. Our instruction is only partially useful if what we teach is not retained. Why engage in educational activities if they do not provide building blocks for learning? By being consciously aware of what we do in the classroom, we can significantly enhance the long-term effects of our teaching.

High-Stakes Learning

The need to maximize our instructional impact has become even more important recently with the focus on testing and standards. Each district and state has made the acquisition of particular knowledge and processes a high priority. With standards for and assessments of those outcomes, students are now being tested on facts and specific knowledge, as well as on their ability to use the processes of learning (reading, writing, speaking, working in groups, and creating products for sharing). Sets of standards list what students should know and be able to do. This focus on specific knowledge that students must possess, especially in social studies, science, and mathematics, makes it important that teachers help students develop strategies for learning and remembering important concepts and knowledge.

Traditionally elementary teachers (or at least primary teachers) were most involved in developing students' language and math processes, and teachers did not attend particularly to retention of knowledge until upper elementary and middle school. Now that is changing. Working with primary teachers in Virginia, we felt their pain as they laid out the standards that were given them for social studies in third grade (see Figure 9.5).

Building a Focus on Retention of Information

To help both students and themselves, teachers need to attend to ways all of the activities in which students engage can be maximized so the information can be easily and enjoyably retained. Learning is and can be fun. Children generally take great pleasure in building their store of knowledge, and they can become more effective learners with some attention from teachers.

How do we do this? In this section, we provide two specific suggestions. First, we need to make the goals of our school activities clear, so students can focus on what they are doing and learning. Second, we need to involve students in their own evaluation. We can do this by helping them collect and evaluate evidence of their own learning; they need to be metacognitively active in thinking about their learning. They need to see evidence of what they have learned and then reflect on their accomplishments. Asking them questions such as "What did you learn? How can you show that you learned this? And what could you do differently next time?" will help them develop reflection.

Making Goals and Standards Explicit

As teachers, we need to begin our learning experiences or units by establishing learning goals or questions, so that students feel they are part of an inquiry. With standards now guiding instruction in many districts, it is even more important for teachers to think about the outcomes we expect as a result of our instructional activities. Then it is possible later to return to these same goals or questions and evaluate changes in students' knowledge. Actually *seeing* the results of their learning activities empowers students to feel more confident. They need to know that their classroom work is purposeful and that their changes in knowledge can be verified by themselves, the learners.

Grade Three

Introduction to History and Social Science

The standards for third-grade students include an introduction to the heritage and contributions of the people of ancient Greece and Rome and the West African empire of Mali. Students should continue developing map skills and demonstrate an understanding of basic economic concepts. Students will explain the importance of the basic principles of democracy and identify the contributions of selected individuals. Students will recognize that Americans are a people who have diverse ethnic origins, customs, and traditions, who all contribute to American life, and who are united as Americans by common principles.

History

3.1 The student will explain how the contributions of ancient Greece and Rome have influenced the present world in terms of architecture, government (direct and representative democracy), and sports.

3.2 The student will study the early West African empire of Mali by describing its oral tradition (storytelling), government (kings), and economic development (trade).

3.3 The student will study the exploration of the Americas by
a) describing the accomplishments of Christopher Columbus, Juan Ponce de Léon, Jacques Cartier, and Christopher Newport;
b) identifying reasons for exploring, the information gained, and the results from the travels.

Geography

3.4 The student will develop map skills by
a) locating Greece, Rome, and West Africa;
b) describing the physical and human characteristics of Greece, Rome, and West Africa;
c) explaining how the people of Greece, Rome, and West Africa adapted to and/or changed their environment to meet their needs.

3.5 The student will develop map skills by
a) positioning and labeling the seven continents and four oceans to create a world map;
b) using the equator and prime meridian to identify the four hemispheres;

c) locating the countries of Spain, England, and France;
d) locating the regions in the Americas explored by Christopher Columbus (San Salvador in the Bahamas), Juan Ponce de Léon (near St. Augustine, Florida), Jacques Cartier (near Quebec, Canada), and Christopher Newport (Jamestown, Virginia);
e) locating specific places on a simple letter-number grid system.

3.6 The student will interpret geographic information from maps, tables, graphs, and charts.

Economics

3.7 The student will explain how producers use natural resources (water, soil, wood, and coal), human resources (people at work), and capital resources (machines, tools, and buildings) to produce goods and services for consumers.

3.8 The student will recognize the concepts of specialization (being an expert in one job, product, or service) and interdependence (depending on others)

in the production of goods and services (in ancient Greece, Rome, the West African empire of Mali, and in the present).

3.9 The student will identify examples of making an economic choice and will explain the idea of opportunity cost (what is given up when making a choice).

(continued)

FIGURE 9.5. Virginia state standards for history and social sciences in third grade. Retrieved October 12, 2007 from *www.pen.k12.va.us/VDOE/Superintendent/Sols/history3.doc.*

Civics

3.10 The student will recognize why government is necessary in the classroom, school, and community by
  a) explaining the purpose of rules and laws;
  b) explaining that the basic purposes of government are to make laws, carry out laws, and decide if laws have been broken;
  c) explaining that government protects the rights and property of individuals.
3.11 The student will explain the importance of the basic principles that form the foundation of a republican form of government by
  a) describing the individual rights to life, liberty, and the pursuit of happiness; and equality under the law;
  b) identifying the contributions of George Washington, Thomas Jefferson, Abraham Lincoln, Rosa Parks, Thurgood Marshall, and Martin Luther King, Jr.;
  c) recognizing that Veterans Day and Memorial Day honor people who have served to protect the country's freedoms.
3.12 The student will recognize that Americans are a people of diverse ethnic origins, customs, and traditions, who are united by the basic principles of a republican form of government and respect for individual rights and freedoms.

FIGURE 9.5. *(cont.)*

One teacher turns the standards she is working on into questions, so that students feel more engaged in their learning. On the board she writes, for example, "Who is Jack Jewett? Why is he important in history?" Then the lesson can begin with brainstorming and active discussion by the class, rather than with the perception of just another fact-filled lesson to be memorized. Teachers need to be creative in how they involve students in learning what is now considered important knowledge. One school in New York City involves students actively in thinking about *why* they are studying what they are. They ask, "What does this matter? Why should we learn this? What would happen if we didn't?" In this way, the natural questions of older students are accepted and serve as a starting point of each new topic or unit.

Once there is some shared understanding of the purposes and direction of the lesson or activity, students will be more focused. However, a second step is also essential. That is, teachers should also engage students in thinking about *how* they will learn the targeted material or concepts. Once the focus on learning about Jack Jewett is clear, for instance, then the next natural question is "How shall we go about learning about Jewett?" The teacher will have prearranged much of this part of the lesson beforehand, but students need to have some participation in this planning, too. They need to learn how to prioritize information, how to make notes that work for them, and how to review and learn the material. If multiple sources are being used, ways to integrate information gained from those sources need to be determined. In one class, for example, students decided to create a web for Jewett and add information about four categories they (with teacher guidance) determined were important: personal life, political and social context, major contributions, and conflicts he had to deal with. They also determined that each student would write a short biographical essay at the end of the lesson arguing either why Jewett either is or is not an important figure in history. As we move toward a more standards-based curriculum, with purposeful outcomes more directly stated, we also need to include a focus on how these outcomes will be achieved by the learners—both as a group and individually.

In addition, within the goals and learning outcomes we teachers ourselves and our districts set, there is much room for students to articulate their own goals and purposes for learning. The more they can take ownership of the learning process, the more likely it is that they will put full energy into it. Therefore, including personal assessments of what they already know and establishing what questions they need to have answered or what areas need to be studied carefully are both important.

Engaging Students in Reflection and Self-Evaluation

When students engage in self-evaluation, they can become more active as learners. They look at what they know and what questions are guiding their learning at the beginning of a unit or project. They also determine how they are going to learn the material or create the project. Usually this takes some reflection and planning time. Then, when they are finished, they look at the changes in their knowledge and see the products they have created. They can then answer these questions of personal evaluation: "How successful was I? Did I achieve my goals? What could I have done better?"

The first step in helping students become focused learners is to keep before them the changes in their level of knowledge and performance. Then they can personally feel the satisfaction that comes from doing well—from learning.

One first-grade team did this very well with their young students. They had a computer program that allowed the teachers to record students while they were reading orally at four times during the first-grade year. The first selection students read was in November. They saved this performance in their individual portfolios (on computer disks) and added pieces of writing (scanned in), and also drew pictures to accompany their pieces on the computer. These were all saved during the year. By May, the students could look back at their portfolio pieces and clearly perceive the changes they had made. They couldn't believe how "bad" they had been as readers just a few months before. Without the voice recordings, the students would not have been able to engage in self-reflection, for they certainly could not recall their level of performance as it had changed over 6 months. Student portfolios are powerful tools; they enable students to reflect on their own performance as learners and to be empowered by knowing that they are learners. With many computer-based programs available teachers can easily help students keep records of their learning across time. Fluency records, numbers of pages read, responses to reading, and vocabulary records are easy ways to show students their progress.

Second, students need to be encouraged to engage in self-testing of what they are learning. Primary-school students can do this as easily as older ones. For instance, in one second-grade classroom where the teacher organizes her instruction around thematic units, the students began a unit on Scandinavia by doing a K-W-L procedure (see Chapter 5). They first listed what they knew (and the teacher wrote down their contributions), and then they listed the major questions they wanted answered. The teacher wrote those questions on strips of poster board, which she later put on the bulletin board. The questions stayed there during the full time of the unit; she used them to guide the development of the unit, but she didn't refer to them often with the children. However, at the end of the unit, she focused the children on the questions they had asked initially. As she took each strip off the board, she handed it to one of the children sitting on the floor in front of her. She then asked each child to read the question and answer it for the class. She said later, "There was not one question the children could not answer, and I didn't pay much attention to which question I handed to each child. The children were amazed at how much they had learned. They knew immediately they were successful! I didn't have to give them grades; they had their own personal verification of their learning."

How had the students progressed to this level of understanding? It certainly didn't just happen. First, the teacher had thought carefully about the unit and had some goals in mind for what she wanted to accomplish. When the students initially discussed what they already knew about Scandinavia (which was very little), the teacher guided them into thinking about a different culture by using the map and telling them the countries were in the North, where it is cold. She then guided them into asking questions about a different culture—what kinds of food the people eat, what they wear, what kinds of schools they have, what kinds of stories they tell and read, and so forth. The list went on and on, once the children began to think of aspects of "culture."

Next, the teacher planned a rich array of activities for the students to engage them deeply in learning the content. She collected plastic crates of resource materials—many books with rich pictures, to help students who were still emergent readers gain access to ideas and information. One crate contained folktales and stories, and another held informational books. Children kept their own learning logs, and each day the class did a "class journal" in which the students reviewed what they had done and what new ideas they had gained. There was much rich learning, and many topics were introduced through a variety of formats—a videotape, a guest speaker, audiotapes of songs and stories, and many books and articles. Each child chose one topic for his or her own research, and the children created reports by writing stories, informational news articles, or poetry. Thus, each child became an "expert" on one aspect of Scandinavia. The teacher reinforced the ideas that to learn new information, the students needed to keep notes in their learning logs, discuss new information, and listen to each other. In all these ways, she helped these young children become self-reliant learners.

These same principles of monitoring learning by establishing goals and questions to guide inquiry and returning to one's initial performance to evaluate change are also important for older students. We must help students become involved in their own evaluation, or else they feel like "pawns" in the educational game. They need to see what they are learning, so they can take pleasure and develop confidence in themselves (Bransford, Brown, & Cocking, 1999; Dembo & Eaton, 2000; Weinstein & Mayer, 1986).

A sixth-grade teacher with whom we work (Ogle, 1992) focuses much of her energy on developing self-evaluation on the part of her students. When they began an integrated science–language arts unit, each student started a personal learning journal. As preassessment, each student made a list of what he or she could recall knowing about insects. Together, the students then clustered that information into a semantic map. Finally, the teacher asked the students to write a table of contents that might come from one of the books they would be reading. (She was also setting up the idea of each student's writing a report and including a table of contents.) After the unit of study, which included a wide variety of activities and a culminating report and creative project—each child created a new insect, drew a picture of it, and described how it functioned (food, protection, senses, and life cycle)—the students returned to their journals. Each student wrote a list of what he or she now knew, clustered that information, and then wrote another table of contents. Then each student compared his or her two sets and wrote answers to these questions?

1. What do you notice about your lists of information?
2. Compare your two semantic maps. What do you notice?
3. What is different or similar about your two tables of contents?
4. What can you say about yourself as a learner now?

Developing Memory Strategies

If students are going to learn new material, we need to help them take ownership of the process of self-monitoring, so they can feel confident that they can learn. This is the beginning. From there, we can help them develop a variety of strategies to make new information and processes their own.

Rehearsal and Practice

For young children, among the first learning strategies that can be used are practice and rehearsal. No one learns something new without practice. Learning how to use a computer keyboard correctly, how to ride a skateboard, or how to use inline skates takes lots of practice. Children who take music lessons know well that they must have schedules and show how many hours they have spent in rehearsal. They do this before lessons and certainly before taking part in a performance. The same is true of everything children learn in school. If it is new and they want to learn it, they need to practice and rehearse.

Students can practice in lots of ways. A key to practice is to do it as quickly after learning as possible. The sooner students practice new learning, the more likely they are to retain it. Immediately after the school day, when students go home, they can tell their families what they are learning in school and practice using new words or concepts. Teachers can help students focus at the end of a class or the end of the school day by refreshing some new concept or skill from the day's activities. Some primary teachers ask students to gather together at the end of the day and create a daily journal of what was done and learned that day. Then when the children go home, their minds are fresh with memories of what they have learned, and they can share this with their eager parents or older siblings.

When teachers involve parents by letting them know what the students are studying each week, parents can have more productive conversations with their children about their school efforts. When children talk with their parents about what they are learning, they are engaging in rehearsal—making the new knowledge their own. To help parents encourage children to talk about their learning, they need to know what areas to probe. The more the parents know about the school curriculum, the more easily they can sustain conversations over time with their children.

To help parents in this effort, many teachers send a newsletter composed by each child home at the end of each week, outlining what the child has done that week and will be working on next week (see Figure 9.6). This short newsletter can be sent in a manila envelope with student work samples from the week, making the home–school connection very real. Another valuable technique is to have the students write weekly reflections on their learning and send these with the work (see Figure 9.7 for two examples). When children even in the primary grades engage in regular self-reflection, they are more likely to take ownership of their school learning and to put much more energy into it.

Creating a home–school journal is another powerful tool for more engaged reflection and sharing. Each week, a student writes a letter to a parent explaining what was done that week and what was interesting (see Figure 9.8). The child also asks the parent one question. When the parent reads the journal, he or she writes a response to the question and adds some comment about the weekly review the child has created. This journal is maintained throughout the year and improves both parents' and children's engagement in the priorities of the school curriculum.

Rehearsal and practice can also be nurtured during the school day in various ways. We can give children time in school to turn to partners and rehearse what

Week #2

Your name: D██████
#29

Parent: M██████████

Write about something you read. I read The BOSSY Gallito. I liked how the rooster needed to say pluse, to get his friends to do things for him.

Write about how you feel about math. Give reasons why. I liked math alot because, I am good with money and working with numbers.

Were you organized this week? Write about it. I don't think I was very organized this week. Next time I need to do my work before I go out to play.

Write about something that happened with your friends. John, Mark, Paul and Trevor and me were playing Super heroes and I was Batman. We were running a lot. I got tired.

Write about how you are doing in the area of listening. What will you work on? I am starting to be a very good listner. I am doing well with my listning Strages.

Parent response (Ideas, Questions) I think that the Friday folders and reading about D███'s work has been very beneficial and exciting. I think it is a great ideas to involve the parents. Thanks. M██████

FIGURE 9.6. A weekly newsletter composed by a child for a parent, with the parent's comments.

Name   *KEVIN*   Date   *2-17*

Thinking about My Learning

1. I'm really good at   *ART*

    because   *I'VE DONE It SISE I WAS 1*

2. I'm getting better at   *WRITING*

    because   *I'M LEARNING LETTERS*

3. I have difficulty with   *SPELLING*

    because   *I FORGET*

FIGURE 9.7a. Two examples (a and b) of student-composed weekly reflections on learning in kindergarten and first grade.

Historical Inquiry Presentation
Reflection

Name *Brandy*   Group *Whales*

The best thing I did in my presentation was *saying the animals and pointing to them.*

I think I should work on *how they eat (have a better explanation)*

because *it was the easyest part.*

because *it sounded a little dumb.*

FIGURE 9.7b.

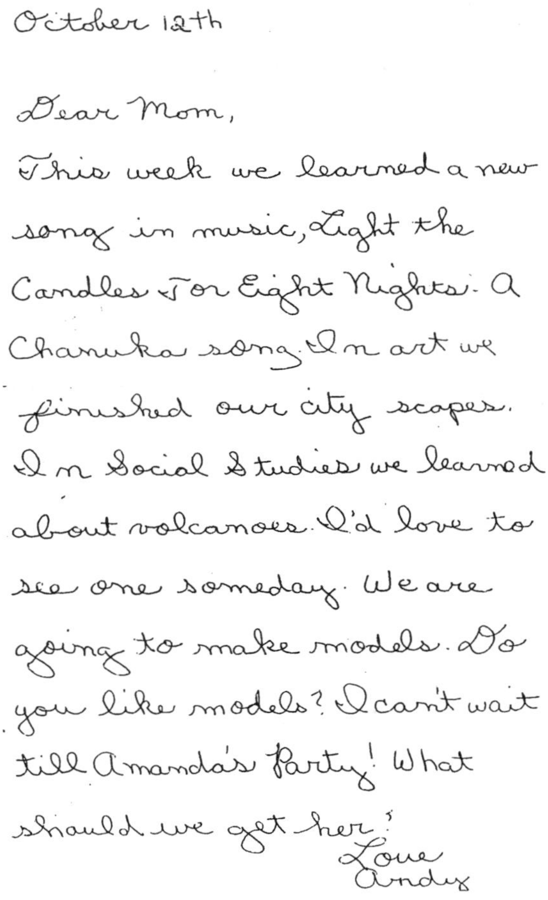

October 12th

Dear Mom,
This week we learned a new
song in music, Light the
Candles For Eight Nights. A
Chanuka song. In art we
finished our city scapes.
In Social Studies we learned
about volcanoes. I'd love to
see one someday. We are
going to make models. Do
you like models? I can't wait
till Amanda's Party! What
should we get her?
                    Love
                    Andy

FIGURE 9.8. A weekly letter written by a child to a parent as part of a home–school journal.

they have been studying. This is the essence of the "Say Something" technique (Short et al., 1996; see Chapter 6). It is a clear check on their comprehension, and it also establishes the expectation that what they are doing is worthwhile and is meant to be learned. A variant of this activity is "Think–Pair–Share" (McTighe & Lyman, 1988), which can be used for review of lessons at the end of a class period. Students first review what they know by writing down ideas during "think" time. Then they "pair" with partners and discuss what they have written. Finally, the whole class gathers, and the students "share" what they know. In this way, children can test out their ideas with partners before they expose their ideas to the whole class. The three-step process also provides even more time for rehearsal and review, and children can both see their ideas in written form and hear these ideas shared and discussed. Teachers can use these times to assess students' levels of understanding and to clarify any misconceptions that remain.

Children can also rehearse ideas individually. Some children practice or review ideas better when they can listen to an audiotape; in such cases, teachers can help them record for themselves what they are studying and take the tapes home for personal listening. For most students, the practice of keeping a learning journal or diary is a powerful tool for memory, because they can return to it and reread it many times. The use of note cards with focused concepts or ideas on them helps many students rehearse new information and terms.

Mnemonics (Association Devices)

A second way to stimulate memory or learning is through various association devices. The word "mnemonics" refers to devices for linking or associating a new item with something familiar. These associations can be made by placing new information in rhymes, or by creating an acronym (a word or sentence made from the first letters in the words being learned). They can also be made by linking new words with similar-sounding ones (key words) and building picture associations.

Some ideas can be learned by thinking of links to other personal associations. Take time in class to build these links for your students. Even learning something like the names of the Scandinavian countries (Sweden, Finland, Denmark, Norway, and Iceland) can be made into a linking activity. The five countries can be represented by the fingers on your hand or by your palm and four fingers. Which country is most like the palm? (Denmark) Which would be the furthest left or west? (Iceland) Which would be the furthest right or east? (Finland) In effect, this is a spatial association device, and many people find thinking of new ideas linked to a familiar room or objects in a room helpful.

Helping students develop key word images is another proven way to learn many new terms and ideas. This strategy works by making associations between a new term and other words that are known, and then creating an image that activates this new term. For example, after a fellow faculty member remarked, "My, you are coruscating today!" and I (Donna Ogle) found out what the word meant, I wanted to learn it. Therefore, I linked the words "chorus at the gate" with "coruscate," and created an image in my mind of a chorus line dancing through a gate. At first I could not always even remember the image, but whenever I saw the word, the association came to me immediately and I knew what the word meant. After some practice with using the word in a variety of situations, it has become a part of my expressive vocabulary. It took a conscious effort and the help of my key word strategy before the word was mine.

Several studies have been conducted using the key word strategy as a memory device for students from intermediate grades through university level, and the power of these associations is clear at all levels. The key words are very easy to use with foreign-language learning, and they also work well with content areas. One of the research studies was done with fourth graders learning about the three basic types of rocks and examples of each. The key words the class developed included "Iggy Pig" ("igneous"), with the image of a pig with a melted chocolate bar triggering the idea of rock formed from melting; "Harry Centipede," with a centipede building a brick wall signifying the layers of sedimentary rock; and "Netta and More Fish" ("metamorphic"), who put both igneous and sedimentary rock in a pressure cooker over a fire (see Williams, Konopak, & Readance, 1989).

If children need to learn something such as the elements of the Linnean classification system, you can develop mnemonics in the form of acronyms (words or sentences formed from the initial letters or parts of the words to be learned) to make the elements memorable. When I (Donna Ogle) was a high school student, I developed the personal name "K. P. Cofgs" to help me recall "kingdom," "phylum," "class," "order," "family," "genus," and "species." Later I read that another memorable association was created by turning the first letters of the words into a sentence acronym: "Kings play cards on fine green sofas." When learning the notes on the musical scale, many of us still use "Every Good Boy Does Fine" as an acronym for the lines on the scale and "FACE" for the spaces. These simple mnemonics make the retention of otherwise meaningless strings possible. As a teacher, you can help students create acronyms (either single-word or sentence acronyms) for important information they need to learn—names of state capitals, geographic information, presidents, scientific concepts, or mathematical terms and relationships.

Turning new information to be learned into poetry, rhymes, and jingles also helps us retain ideas. How many of us haven't used the sing-song way of learning how to spell "Mississippi" for instance? Current students have done amazing work creating raps to learn new content. For example, the son of a colleague of ours has developed a rap to help him remember explorers of Central and North America. Many of us began learning foreign languages by singing songs with a strong beat and repeating rhymes. There is something about rhythm that helps lock new ideas in our memories. Another interesting way to remember new concepts is to turn the ideas into "cinquains" (five-line poems).

Writing, Drawing, and Imaging to Remember

One of the easiest ways to recall new information and concepts is to make personal connections through writing in personal journals and logs and then to reread those notes periodically. Double-entry journals help students keep key ideas from texts as well as respond personally. (See Figure 2.3 in Chapter 2.)

Drawing and imaging are also good tools for remembering. Students who learn to create "mind maps" have yet another memory device for learning and retention. After making an original drawing, a student then visualizes this drawing as a reinforcement tool, so the ideas become rehearsed in relation to the drawing or image. We have found many students who can recall ideas and terms much more easily after they have created their own pictures for the new ideas or terms.

Cooperative Discussion and Review

Children, like adults, need to use new ideas and information regularly to make these their own. Often in elementary grades, the use of cooperative groups or partner activities helps students review and practice what they are learning. Some of these activities have been described above under "Rehearsal and Practice," but they are worth reiterating here.

Some teachers take just a few minutes after students study a new concept to ask students to turn to partners and tell them what they just learned. Putting the ideas into one's own words is important. Other teachers use the first 3 minutes of a class session as a refresher time for reviewing what was done or studied the day previously: "With your partner, write down what you remember from yesterday." The combination of talk and writing can be a powerful activator for learning and can give students an opportunity for self-rehearsal and self-evaluation.

Many studies of older learners have shown that the opportunity to talk with someone about what is being learned, as well as to discuss *how* they go about learning, is very beneficial. Especially for less secure learners, the ability to put the ideas being learned into one's own words is important.

It is also very important for second-language learners to have regular opportunities to talk about and express ideas being learned. Providing time for small-group and partner activity specifically geared to review and rehearsal is essential. These learners need to hear content terminology used in settings that are not stressful. They also need to be able to try out their use of these ideas and terms in safe environments. By putting such students in small groups, teachers can enhance the risk taking and practice of these less secure learners and English speakers.

Preparing for Examinations

The first step in helping students prepare for examinations is to focus on the kinds of tests that are given and to think about their demands. A multiple-choice test, for example, does not require the same kind of study as an essay test does. Yet these tests require that students review a wide range of materials. Recognition of items for multiple-choice tests is easier in most cases than is production of ideas from memory. For essay exams, students need to develop arguments and then to bring in strong supporting evidence from memory to support the key ideas being developed. The time frame for exams also influences how students both study and take these tests. For example, if the time is short, students should answer the questions they are most sure of first and then tackle the less sure items later. Because children are being given such a variety of tests now, it is important to prepare them for the demands of each and help them become "test-wise."

When multiple-choice tests are given, students need to think about the kinds of answers that are most likely to be considered "right" by the test makers. One good way to help students "think like the testers" is to use the framework provided by QARs (question, answer, relationship; see Figure 5.13 in Chapter 5). You can explain to students that this type of testing can't permit "on my own"-type questions, as answers are machine scored. Therefore, all answers will be "right there" or "think and search." Only infrequently are there "author and you" items. It is best to try to locate information to answer questions in the text.

With some discussion of actual tests, students can learn more about how these different test formats function, and testing doesn't have to seem so scary or unpredictable. It also helps to suggest that children prepare for tests physically by getting enough rest before a test, by bringing snacks if the testing is long, and by having pencils and whatever other equipment is allowed ready. Parents can easily be involved, too, in helping students come rested and ready.

Putting It All Together

In this chapter, we have covered a wide variety of strategies students need to develop to become those complete "comprehenders" that we want to see them become. Much of what is required in reading to perform tasks and in reading to learn is similar: Readers must attend carefully to the text and be able to retain or use the information in new ways. Vocabulary is often critical in both cases, and we need to connect this chapter with Chapter 7 in how we teach and assist students in learning.

The more we can help students enjoy learning and develop a set of strategies they can test out and use independently, the more likely they are to use reading fully in school and beyond.

CHAPTER 10

Strategies That Encourage Lifelong Reading

In the chapters preceding this one, we have shared ideas for helping students acquire the skills and strategies to become effective comprehenders. Looking back at the model presented in Chapter 2 reminds us that there is more to developing good comprehenders than skills and strategies, however. Readers need to develop reading interests; need to be able to interact with a variety of texts; need to talk and interact with others about what and why they read; need persistence to keep at their reading; need to have all sorts of knowledge about reading, as well as a variety of reading experiences; and need to have self-awareness and confidence as readers. In addition, they need to be flexible readers who read for home, school, work, community, and other purposes.

If we think back to the discussion of Nikki and Maria in Chapter 2, we can remember that they talked with each other about what and why they read; they had persistence to keep at their reading to learn about butterflies; they used their knowledge about books and other informational sources to learn more about butterflies; and they had self-awareness and confidence as readers. All of the reading they did reflected the model we have presented in Chapter 2 as well. Becoming a reader was a social process for both girls, but each girl had her own style of reading and her own self-perception as a reader.

In the process of students' becoming lifelong readers, interest (which drives purpose) and self-awareness and confidence as readers are big keys. How useful will well-developed reading strategies be if students leave our classrooms not wanting to read? Statistics suggest that many highly educated adolescents and adults who can read don't read. A Gallup poll on readership reported that the number of Americans who had not read a book in the previous year doubled from 8% in 1978 to 16% in 1990. Three out of four people 55 and older read a daily paper, but only 50% of those 18–24 years of age did so (Heath, 1997). Further, there is compelling research that supports the importance of volume of reading as significant to a learner's growth (Cunningham, 2005). So in this, our final chapter, we want to focus on classroom strategies for building the habits of readership with our students (see the graphic organizer in Figure 10.1). Because we have started this book with reflections on good readers, let's begin this last chapter by thinking about what lifelong readers look like. Stop for a moment and think about yourself, or someone you know, who would fall into this category. What do such readers look like? How do they embody the notion that reading and comprehending are both social and individual processes?

What Lifelong Readers Are Like

Bud and Jim, our husbands, like our friends Terry and Monica, start out each day with the newspapers, no matter how much of a rush they're in to get out the door. On Sunday, they love to linger over the local paper and *The New York Times*; when they travel, the *International Herald Tribune* or local papers in languages they are trying to master are a must. *Newsweek, Time, Harper's, Archaeology, National Geographic, Science News*, and many other magazines, along with professional journals, find their ways into our houses and seem to be piled in every corner, bathroom, and kitchen basket. The library reference room is a repository, thankfully, for those magazines and journals that are consulted now and then— *Consumer Reports* before a big purchase, for example, or *Travel and Leisure* prior to a trip. Now and then an exotic magazine, such as *Mercator's World* for the lover of maps, makes its way in through the newsstand. An avid readership of periodicals is one mark of a lifelong reader. These readers subscribe to magazines and newspapers, know where to find them in the library and newsstand, and give subscriptions to others for gifts. Jake, Jim's son, has emulated his father in his love of news and niche magazines, requesting subscriptions to a news magazine, *Guitar*, and *Rolling Stone* to have at college.

Jesse and her friend Cara are two teens who love to follow the books recommended by Oprah Winfrey, watching the newly listed books and choosing one to read at the same time and talk about. Diana and her friends have a formal book club with a paid leader to nurture and guide their discussions; Esther dips in and out of book discussions at the local bookstore, signing up when she sees one she likes. Bonnie moderates an Internet book club, whose members do their chatting electronically. Danny, Matt, and Patrick, brothers in elementary school, rotate books. Each boy in turn reads a classic as he is deemed "old enough," and the

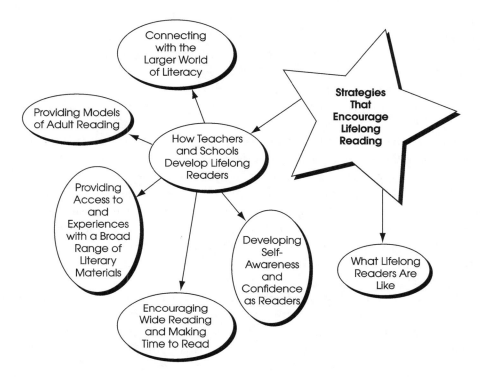

Resource Locator—Strategies and Resources Discussed in Chapter 10

FIGURE 10.1. Graphic organizer for Chapter 10.

family bookshelf reflects their fraternal reading. These readers know books and authors; follow the book sections in local and national papers; watch book shows on TV; prowl the bookstores for new arrivals; and attend the used-book sales at the public library, local colleges, and other organizations for their reading material. They own books, trade books, and use the library to "feed" their habits. They love the social interaction of talking about and sharing books in many different venues.

Tom, Andrew, Junko, and Donna rely on books on tape when they jog and travel. They relish a long car trip or a daily jog, as well as short jaunts for work, when they know a new book is waiting. They utilize the lending capability of their local libraries to make it possible for them to be "cassette junkies" without spending lots of money, though they buy favorite tapes for repeated listening and for loaning. They use electronic catalogs to find out about the newest tapes; many of the "new" tapes are classics that they have already read and want to revisit through listening. Alternatively, they often read books after they have listened to the taped versions.

Kathleen, Camille, Jesse, and John Paul all survived a year's posting in Europe by writing e-mails back and forth. When they took a trip together during that year, they kept journals and shared them with one another. Another time, they wrote an account of a trip they shared, which was published (usually, the "publication" is just for family and friends). They collected artifacts of their trip and logged them in journals. Jesse kept a diary. And they all collected jokes, sayings, incidents, and lists of books that related to travel.

Marilou, Sam, Mitch, and Anne are all film buffs. They read film magazines, movie reviews, articles and magazines about film, books about directors and stars, and *TV Guide* with relish and gusto. Their reading is often driven by this hobby and interest, and Marilou and Mitch have done lots of reading in pursuit of their degrees in popular culture and film. Sam pores over technical manuals on animation, and Anne's "radar" leads her to news on design for her work in set dressing for movies. Like that of so many people, their reading is fueled by a specific interest, a passion.

All of these relatives and friends, whose ages range from 9 to 60, talk about books at home, on the phone, in formal groups, over coffee at the local coffee shop or bookstore, and over dinner. Dinner table conversations often revolve around what someone has read (either a book, a news item, or a magazine article), and new topics frequently send someone upstairs to the bookshelf, the dictionary, or the Web. The interest and ability to talk about books and literature—the base of "cultural literacy" with respect to books that allows people to do this—is another type of lifelong reading.

We could go on and on with descriptions of lifelong readers: Herb at the gas station with his daily quote from *The Wall Street Journal*; Diane with her latest education book of the month; Jim, the limousine driver, who always has a book on the seat for "down"times; Joe, whose poetry and Buddhist quotes engage and mystify; Doris and Gary with the newest technological Web sites . . . the list is endless. All of these lifelong readers have individual interests, have personal styles of interacting with what they read, use their knowledge and experience when they read, and have confidence in themselves as readers. They also use reading for social purposes; for work; for home, school, and community needs; and for their roles as members of various groups.

We see by their actions that they perceive themselves as literate people—people for whom print is pleasurable, accessible, and friendly. They are aware of the variety and diversity of things in print; they know where and how to locate what they need; and they turn to text resources when they have a question, as well as when they are looking for enjoyment. They have the skills they need to locate and understand various forms of print media, and they embrace new technologies that make more text available to them (whether through conventional print, telecommunications, audio, or other media). They use all these skills, perceptions, and knowledge in social settings, as well as in private learning and reading. Finally, they have an awareness of themselves as avid readers and writers.

All these characteristics relate directly to the model presented in Chapter 2 of this book, where comprehension is characterized as a process with social dimensions (at use and developed not only at school, but at work in our affinity groups and in our community), as well as individual dimensions (relating to style, awareness, confidence, knowledge, and experience; the ability to persist even when some others flag; and a purposeful process in which meaning is built).

Now the question is this: How do we get our students to this point? How can we as teachers build lifelong readers who are constructive, motivated, purposeful, skillful, and strategic about their reading; who monitor their own reading; and who read for both individual and social purposes?

How Teachers and Schools Develop Lifelong Readers

There are many avenues toward ensuring that our students become lifelong readers. As teachers, we need an understanding of reading, the reading process, and the development of strategies and skills to help our students become good comprehenders. In Chapters 5–9 we have focused on the instructional strategies that develop effective comprehension. To get our students to go beyond "I can read" to "I want to read," however, research and best practices tell us that students must also have and do the following:

- Have models of literate behavior—in the classroom, home, school, community, and beyond. If students are to develop the ability to use reading for the purposes of home, work, school, community, and interest groups, they must have models of how mature reading looks.

- Have a personal self-awareness as readers and writers. If students are to develop the individual persistence and strategies needed to emulate these mature readers, they must develop an awareness and confidence of *themselves* as readers, whatever their age and developmental level. These methods must take into account the driving forces of interest and choice in children's becoming readers.

- Have access to materials, and experiences in using these materials, that reflect a broad view of literacy and that help them embrace new technologies and literacies as well. We will look at each of these, what they mean, and the ways they interact. The meaning of "literacy" in today's world has changed from its meaning in earlier decades, and it will continue to change. Students need to build knowledge that will help them not only cope with change but embrace changing types of literacy in a positive and confident fashion. A broad view of literacy prepares them to operate individually, socially, and strategically as readers.

- Have a wide variety of reading materials available, as well as ample time to read them. All the skills and strategies in the world won't produce a good reader unless he or she has time to utilize them. Like any other ability, reading takes practice.

- Make conscious literacy connections from school to home, community, the world of work, and affinity groups. If literacy is to be developed and used in a social setting, facilitating those links will help the process and help students see the value of their literacy.

Providing Models of Adult Reading: "Cool Adults Read"

Students need to see both that reading is an important adult activity and that it can be a "cool" activity. In Chapters 5 and 6, we discussed the importance of the teacher's modeling literacy practices and reading and talking about books with students. Some other ideas for providing adult models are presented below.

A "Visiting Reader" Program

Invite people from outside the school to read to your students. The police chief, the high school or college basketball coach, the manager of the sporting-goods shop or the bike store, the owner of the ice cream shop—all these can be great models. Invite them to come in and bring something they like to read, or to read something that you have chosen. Let them talk about reading in their own lives. Visiting readers don't have to be famous, even locally; parents make great visiting readers, as do older siblings and other relatives. Many times visiting readers are a bit anxious, so be sure to be there to introduce them, to support them, and to help with the question and answers. Keeping a photo gallery of all the visiting readers in a school, along with pictures of the books they have chosen, is a great way to "spread the word" as well. The more these visiting readers can represent different life paths, cultural groups, and age groups, the fuller the picture of lifelong reading that students can develop.

"What Are You Reading?" Interviews

If visitors are hard to come by, "What are you reading?" interviews may be easier. Patterned after common inserts in newspapers and magazines, these ask simple questions of well-known, and not-so-well known people (see Figure 10.2). This is

What's Hot . . . Books for Teens

Athena Lamberis
Sophomore, Evanston Township High School

The Joy Luck Club
by Amy Tan
(Ivy Books, NY)

"This novel portrays the detailed realities of mother–daughter relationships through tragedy, hope, and love."

Jesse Blachowicz
Sophomore, Evanston Township High School

She's Come Undone
by Wally Lamb
(Pocket Books, NY)

"Though it's slow at first, you won't be able to put this book down as Delores's life unfolds and captures you."

FIGURE 10.2. Two "What are you reading?" interviews.

an excellent reading and writing activity; it can also be an excellent use of telecommunication ability.

Books as Models of Mature Readership

Biographies and other books in which reading and writing play a prominent part present other models of mature readership. Such books as *More Than Anything Else* (Bradby, 1995), which includes a moving vignette about literacy in the life of Booker T. Washington, and the more sophisticated *The Road from Coorain*, Jill Ker Conway's (1989) story of moving from a childhood in the Australian outback to become president of a university, movingly recount the important role reading and writing can play in life development.

Authors' Biographies; Author/Illustrator Websites

Author biographies are another great way to learn about living authors, and many authors (and book illustrators too) have websites for contacting them directly. An author's biography or website usually focuses on the part reading and writing play in the author's life, and a favorite author is often a good model for a student. There are many fine references about authors and illustrators in texts on juvenile literature (Norton, 1999; Temple, Martinez, Yokota, & Naylor, 1996). For constantly updated and new information, Yokota, Anderson, and McFarlane (1999) have singled out a number of excellent websites for locating information about authors and illustrators, such as the following:

• Index to Internet Sites: Children's and Young Adults' Authors and Illustrators (*www.falcon.jmu.edu/~ramseyil/biochildhome.htm*). This comprehensive site is the Internet School Library Media Center's index to websites of authors and illustrators, as well as to other directory sites for authors and illustrators. Also included are links to teacher resource files of biographical information and lesson plans for particular books, as well as online resources for some of the authors.
• The Scoop (*www.friendly.net/scoop*). This online magazine features reviews of children's books, activities for children, and information for teachers. Also included are interviews with authors and illustrators, as well as links to related sites.
• Telling Stories with Pictures: The Art of Children's Book Illustration (*www. decordova.org/decordova/exhibit/stories/index.html*). This website describes different styles and techniques illustrators use, as well as the steps an illustrator takes from start to finish when illustrating a book. Other author and illustrator sites are linked from here.
• Yahoo: Links to Children's Author/Illustrator websites (*www. dir.yahoo. com/arts/humanities/literature/genres/children_s/authors/*). This site offers links to

Web pages for many authors and illustrators, ranging from creators of classics (e.g., A. A. Milne and Beatrix Potter) to well-known contemporary authors and illustrators, as well as many who are less widely known. The links connect multiple sites for certain authors, as well as the commercial sites of authors' publishers.

• Yahooligans Collection of Author and Illustrator Sites (*www. yahooligans. com/Art_Soup/Books_and_Reading/Authors/*). This site has links to many authors and illustrators. It overlaps somewhat with the one just described. However, as Yahooligans is meant to be accessed by children, it emphasizes student appeal and student user-friendliness.

Developing Self-Awareness and Confidence as Readers

Whereas models of good readership encourage a student to say "I want to do that," self-awareness as a reader is the student's answering, "I *can* do that. I *am* a reader." In the preceding chapters, we have shared many ideas for engaging students in reading and comprehending. There are many other classroom-tested ideas that highlight a student's identity as a reader. Some that are widely used are discussed below.

Book Journals

Keeping a book list or book journal is a perfect way for students to record the growing number of books they have read, to make notes about favorite authors, to keep a personal "new and interesting word" list, to jot down quotes that strike their fancy, and so forth. These can be simple (see Figure 10.3) or more elaborate (see Figure 10.4). They also lend themselves to the computer for record keeping; hypercard design is a possibility for the very technically minded (see Figure 10.5).

Book Ownership

Book ownership is another way to say, "I am a reader." Even children who are not avid readers may be excited by a shiny, new-smelling book or a real treasure find in a used-book sale. There are many book-purchasing clubs for students of all ages. These not only provide low-cost, high-quality new books; they have bonus point features that allow a teacher to assemble a classroom library at low cost. Two well-known companies that host book-purchasing clubs for all ages are the following:

• Scholastic (*www.scholastic.com/bookclubs*). Clubs are available at these levels: Preschool (Firefly), K–1 (Seesaw), 2–3 (Lucky), 4–6 (Arrow), and 7–8 (Tab).
• Troll (*www.troll.com*). Clubs are available at these levels: Pre K–K, K–1, 2–3, 4–6, and 6–9.

Date finished	Title	Author	Comment

FIGURE 10.3. A simple book list.

Book Record		
Title _____ Author _____		
Favorite Part (Pages _____)	Drawing Inspired by Book (explain)	
Recommendations: Who would like this book and why?		

FIGURE 10.4. A more elaborate book record.

Title and Author:		
Type (Genre):		
Short Summary:		
Other Books Like This:	Other Books by Same Author:	New Vocabulary:

FIGURE 10.5. A Hypercard format for book records.

In cases where money for book ownership is a problem, book sales can often be a real boon. Most libraries conduct one or more annual sales where inexpensive paperbacks can be had for a song. Taking a book sale field trip can be a great way to build an inexpensive library. Some library book sales have bag sales on the final day, or will donate some books to schools in exchange for help with cleanup. Garage sales are also a fine and inexpensive source of books.

Book Swaps

Book swaps are fun and cost nothing. Students each bring in at least one book, but as many as they like, and are given a ticket for redeeming another book. Having extra books is always a good thing, as some students may forget. Then the swap room can be open for a new selection at regular intervals, and students can reswap a book after it has been read. Pasting an index card in the back of each book can allow each swapper/reader to add his or her name and a small comment.

Other Sources for Books

Awareness that readers read a variety of things can be encouraged by pursuing the ideas mentioned above, and also by visiting libraries, bookstores, used bookstores, and online book sellers. They make it possible to locate books on every conceivable interest and level.

Book Clubs

Being a member of a book discussion club is one way we adults continue our habit of reading. Being able to discuss books in a social setting, to share our ideas and hear new ideas, and to browse books and choose what to read—these are all ways in which reading as a social process helps us grow and mature. We talked about classroom book clubs in Chapter 6.

Many schools are developing new models for book clubs. For instance, Sandy Olson's third-grade class at Grove Elementary School in Northbrook, Illinois, observed that Oprah Winfrey's book club on the *Oprah* TV show never included books for them ("The Little O's Book Club," 1998). Student Andrew Pines noted, "We decided to form a club of our own. We called it the Little O's Book Club" (1998, p. 22). They chose books such as biographies of Louis Braille, books by Roald Dahl, and others for their reading; they ultimately wrote to Oprah Winfrey, who invited them to appear on her show. In their school, the club continued to meet the next year and inspired the incoming group of third graders to form a similar club. The superintendent of the district remarked that the formation of the book club was just one step in the students' development as lifelong readers.

A second example involves older students. Reading specialist Christine Bogue and librarian Gail Bush, who work with older readers in a departmentalized setting, started the Reader's Society as an extracurricular school activity (Bogue & Bush, 1999). Cosponsored by the school's English department and the library, the Reader's Society meets weekly in the morning before school for "breakfast meetings" or in homeroom time set aside for extracurricular activities. Generally, a year of the Reader's Society involves a cycle of reading and discussing a book or two and then taking a field trip on a weekend afternoon to a chain bookstore (with a cafe!). Students read an average of six books a year, discussing selected chapters each day. Along with discussion, students have submitted reviews to *amazon.com*.

Students lead the discussions; the Reader's Society is a student-led group. Teachers facilitate the group by scheduling the discussions, planning field trips, and driving the van for field trips. Student participants come from all four grades represented in the school, and from accelerated to special education curricula. One of the participants noted, "As my class time had become more saturated with homework and activities, I have continued to read for pleasure during the school year due to my involvement in Reader's Society" (quoted in Bogue & Bush, 1999, p. 15). This and the Little O's Book Club are just two examples of book clubs where membership helps students expand their picture of themselves as readers and writers.

Providing Access to and Experience with a Broad Range of Literacy Materials

The Importance of a Wide Range of Materials

In a fascinating book, *Voices of Readers* (Carlsen & Sherrill, 1988), the authors asked college students what most affected their becoming (or not becoming) readers. Over and over again, the young adults responded that the reading and overanalyzing of literature that took place in their classrooms turned them away from reading, squeezed all the enjoyment out of it, and led to their rejection of reading as a personal activity. One of our young teachers in training responded to *Voices of Readers* by noting that English classes and reading in school always seemed aimed toward "making us all be English majors." Another young man commented, "I wanted to read about *real* things, not stories. And I wanted to read manuals for fixing my car when I was in high school." A third young teacher noted, "Even those of us who *are* English majors don't want to read *War and Peace* all the time!"

Like being all dressed up and having no place to go, having the desire and confidence to read is frustrating if we do not have a wide variety of good things to read—things that both feed and expand our interests—and the time to read them. Attention to developing literacy in school needs to acknowledge that students become literate in a wide variety of ways. Certainly teachers need to know the best sources of classic literature for students of all ages, but they also need to keep aware of newly emerging authors and books (the classics of the next century), as well as other popular fiction and nonfiction for children, adolescents, and young adults.

Informational books need to form a substantial part of the literacy materials in schools as well. Much of adults' reading is reading for information. The average American spends about 165 hours a year with newspapers, 99 hours with books, and 84 hours with magazines (Heath, 1997); much of all of this time is spent reading for information. The new state standards and assessments are also making new demands on informational reading. Teachers need resources for finding a variety of materials suitable for the classroom, and strategies for encouraging their use. Beverly Kobrin's resource books, *Eyeopeners!* and *Eyeopeners II!* (Kobrin, 1988, 1995), are excellent starting points for informational reading material for schools.

Magazines, so-called 'zines (those small-press magazines), and newspapers bring up-to-the-moment news into the classroom, if money is available for purchasing they can also be either archived for reference use or cut apart for various purposes. There are several excellent guides to periodicals for children, and the depth and breadth of the selection possible may surprise you (Richardson, 1991; Stoll, 1997).

Other reading material in the classroom might include the following:

Specialized dictionaries and encyclopedias.
Catalogues and brochures.
Manuals for computers and other machines.
Games and their directions.
Cookbooks and recipe collections.
Reference books.
Books on tape.
Books on film.
Books and references on CD-ROMs and the Internet.
Electronic books. (For those students who are deeply and truly into technology, electronic books may draw them in.)

Web-Based Resources for Children's Literature

There are many classic resources for finding out about children's literature. You may wish to update these traditional resources with Web-based resources such as the following (Yokota et al., 1999):

• Children's Literature Web Guide (*www.acs.ucalgary.ca/~dkbrown/index. html*). This is the most comprehensive guide to Internet resources related to books for children and young adults. It contains links to high-quality sites through the "Web-Traveler's Toolkit: Essential Kid Lit Websites." Discussion boards offer visitors opportunities to read and contribute their thoughts on special topics, to comment on specific titles, or to request information and post news. Quick references to award-winning books, lists of "best books," best-seller lists, and teaching ideas for specific books can also be found. There are links to resources for teachers, parents, and librarians, including links to author/illustrator websites.

• American Library Association: Young Adult Library Services Association (*www.ala.org/yalsa/*). The Young Adult Library Services Association of the American Library Association is committed to providing high-quality library service to young adults, focusing on the need to "understand and respect the unique informational, educational and recreational needs of teenagers." This site provides general information about the organization and its work, including an extensive set of book lists, awards, and programs.

• Center for the Study of Books in Spanish for Children and Adolescents (*www.csusm.edu/campus_centers/csb/*). This center's information can be viewed in

English or in Spanish. There are weekly updates of recommended books, as well as a feature that creates a customized book list. Information about the work of the center (e.g., workshops, conferences, and publications) and links to related sites can also be found.

Encouraging Wide Reading and Making Time to Read

With all this wealth of reading materials, teachers need to make sure students have time to use them—to savor, to browse, and to read carefully. Having a classroom collection is essential to this kind of "book walking." Waiting until the scheduled library time is a sure interest killer. In Chapter 3, we talked about the importance of a classroom library. For older students, especially adolescents, having paperbacks that can fit into a pocket is another inducement for reading.

Time for Self-Selected Reading

Along with having a wide variety of materials to read, *time* to read is critical. Time for some form of self-selected reading—SILR (scaffolded independent-level reading) and Read and Relax (as we described in Chapter 3), SSR (sustained silent reading), DEAR (drop everything and read), or one of many other names for such reading—is important to building the habit of reading. But "reading time" requires careful preparation and input by a teacher; the teacher can't just say, "You kids all go read now." Each student must have several items for reading available and ready to go. Spending all of the "reading time" looking for something to read is counterproductive.

One school of thought is that each of us should have a "stretcher" and a "coaster" as well as a "just right" book or magazine at all times. This is sometimes called the "bedside" model for selecting reading materials. Think about the basket or end table next to your bed. Chances are that you have some professional reading there, a book or magazine on a hobby or interest, a bit of fluff (who buys all those copies of *People* magazine anyhow?), and the latest novel or informational book we never have enough time for. Students' desks should have the same selection.

For reluctant readers, teachers may have to come up with constant "temptations" to get the reading going. Short, varied pieces often help such a student ease into reading longer things. Using paired reading or supported reading is another method for making self-selected reading time more productive for younger readers or readers who need more support of either a social or an intellectual nature. Self-selected reading does not necessarily have to be individual or silent. Quiet partner reading is often a wonderful way to proceed.

For middle school or departmentalized students, finding the time for self-selected reading is often difficult. If this time cannot be built into the advisory or homeroom period, you might want to try "Backpack Books." The team responsible for a group of students takes responsibility for seeing that each student has a book in his or her backpack at all times. Each classroom must also have a selection of magazines, or magazines for the group can circulate. The understanding is that the last 5 minutes of each departmentalized class will be time for "backpack reading," and also that at any point when there is extra time or a waiting period, this too is "Backpack Book" time. Teachers must work as a team to encourage, monitor, and reward students who use this time well. Teachers who use "Backpack Books" find that students get in the habit of whipping out a book whenever there are a few minutes to spare, and some have even seen students reading voluntarily on school buses!

Having good models, access to excellent materials, and adequate time for reading is still not enough to get all students into reading, however. To have a good "fit" between students and materials, teachers need to know what their students' interests are, and to create new interests as well as providing for current interests.

Assessing Students' Interests

Interest inventories are a quick way for teachers to learn about students' interests early in the year. Using a survey (Johns & Lenski, 1997; see Figure 10.6), students can indicate their interests. They can do this with pen and pencil, can enter their answers into a computer database for comparative charting, or can respond in a variety of other ways.

One interesting and interactive method of inventorying interests is having students use an interest inventory as a framework for interviewing each other. Each interviewer can then write a profile of his or her interviewee as a reader (see Figure 10.7).

The teacher can have each student interviewer write the interview without giving the interviewee's name and can then post all of the interviews and ask the rest of the class to guess who is being described. These activities not only let the teacher know what the interests in the class are; it helps students come to know their classmates better and find others with similar interests.

An interactive and physical type of interest inventory is called "book stacking" (Blachowicz & Wimett, 1994). Each student is asked to bring three things he or she likes to read to class (these can be books, magazines, etc.). In a school where students might not own books, they can go to the library and select three items. Then these are placed on chairs, and the students circulate among the chairs and look for something new that they might like to read. They can leave notes for the other students indicating similar interests. While the students are circulating, the teacher also circulates and makes notes of interests and similarities.

Interest Inventory

Name _____   Class _____

1. What do you like to do after school?
2. What activities do you like to do on weekends?
3. What are your hobbies?
4. What do you like to do in your free time?
5. When you are really tired, what do you like to do?
6. What shows or sports do you like to watch on TV?
7. What is a good movie you have seen?
8. What kind of movies do you like?
9. What is a good book you have read?
10. What kinds of books do you like to read?
11. What is your favorite magazine?
12. What is your favorite game?
13. What is your favorite class at school? Least favorite?
14. Where would you like to go on vacation?
15. What is something you would like to learn to do or do better?
16. If you could talk to anyone living or dead, who would you choose to talk to? What would you want to ask them?

FIGURE 10.6. An inventory for assessing students' interests. From *Improving Reading: A Handbook of Strategies, 2nd Edition* (pp. 18–19), by Jerry L. Johns and Susan Davis Lenski. Copyright 1997 by Kendall/Hunt Publishing Company. Used with permission.

Creating New Interests

Either students or teachers can give book talks to share interesting books with others. The presenter picks a book he or she likes and describes it to the group, without "giving away" things that would spoil the plot or making a dull list of informational categories. Presenters can focus on character, plot, informational questions, art, descriptive language—anything that will "sell" their books. Reading aloud a short passage from a book is a useful way to share the level of difficulty with others. Teams can give book talks, using drama, reading, drawing on the overhead projector, and/or musical background.

Using technology for recommendations is also excellent. Commercial sites such as *amazon.com* have excellent listings by titles, authors, and subjects, along with reviews. Your students can add reviews themselves and see themselves as

---

My Secret Reader
by Jamie J.

My secret reader has 2 brothers and no sisters. He likes to go swimming with this family and play cards at home. He has a cat named Sissy which he and his brothers take turns taking care of.

The <u>Harry Potter</u> books are my reader's favorites but the best book he ever read was <u>Encyclopedia Brown</u>. He uses the library mostly in the summer and uses the class or school library during school. His best friend and him plays Nintendo and basketball. When he grows up he would like to be a lawyer like his mom and dad, or maybe a fisherman.

Can you guess who my secret reader is?

FIGURE 10.7. A student-to-student interview, based on an interest inventory.

readers and critics on the Internet. Some classrooms create their own review file, either on a hypercard stack, in a database, or in a plain old card file. Students love to find a book recommended by a friend, by an older student or sibling who read it another school year, or by someone far away.

The Internet Book Club and the Biography Project (access through *www. collaboratory.acns.nwu.edu/neighborhood/mediaspace/*) are two other excellent ways in which students can share book reviews across time and space.

Connecting with the Larger World of Literacy

Connecting beyond the classroom helps students see that literacy is embedded in the everyday life beyond school. Teachers can facilitate this connection by consciously trying to do something each week or each month that draws on and draws in the wider world of literacy.

Home–School Ideas

The connection between home and school is an essential ones. Try the following activities to strengthen that bond:

1. Have students collect family stories. Most families have some often-told funny or dramatic story. Have students take dictation from their parents, grandparents, or other relatives and report stories to the class. These can be collected into a book for the class.

The same thing can be done with family sayings. Don't all of us have some often-repeated saying that we associate with a parent, grandparent, or other favorite adult? "It's easier to catch flies with honey than with vinegar" is one we remember. Have students collect these and share them with the class. In one class, a favorite one was "She's got too much sour cream on that taco," which meant the person being described was too loud and "show-offy." These are wonderful multicultural activities as well, because many cultures have different sayings for the same essential truth.

2. Have students do a narrative photo album. Encourage them to collect photos and write captions to introduce their families or communities. Photos can be photocopied and returned, and the narratives can be handwritten or typed in.

3. Have children write letters or do a class newsletter to let parents know what is going on in the class. Asking the parents to write back is an excellent way to keep the project going.

Community–School Ideas

Schools also need to make visible the connection between what is done in school and what goes on in the wider community. A "visiting reader" program (described above) is a wonderful way to bring the community into the classroom. Another tactic is to encourage students to ask, on every field trip or excursion, "What reading do you do here? What's important to read and write for your work?" This beings the variety of reading and writing home to students.

Having your students keep an observation list on every field trip of things to read is another way to emphasize them. Along with collecting samples of brochures, memos, newsletters, and other reading materials from businesses, museums, zoos, and so on, students can make posters and collections of "reading at the museum" or "reading at the grocery store."

Encouraging students to participate in summer reading games or other activities at their local library opens up another avenue of literacy. Most libraries have summer and after-school programs. Some schools send home summer reading lists but allow the option of students' participating in a library program instead.

Many newspapers and magazines have "kids' pages." Having students read and contribute to these pages can open up the world of journalism to them at a young age. Nothing is so rewarding to young writers as seeing their work in print for others to read.

District and community contests are another way to make reading and writing exciting and rewarding. Science fairs, history fairs, and the like are great motivators for writing. Similarly, projects for Boy and Girl Scouts, 4-H, Boys' and Girls' Clubs, and similar groups often involve writing and reading. Contact these groups to find out what appeals to your students.

School sports loom large in the lives of many students. Some judicious networking with physical education teachers and coaches can sometimes bear fruit for literacy. Something as simple as asking a physical education teacher to read his or her students some short item from the sports pages each day can pique interest and emphasize that sports people read. One teacher who served as her daughter's "soccer mom" found easy-to-read soccer items, which she photocopied and provided to the coach as handouts each week.

One middle school coach emulates Coach Phil Jackson, formerly of the Chicago Bulls and now of the Los Angeles Lakers, who gives a book to each of his players at the start of each season; each book is chosen individually for that person. Working in collaboration with the middle school's booster club, which funds the project, and the school librarian, who helps with the selections, the coach provides a gift book for each player at the end of each season. Another coach, working with the same resources, keeps a bag of magazines on the bus for long trips. He has also purchased small snap-on lights for bus reading. In a school setting, having every teacher think about literacy is one way to spread the word that reading is a real-world skill.

Putting It All Together

Encouraging lifelong literacy takes attention beyond the development of skills and strategies for good comprehension. And this most important goal of literacy instruction requires the same attention as all other instruction. To encourage students to want to read and to consider reading as a tool for almost every life activity, we need to provide models of adult reading and help them develop an awareness of themselves as readers and confidence in their own abilities. We need to make reading readily available to them by guiding them through a variety of types of literature. Also, we need to ensure that all students have broad experiences with literacy, to encourage wide reading and provide time for reading, and to help them make the connection between school literacy and literacy in the larger world. Achieving these goals takes attention, intervention, support, and (to a certain degree) seduction. The rewards of drawing students into lifelong literacy, however are well worth the effort.

References

Abromitis, B. (1992). *New directions in vocabulary*. Rolling Meadows, IL: Blue Ribbon Press.

Allington, R. L., & Walmsley, S. A. (Eds.). (1995). *No quick fix: Rethinking literacy programs in America's elementary schools*. New York: Teachers College Press.

Almasi, J. (1995). The nature of fourth graders' sociocognitive conflicts in peer-led and teacher-led discussions of literature. *Reading Research Quarterly, 30*, 314–351.

American Institute of Research. (2007). *National Assessment of Educational Progress*. Washington, DC: Author.

Amery, H., Kinienko, K., & Cartwright, S. (1989). *The first thousand words in Russian*. London: Usborne.

Anderson, L. W., & Krathwohl, D. R. (Eds.). (2001). *A taxonomy of learning, teaching and assessing: A revision of Bloom's taxonomy of educational objectives*. New York: Longman.

Anderson, R. C. (1972). How to construct achievement tests to assess comprehension. *Review of Educational Reasearch, 42*, 145–170.

Anderson, R. C., Hiebert, E., Scott, J., & Wilkinson, J. (1985). *Becoming a nation of readers: The report of the Commission on Reading with contributions from members of the Commission on Reading*. Washington, DC: National Academy of Education.

Anderson, R. C., Wilson, P., & Fielding, L. (1988). Growth in reading and how children spend their time outside of school. *Reading Research Quarterly, 23*, 285–303.

Atwell, N. (1987). *In the middle: Writing, reading and learning with adolescents*. Portsmouth, NH: Boynton/Cook.

Baker, L., & Brown, A. (1984). Metacognitive skills of reading. In P. D. Pearson, M. Kamil, P. Mosenthal, & R. Barr (Eds.), *Handbook of reading research* (pp. 353–394). New York: Longman.

Barr, R., Blachowicz, C. L. Z., Bates, A., Katz, C., & Kaufman, B. (2007). *Reading diagnosis for teachers: An instructional approach* (5th ed.). New York: Allyn & Bacon.

Bash, B. (1990). *Urban roosts: Where birds nest in the city.* San Francisco: Sierra Club Books.

Baumann, J. F., Jones, L. A., & Seifert-Kessell, N. (1993). Using think alouds to enhance children's comprehension monitoring abilities. *Journal of Reading Behavior, 24,* 143–172.

Beck, I. L., & McKeown, M. G. (1981). Developing questions that promote comprehension: The story map. *Language Arts, 58,* 913–918.

Beck, I. L., McKeown, M. G., Hamilton, R. L., & Kucan, L. (1997). *Questioning the author: An approach for enhancing student engagement with text.* Newark, DE: International Reading Association.

Beck, I. L., McKeown, M. G., & Kucan, L. (2002). *Bringing words to life: Robust vocabulary instruction.* New York: Guilford Press.

Beck, I., Perfetti, C., & McKeown, M. (1982). The effects of long-term vocabulary instruction on lexical access and reading comprehension. *Journal of Educational Psychology, 74,* 506–521.

Bender, L. (1989). *Island.* New York: Watts.

Betts, E. A. (1946). *Foundations of reading instruction.* New York: American Books.

Blachowicz, C. L. Z., Cieply, C., & Sullivan, D. (2001). Get the picture?: Classroom fluency snapshots. *Reading Psychology.*

Blachowicz, C. L. Z., & Fisher, P. J. L. (2006). *Teaching vocabulary in all classrooms* (3rd ed.). Columbus, OH: Pearson/Merrill-Prentice Hall.

Blachowicz, C. L. Z., Fisher, P. J. L., Costa, M., & Pozzi, M. (1993). *Researching vocabulary learning in middle school cooperative reading groups: A teacher–researcher collaboration.* Paper presented at the Tenth Great Lakes Regional Reading Conference, Chicago.

Blachowicz, C. L. Z., & Obrochta, C. (2005). Vocabulary visits: Developing primary content vocabulary. *The Reading Teacher, 59*(3), 262–269.

Blachowicz, C. L. Z., & Obrochta, C. (2007). *"Tweaking Practice": Modifying read-alouds to enhance content vocabulary learning in grade 1.* National Reading Conference Yearbook, 111–121. Oak Creek, WI: National Reading Conference.

Blachowicz, C. L. Z., & Wimett, C. (1994). Response to literature: Models for new teachers. In E. Cramer & M. Castle (Eds.), *Fostering a life-long love of reading* (pp. 183–196). Newark, DE: International Reading Association.

Blachowicz, C. L. Z., & Zabroske, B. (1990). Context instruction: A metacognitive approach for at-risk readers. *Journal of Reading, 33,* 504–508.

Bloom, B. (1956). *Taxonomy of educational objectives: Handbook I. Cognitive domain.* New York: McKay.

Blumberg, R. (2001). *Shipwrecked!: The true adventures of a Japanese boy.* New York: HarperCollins.

Bogue, C. A., & Bush, G. (1999). Come join the Reader's Society: A student-directed book discussion group. *Illinois Reading Council Journal, 27*(1), 8–15.

Booth, J. (1994). *Big bugs.* San Diego: Harcourt, Brace.

Bortnick, R., & Lopardo, G. (1973). An instructional application of the cloze procedure. *Journal of Reading, 16,* 296–300.

Boyd, F. B., & Ikpeze, C. H. (2007). Navigating a literacy landscape: Teaching conceptual understanding with multiple text types. *Journal of Literacy Research, 39*(2), 217–248.

Bradby, M. (1995). *More than anything else.* New York: Orchard Books.

Bransford, J. D., Brown, A. L., & Cocking, R. R. (1999). *How people learn: Brain, mind, experience and school.* Washington, DC: National Research Council.

Bridge, C. A., & Tiemey, R. J. (1981). The inferential operations of children across text with narrative and expository tendencies. *Journal of Reading Behavior, 13,* 201–214.

Buikema, J. L., & Graves, M. F. (1993). Teaching students to use context clues to infer word meanings. *Journal of Reading, 36,* 450–457.

Bush, G. (2003). *The school buddy system.* Chicago: American Library Association

Calkins, L. (1994). *The art of teaching writing.* Portsmouth, NH: Heinemann Educational Books

Carlsen, G. R., & Sherrill, A. (1988). *Voices of readers: How we come to love books.* Urbana, IL: National Council of Teachers of English.

Carr, E., & Ogle, D. M. (1987). A strategy for comprehension and summarization. *Journal of Reading, 30,* 626–631.

Cassie, B., & Pallotta, J. (1995). *The butterfly alphabet book.* Watertown, MA: Charlesbridge.

Carwardine, M. (2002). *Whales, dolphins and porpoises.* Washington, DC: Smithsonian Handbooks.

Chicago Public Schools, Office of Literacy. (2004). *Mid-tier reading project.* Integrated units. Chicago: Author.

Chicago Public Schools, Office of Literacy. (2006). *Nonfiction leveled text sets. Grades 5–8.* Chicago: Author.

Clay, M. (1993). *Reading recovery: A guidebook for teachers in training.* Portsmouth, NH: Heinemann.

Cleary, B. (1983). *Dear Mr. Henshaw.* New York: Morrow.

Cole, J. (1995). *The magic school bus inside a hurricane.* New York: Scholastic.

Conway, J. K. (1989). *The road from Coorain.* New York: Knopf.

Cunningham, A. E. (2005). Vocabulary growth through independent reading and reading aloud to children. In E. H. Hiebert & M. Kamil (Eds.), *Teaching and learning vocabulary: Bringing research to practice* (pp. 45–68). Mahwah, NJ: Erlbaum.

Cunningham, A. E., & Stanovich, K. E. (1997). Early reading acquisition and its relation to reading experience and ability 10 years later. *Developmental Psychology, 33*(6), 934–945.

Cunningham, A. E., & Stanovich, K. E. (1998, Spring–Summer). What reading does for the mind. *American Educator,* pp. 8–17.

Curtis, C. P. (1995). *The Watsons go to Birmingham—1963.* New York: Delacorte Press.

Dahl, R. (1982). *The BFG.* New York: Farrar, Straus & Giroux.

Dale, E., & O'Rourke, J. P. (1981). *The living word vocabulary: A national vocabulary inventory.* Chicago: World Book–Childcraft International.

Daniels, H. (1996). *Literature circles: Voice and choice in the student-centered classroom.* York, ME: Stenhouse.

Daniels, H., & Bizar, M. (1999). *Methods that matter: Six structures for best practice classrooms.* York, ME: Stenhouse.

Dembo, M. H., & Eaton, M. J. (2000). Self-regulation of academic learning in middle-level schools. *Elementary School Journal, 100*(5), 473–490.

Dorn, L. J., & Soffos, C. (2001). *Shaping literate minds: Developing self-regulated learners*. Portland, ME: Stenhouse.

Downing, J., & Leong, C. K. (1982). *Psychology of reading*. New York: Macmillan.

Duke, N. K. (2000). 3.6 minutes per day: The scarcity of informational texts in first grade. *Reading Research Quarterly, 35*, 202–224.

Duke, N. K. (2004a). The case for informational text. *Educational Leadership, 61*(6), 40–44.

Duke, N. K. (2004b). Reading to learn has no minimum age: Nonfiction books for K–3. *Children's Book Council Features, 57*(2).

Duke, N. K., & Moses, A. M. (2004). On what crosses our desks and what does not [Review of the book *Language, literacy and cognitive development: The development and consequences of symbolic communication*.]. *Reading Research Quarterly, 39*, 360–366.

Durrell, D. (1956). *Durrell analysis of reading difficulty*. New York: Harcourt, Brace & World.

Echeverria, J., Vogt, M. E., & Short, D. J. (2008). *Making content comprehensible for English learners: The SIOP model*. Boston: Allyn & Bacon.

Eller, G., Pappas, C., & Brown, E. (1988). The lexical development of kindergartners: Learning from written context. *Journal of Reading Behavior, 20*, 5–24.

Elley, W. B. (1988). Vocabulary acquisition from listening to stories. *Reading Research Quarterly, 24*, 174–187.

Erlbach, A. (1997). *Sidewalk games around the world*. Brookfield, CT: Millbrook Press.

Espy, W. R. (1975). *An almanac of words at play*. New York: Potter.

Evans, K. (1966). A closer look at literature discussion groups: The influence of gender on student response and discourse. *New Advocate, 9*, 183–196.

Fleischman, P. (1985). *I am Phoenix*. New York: Harper & Row.

Fleischman, P. (1988). *Joyful noise: Poems for two voices*. New York: Harper & Row.

Fountas, I., & Pinnell, G. S. (2001). *Guiding readers and writers: Teaching comprehension, genre, and content literacy*. Portsmouth, NH: Heinemann.

Freedman, R. (2005). *Children of the Great Depression*. New York: Clarion Books.

Freeman, D. E., & Freeman, Y. S. (2000). *Teaching reading in multilingual classrooms*. Portsmouth, NH: Heinemann.

Gambrell, L., & Almasi, J. F. (1996). *Lively discussions: Fostering engaged reading*. Newark, DE: International Reading Association.

Gambrell, L., Block, C., & Pressley, M. (2002). Improving comprehension instruction: An urgent priority. In C. Block, L. Gambrell, & M. Pressley (Eds.), *Improving reading comprehension* (pp. 3–16). Newark, DE: International Reading Association.

George, J. C. (1972). *Julie of the wolves*. New York: HarperCollins.

Gildea, P. M., Miller, G. A., & Wurtenberg, C. L. (1990). Contextual enrichment by videodisk. In D. B. Nix & R. Spiro (Eds.), *Multimedia: Exploring ideas in high technology*. Hillsdale, NJ: Erlbaum.

Golden, J., & Pappas, C. (1987). *A critical review of retelling procedures research or children's cognitive processing of written text*. Paper presented at the annual meeting of the National Reading Conference. St. Petersburg, FL.

Graves, D. (1994). *A fresh look at writing*. Portsmouth, NH: Heinemann.

Graves, M., & Hammond, H. K. (1980). A validated procedure for teaching prefixes and its effect on students ability to assign meanings to novel words. In M. Kamil & A. Moe (Eds.), *Perspectives on reading research and instruction* (pp. 184–188). Washington, DC: National Reading Conference.

Guszak, F. J. (1967). Teacher questioning and reading. *The Reading Teacher, 21*, 227–234.

Gwynne, F. (1970). *The king who rained*. New York: Simon & Schuster.

Haggard, M. R. (1985). An interactive strategies approach to content reading. *Journal of Reading, 29*, 204–210.

Harvey, S., & Goudvis, A. (2007). *Strategies that work*. Portland, ME: Stenhouse.

Heath, R. P. (1997). In so many words: How technology reshapes the reading habit. *American Demographics, 19*(3), 11–14.

Heimler, C. H., Daniel, L., & Lockard, J. D. (1984). *Focus on life science*. Columbus, OH: Merrill.

Helfgott & Westhaven. (1997). *Inspiration* [Computer software].

Herman, P. A., & Dole, J. (1988). Theory and practice in vocabulary learning and instruction. *Elementary School Journal, 89*, 43–54.

Hiebert, E. H., & Kamil, M. L. (Eds.). (2005). *Teaching and learning vocabulary: Bringing research to practice*. Mahwah, NJ: Erlbaum.

Hitte, K., & Hayes, W. D. (1970). *Mexicali soup*. New York: Parents' Magazine Press.

Hoffman, J. V. (1992). Critical reading and thinking across the curriculum. *Language Arts, 69*, 121–124.

Hughes, L. (1997). Thank you, Ma'm. In E. Current-Garcia (Ed.), *American short stories* (6th ed.). Montgomery, AL: Auburn University Press.

Hyerle, D. (2000). *A field guide to using visual tools*. Alexandria, VA: ASCD.

Illinois State Educational Standards. (1997). Illinois State Board of Education Website. Available at *www.ISBE.org*.

Jensen, E. (1998). How Julie's brain learns. *Educational Leadership*.

Johns, J. L. (1993). *Basic reading inventory* (5th ed.). Dubuque, IA: Kendall/Hunt.

Johns, J. L., & Lenski, S. D. (1997). *Improving reading: A handbook of strategies* (2nd ed.). Dubuque, IA: Kendall/Hunt.

Kalman, B., & Reiach, M. A. (2002). *The life cycle of a butterfly*. St. Catherine, Ontario: Crabtree Publishers.

Katz, C., Polkoff, L., & Gurvitz, D. (2005). "Shhh . . . I'm reading": Scaffolded independent-level reading. *School Talk, 10*(2), 1–3.

Kobrin, B. (1988). *Eyeopeners!: How to choose and use children's books about real people, places, and things*. New York: Viking.

Kobrin, B. (1995). *Eyeopeners II: Children's books to answer children's questions about the world around them*. New York: Scholastic.

Koren, S. (1999). Vocabulary instruction through hypertext: Are there advantages over conventional methods of teaching? *Teaching English as a Second or Foreign Language, 4*(1), 1–13.

Larson, R. E., Boswell, L., & Stiff, L. (1997). *Heath passport to mathematics, Book 2*. Evanston, IL: Heath.

Lasky, K. (1993). *Monarchs*. San Diego: Harcourt, Brace.

Lawrence, J. (1968). *Harriet and the promised land*. New York: Windmill Books.

Leal, D. J. (1992). The nature of talk about three types of text during peer group discussions. *Journal of Reading Behavior, 24,* 265–287.

Leal, D. J. (1996). Transforming grand conversations into grand creations: Using different types of text to influence student discussion. In L. Gambrell & J. F. Almasi (Eds.), *Lively discussions! Fostering engaged reading* (pp. 149–168). Newark, DE: International Reading Association.

Leal, D., & Moss, B. (1999). Exploring the realm of the gifted reader: Encounters with informational text. *Reading Horizons, 40*(2), 81–101.

Little O's Book Club. (1998). *Reading Today, 16*(2), 1–22.

Lytle, S. L. (1982). *Exploring comprehension style: A study of twelfth grade readers' transactions with text.* Unpublished doctoral dissertation, University of Pennsylvania.

Makine, A. (1997). *Dreams of my Russian summers.* New York: Aracde/Little, Brown.

Mallory, K., & Conley, A. (1989). *Rescue of the stranded whales.* New York: Simon & Schuster.

Many, J. E. (1996). Traversing the topical landscape: Exploring students' self-directed reading–writing–research processes. *Reading Research Quarterly, 31*(1), 12–35.

Many, J. E., Fyfe, R., Lewis, G., & Mitchell, L. (2004). Traversing the topical landscape: Exploring students' self-directed reading–writing–research processes. In R. B. Ruddell & N. J. Unrau (Eds.), *Theoretical models and processes of reading* (5th ed., pp. 684–719). Newark, DE: International Reading Association.

Maro, N. (2001). Reading to improve fluency. *Illinois Reading Council Journal, 29*(3), 10–18.

Martin, B. (1967). *Brown bear, brown bear, what do you see?* New York: Holt, Rinehart & Winston.

Martin, J. B. (1998). *Snowflake Bentley.* Boston: Houghton Mifflin.

Marzano, R. J., & Marzano, J. S. (1988). *A cluster approach to elementary vocabulary instruction.* Newark, DE: International Reading Association.

McConoughy, S. (1980). Using story structure in the classroom. *Language Arts, 57,* 157–165.

McGinley, W. J., & Denner, P. R. (1986). *The use of semantic impressions as a previewing activity for providing clues to a story's episodic structure.* Paper presented at the annual meeting of the Northern Rocky Mountains Educational Research Association, Jackson, WY.

McGinley, W. J., & Denner, P. R. (1987). Story impressions: A prereading/writing activity. *Journal of Reading, 31,* 248–253.

McKee, J., & Ogle, D. (2005). *Integrating instruction: Literacy and science.* New York: Guilford Press.

McKenna, M. (1978). Portmanteau words in reading instruction. *Language Arts, 55*(3), 315–317.

McKeown, M. G. (1985). The acquisition of word meaning from context by children of high and low ability. *Reading Research Quarterly, 20,* 482–496.

McKeown, M. G., Beck, I. L., & Worthy, M. J. (1993). Grappling with text ideas: Questioning the author. *The Reading Teacher, 46,* 8.

McLachlan, P. (2004). *Sara, plain and tall*. New York: HarperCollins.

McTighe, J., & Lyman, F. T., Jr. (1988). Cueing thinking in the classroom. *Educational Leadership, 45*(7), 18–24.

Mehan, J. (1979). *Learning lessons*. Cambridge, MA: Harvard University Press.

Milton, J. (1989). *Whales: The gentle giants*. New York: Random House.

Montgomery, S. (2006). *Quest for the Tree Kangaroo: Expedition to the Cloud Forest of New Guinea*. Boston: Hougton Mifflin.

Mora, J. K. (2006). Differentiating instruction for English learners: The Four by Four Model. In T. A. Young & N. L. Hadaway (Eds.), *Supporting the literacy development of English learners: Increasing success in all classrooms* (pp. 24–40). Newark, DE: International Reading Association.

Morris, D. (1999). *The Howard Street tutoring manual: Teaching at-risk readers in the primary grades*. New York: Guilford Press.

Morris, L. (1988). Retelling stories as a diagnostic tool. In S. M. Glazer, L. W. Searfoss, & I. M. Gentile (Eds.), *Reexamining reading diagnosis: New trends and procedures* (pp. 128–149). Newark, DE: International Reading Association.

Nagy, W. E. (1988). *Teaching vocabulary to improve reading comprehension*. Newark, DE: International Reading Association.

Nagy, W. E., & Anderson, R. C. (1984). How many words are there in printed school English? *Reading Research Quarterly, 19*, 303–330.

National Assessment of Educational Progress. (2005). The nation's report card on reading. Retrieved January 2008 from *nationsreportcard.gov/tuda_reading_mathematics_ 2005*.

National Assessment of Education Progress Frameworks for Comprehension. (2007). Retrieved August 4, 2007, from *www.nagb.org/pubs/r_framework_05/ch2.html#3*.

Nist, S. L., & Olejnik, S. (1995). The role of context and dictionary definitions on varying levels of word knowledge. *Reading Research Quarterly, 30*, 172–193.

North Carolina Rubric. Retrieved January 2007 from *intranet.cps.k12.il.us/assessments/ ideas_and_rubrics/rubric_bank/rubric_bank.html*.

Northfield Township Public Schools. (1999). *Language arts reference handbook*. Northfield, IL: Author.

Norton, D. E. (1999). *Through the eyes of a child: An introduction to children's literature*. Upper Saddle River, NJ: Merrill.

Norwood Park Rubric. Retrieved January 2007 from *intranet.cps.k12.il.us/assessments/ ideas_and_rubrics/rubric_bank/rubric_bank.html*.

O'Dell, S. (1960). *Island of the blue dolphins*. Boston: Houghton Mifflin.

Ogle, D. M. (1986). K-W-L: A teaching model that develops action reading of expository text. *The Reading Teacher, 40*, 564–570.

Ogle, D. M. (1992). Developing problem-solving through language arts instruction. In C. Collins & J. N. Mangieri (Eds.), *Teaching thinking: An agenda for the twenty-first century* (pp. 25–39). Hillsdale, NJ: Erlbaum.

Ogle, D. M. (2000a). Make it visual. In M. McLaughlin & M. E. Vogt (Eds.), *Creativity and innovation in content reading and learning* (pp. 103–114). Norwood, MA: Christopher-Gordon.

Ogle, D. M. (2000b). Multiple intelligences and reading instruction. In B. Lightner (Ed.), *Teaching for intelligence II: A collection of articles*. Arlington Heights, IL: Skylight.

Ogle, D. M. (2007). *Coming together as readers* (2nd ed.). Thousand Oaks, CA: Corwin Press.

Ogle, D. M., & Correa, A. (2006, November). *Partner reading for English learners.* Paper presented at the National Reading Conference, Austin. TX.

Ogle, D. M., & McKee, J. (1996). Science journals in an integrated second-grade classroom. *Illinois Reading Council Journal, 24*(2), 7–22.

Ogle, L. T., Sen, A., Pahlke, E., & Jacelyn, L. (2003). *International comparisons in fourth grade reading literacy: Findings from the Progress in International Reading Literacy Study (PIRLS) of 2001.* Washington, DC: National Center for Educational Statistics, U.S. Department of Education.

Palincsar, A. S., & Brown, A. L. (1984). Reciprocal teaching of comprehension-fostering and monitoring activities. *Cognition and Instruction, 1*(2), 117–175.

Palincsar, A. S., & Brown, A. L. (1986). Interactive teaching to promote independent learning from text. *The Reading Teacher, 39*, 771–777.

Palmer, G. A. (2006). *Education in hand: Reading, writing and podcasting.* Available at *www.disrictadministrator.com/viewarticle.aeps?*

Paris, S. G., Lipson, M. Y., & Wixson, K. K. (1983). Becoming a strategic reader. *Contemporary Educational Psychology, 8*, 293–316.

Paris, S. G., & Oka, E. R. (1986). Self-regulated learning among exceptional children. *Exceptional Children, 53*(2), 103–108.

Parish, P. (1963). *Amelia Bedelia.* New York: Harper & Row.

Paterson, K. (1977). *Bridge to Terabithia.* New York: Crowell.

Paulsen, G. (1987). *Hatchet.* New York: Bradbury Books.

Pawling, E. (1999). Modern languages and CD-ROM-based learning. *British Journal of Educational Technology, 30*, 163–176.

Pearson, P. D. (1985). Changing the face of comprehension instruction. *The Reading Teacher, 38*, 724–738.

Pearson, P. D., & Gallagher, M. C. (1983). The instruction of reading comprehension. *Contemporary Educational Psychology, 8*(3), 317–344.

Pinnell, G. S., & Fountas, I. (1996). *Guided reading: Good first teaching for all children.* Portsmouth, NH: Heinemann.

Plecha, J. (1992). Shared inquiry: The Great Books method of interpretive reading and discussion. In C. Temple & P. Collins (Eds.), *Stories and readers: New perspectives on literature, the elementary classroom* (pp. 103–114). Norwood, MA: Christopher-Gordon.

Pressley, M. (2000). *Reading instruction: What works.* New York: Guilford Press.

Pressley, M., & Harris, K. R. (1990). What we really know about strategy instruction. *Educational Leadership, 48*(1), 31–34.

Pressley, M., & Woloshyn, V. (1995). *Cognitive strategies: Instruction that really improves children's academic performance* (2nd ed.). Cambridge, MA: Brookline Books.

Pringle, L. (1997). *An extraordinary life: The story of a monarch butterfly.* New York: Orchard Books.

Raphael, T. *www.planetbookclub.com.*

Raphael, T. (1986). Teaching question–answer relationships, revisited. *The Reading Teacher, 39*, 516–522.

Raphael, T. (2004). *Super QAR for test-wise students*. New York: Wright Group/McGraw-Hill.

Raphael, T., & McMahon, S. I. (1994). Book club: An alternative framework for reading instruction. *The Reading Teacher, 48*, 102–116.

Readence, J. E., Bean, T. W., & Baldwln, R. S. (1995). *Content area literacy: An integrated approach* (5th ed.). Dubuque, IA: Kendall/Hunt.

Richardson, S. (1991). *Magazines for children: A guide for parents, teachers, and librarians*. Chicago: American Library Association.

Rosenblatt, L. M. (1985). Viewpoints: Transaction versus interaction—A terminological rescue operation. *Research in the Teaching of English, 19*, 96–107.

Rumelhart, C. E. (1975). Notes on a schema for stories. In D. G. Bobrow & A. Collins (Eds.), *Representation and understanding: Studies in cognitive science*. New York: Academic Press.

Ryder, J. (1989). *Where butterflies grow*. New York: Lodestar Books.

Sadoski, M., & Paivio, A. (2004). A dual coding theoretical model of reading. In R. B. Ruddell & N. J. Unrau (Eds.), *Theoretical models and processes of reading* (5th ed., pp. 1329–1362). Newark, DE: International Reading Association.

Sadoski, M., & Willson, V. L. (2006). Effects of a theoretically based large-scale reading intervention in a multicultural urban school district. *American Educational Research Journal, 43*, 135–152.

Sanders, N. M. (1966). *Classroom questions: What kind?* New York: Harper & Row.

Sandved, K. B. (1997). *The butterfly alphabet*. New York: Scholastic.

Schreiber, J. E., & Kain, K. (1985). *Regions of our country and our world* (Scott, Foresman Social Studies Grade 4). Glenview, IL: Scott, Foresman.

Schwartz, R. M., & Raphael, T. E. (1985). Concept of definition: A key to improving students' vocabulary. *The Reading Teacher, 39*, 198–205.

Short, K. G., Harste, J., with Burke, C. (1996). *Creating classrooms for authors and inquirers* (2nd ed.). Portsmouth, NH: Heinemann.

Short, K. G., & Klassen, C. (1995). So what do I do? The role of the teacher in literature circles. In N. Roser & M. Martinez (Eds.), *Book talk and beyond: Children and teachers respond to literature* (pp. 97–108). Newark, DE: International Reading Association.

Smith, M. C. (2000). The real world reading practices of adults. *Journal of Literacy Research, 32*, 25–32.

Snow, C. E. (2002). *Reading for understanding: Toward an R&D program in reading comprehension*. Report of the RAND Reading Study Group. Santa Monica, CA: RAND/Science and Technology Policy Institute.

Snow, C. E., Hemphill, L., & Barnes, W. S. (1991). *Unfulfilled expectations: Home and school influences on literacy*. Cambridge, MA: Harvard University Press.

Snowball, D. (1995, May). Building literacy skills through nonfiction. *Teaching K–8*, pp. 62–63.

Spector, K., & Jones, S. (2007). Constructing Anne Frank? Critical literacy and the Holocaust in eighty-grade English. *Journal of Adolescent and Adult Literacy, 51*(1), 36–48.

Spiro, R. J., Coulson, R. L., Feltovich, P. J., & Anderson, D. K. (2004). Cognitive flexibility theory: Advanced knowledge acquisition in ill-structured domains. In R. B. Ruddell &

N. J. Unrau (Eds.), *Theoretical models and processes of reading* (5th ed., pp. 640–653). Newark, DE: International Reading Association.

Stahl, S. A. (1999). *Vocabulary development: Vol. 2. From reading research to practice.* Cambridge, MA: Brookline Books.

Stauffer, R. G. (1969). *Directing reading maturity as a cognitive process.* New York: Harper & Row.

Stein, N. I., & Glenn, C. (1979). *The language experience approach to the teaching of reading.* New York: Harper & Row.

Still, J. (1991). *Amazing butterflies and moths.* New York: Knopf.

Stoll, D. R. (1997). *Magazines for kids and teens.* Newark, DE: International Reading Association.

Tatler, D. (1996). *Polka dots.* Glenview, IL: Celebration Press/Scott, Foresman.

Temple, C. A., Martinez, M., Yokota, J., & Naylor, A. (1996). *Children's books in children's hands: An introduction to their literature.* Boston: Allyn & Bacon.

Templeton, S. (1983). Using the spelling/meaning connection to develop word knowledge in older students. *Journal of Reading, 27,* 8–14.

Thaler, M. (1988, April–May). Reading, writing, and riddling. *Learning,* pp. 58–59.

Tharp, R., & Gallimore, R. (1988). *Rousing minds to life: Teaching, learning and school in social context.* Cambridge, MA: Cambridge University Press.

Tierney, R. J., Readence, J. E., & Dishner, E. K. (1995). *Reading strategies and practices: A compendium.* Boston: Allyn & Bacon.

Tierney, R. J., Schallert, D. & LaZansky, J. (1982). *Secondary students' use of social studies and biology texts.* (Report prepared in conjunction with NIE grant). Garden City, NY: National Institute of Education.

"Twiga's first days." (1976). *Ranger Rick, 10*(6), pp. 3–8.

U.S. Department of Labor. (1991). *Secretary's Commission on Achieving Necessary Skills: What work requires of schools.* Washington, DC: U.S. Department of Labor.

Vacca, R. T., & Vacca, J. L. (1999). *Content area reading: Literacy and learning across the curriculum.* Boston: Longman.

Vaughan, J. L., & Estes, T. H. (1986). *Reading and reasoning beyond the primary grades.* Boston: Allyn & Bacon.

Viorst, J. (1972). *Alexander and the terrible, horrible, no good, very bad day.* New York: Atheneum.

Vygotsky, L. S. (1978). *Mind in society.* Cambridge, MA: Harvard University Press.

Weaver, C. A., & Kintsch, W. (1991). Expository text. In R. Barr, M. Kamil, P. Mosenthal, & P. D. Pearson (Eds.), *Handbook of reading research* (Vol. 2, pp. 230–245). New York: Longman.

Weinstein, C. E., & Mayer, R. E. (1986). The teaching of learning strategies. In M. C. Wittrock (Ed.), *Handbook of research in teaching* (pp. 315–327). New York: Macmillan.

White, E. B. (1952). *Charlotte's web.* New York: Harper.

White, T. G., Sowell, J., & Yanagihara, A. (1989). Teaching elementary students to use word-part clues. *The Reading Teacher, 42,* 302–308.

Winthrop, E. (2000). *Castle in the attic.* New York: Random House.

Williams, N., Konopak, B., & Readance, J. (1989). *NREC yearbook: Cognitive and social perspectives for literary research and instruction.* Chicago: National Reading Conference.

Wood, A. (1985). *King Bidgood's in the bathtub.* San Diego: Harcourt Brace Jovanovich.

Xin, J. F., & Rieth, H. (2001). Video-assisted vocabulary instruction for elementary school students with learning disabilities. *Information Technology in Childhood Education Annual,* 87–104.

Yokota, J., Anderson, S., & McFarlane, D. (1999). Web sources for children's literature. *Illinois Reading Council Journal, 27*(2), 66–76.

Index